CHURCHILL'S ADMIRAL IN TWO WORLD WARS

ADMIRAL OF THE FLEET LORD KEYES OF ZEEBRUGGE AND DOVER GCB KCVO CMG DSO

This book is dedicated to my wife Anne who diligently read proofs and encouraged my work in writing it.

By the same author

Something Wrong with Our Ships (F.J. Crossley, 2008)

British Destroyers 1892-1918 (Osprey Publishing, Botley, Oxford, 2009)

Bismarck: the Epic Chase: The Sinking of the German Menace (Pen & Sword Books, Barnsley, 2010)

The Hidden Threat: The Story of Mines and Minesweeping (Pen & Sword Books, Barnsley, 2011)

Monitors of the Royal Navy: How the Fleet brought the Great Guns to Bear (Pen & Sword Books, Barnsley, 2016)

Voices from Jutland: A Centenary Commemoration (Pen & Sword Books, Barnsley, 2016)

CHURCHILL'S ADMIRAL IN TWO WORLD WARS

ADMIRAL OF THE FLEET LORD KEYES OF ZEEBRUGGE AND DOVER GCB KCVO CMG DSO

Jim Crossley

PEN & SWORD
MARITIME

First published in Great Britain in 2020 by
PEN AND SWORD MARITIME
an imprint of
Pen and Sword Books Ltd
Yorkshire – Philadelphia

ISBN 978 1 52674 839 3

Typeset in Times New Roman 11/13.5 by
Aura Technology and Software Services, India.
Printed and bound in the UK by TJ International.

Pen & Sword Books Ltd incorporates the imprints of Pen & Sword
Archaeology, Atlas, Aviation, Battleground, Discovery,
Family History, History, Maritime, Military, Naval, Politics, Railways,
Select, Social History, Transport, True Crime, Claymore Press,
Frontline Books, Leo Cooper, Praetorian Press, Remember When,
Seaforth Publishing and Wharncliffe.

For a complete list of Pen & Sword titles please contact
PEN & SWORD BOOKS LIMITED
47 Church Street, Barnsley, South Yorkshire, S70 2AS, England
E-mail: enquiries@pen-and-sword.co.uk
Website: www.pen-and-sword.co.uk

Or

PEN AND SWORD BOOKS
1950 Lawrence Rd, Havertown, PA 19083, USA
E-mail: Uspen-and-sword@casematepublishers.com
Website: www.penandswordbooks.com

Contents

Introduction

Keyes was a hero, not a mighty victor like Nelson, St Vincent or Rooke, but a hero nevertheless, fearless, resourceful, decisive and unfailingly decent in his treatment of his own men, a defeated enemy, or a rival. It is common for biographers of such men, especially of soldiers and sailors of the Imperial era, to look for faults, examine weaknesses and generally poke fun at their subjects. In Keyes's case this just won't do. Certainly, he was a staunch supporter of the British imperialism – so were the vast majority of his contemporaries – and such views are not fashionable now. He liked to move smoothly through the very highest echelons of European society; in those days progress in the Royal Navy almost demanded a certain amount of social climbing. One cannot, however, study his life without recognising his fine seamanship, his loyalty to friends, his outstanding qualities of leadership and, above all, his utter contempt of danger.

He was not an intellectual and, unlike his hero Nelson, he was incapable of penning a memorable phrase. Probably dyslexic, he never learnt to spell, to deliver a fluent speech or to write concisely, but he could transform a ship's crew from a mediocre time-serving 'shower' into a keen, lively band of brothers, each man eager to do that little extra to earn a word of praise from his captain. As a public speaker in parliament he was an utter disaster; he stumbled, stuttered and his arguments were prolix and muddled, but he could stand in front of a band of discontented dockyard workers and win their respect and even, sometimes, co-operation. Pictures of him, even when he was uniformed as an admiral, show a slender, even slight, build. He retained the boyish face, the bright alert eyes and the trim figure of a schoolboy, but he was as ferocious as a tiger and possessed of an iron will.

He was to win no great naval victory and his proudest achievement, the Zeebrugge Raid, was at best a partial success, but his achievements, character and daring made him stand out as a beacon among naval officers of his time and as an example to future generations.

INTRODUCTION

Churchill was quick to recognise the outstanding qualities of this young naval officer and shared with him the triumphs and the tragedies of the first years of the Great War, in particular the disastrous Gallipoli campaign. Their friendship endured bitter disagreements during the inter-war years and crushing disappointments in the 1940s. Both men were big enough to put conflict and jealousies aside and celebrate each other's achievements.

Map 1 – Approaches to Tientsin

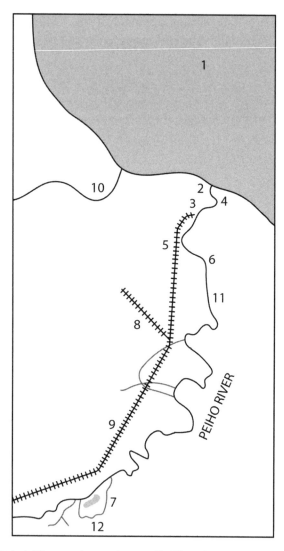

1. Gulf of Bohai (Fleet anchorage)
2. North Fort
3. North Fort
4. South Fort
5. Tonku
6. Taku
7. Tientsin
8. Branch Line to Lutai
9. Railway to Tientsin and Peking
10. Peh-Tang
11. Hsi-Cheng Fort
12. Ha River

Map 2 – Tientsin to Peking

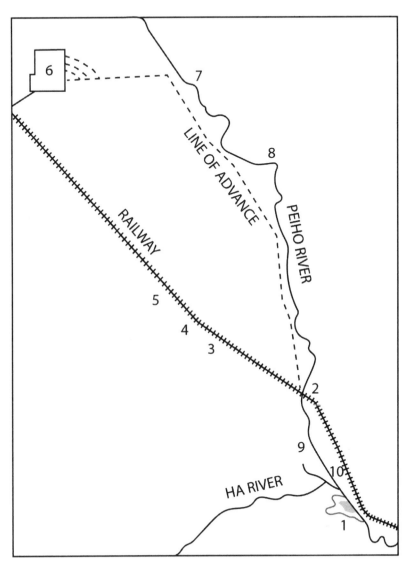

1. Tientsin
2. Yang-Tsun
3. Lofa
4. Lang-Fang
5. Antung

6. Peking
7. Tung-Chau
8. Ma-Tau
9. Pei-Tsung
10. Hsi-Ku Arsenal

Map 3 – Peking

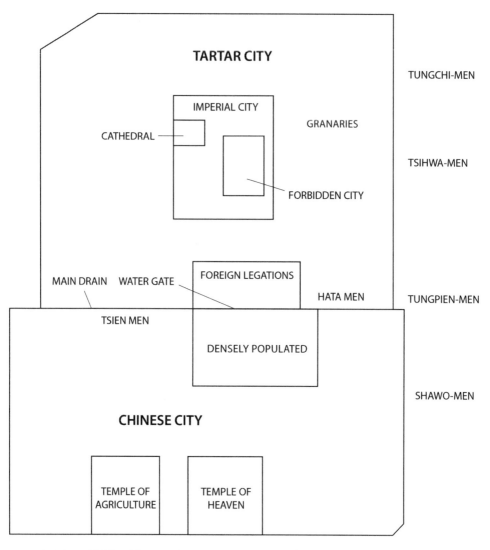

TARTAR CITY

TUNGCHI-MEN

IMPERIAL CITY

GRANARIES

CATHEDRAL

TSIHWA-MEN

FORBIDDEN CITY

FOREIGN LEGATIONS

MAIN DRAIN   WATER GATE

HATA MEN

TUNGPIEN-MEN

TSIEN MEN

DENSELY POPULATED

SHAWO-MEN

CHINESE CITY

TEMPLE OF AGRICULTURE

TEMPLE OF HEAVEN

1. Tungchi-Men (Japanese)
2. Tsiawa-Men (Russian)
3. TungPien-Men (American)
4. Shawo-Men (British)
5. Densely Populated Chinese Area
6. Sewage Outfall
7. Foreign Legations
8. Imperial City
9. Catholic Cathedral
10. Dividing Wall
11. Granaries

Map 4 – Gallipoli

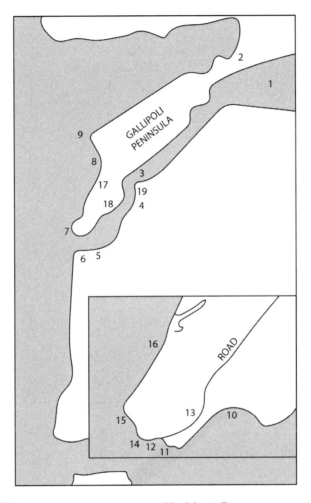

1. Sea of Marmara
2. Bulair
3. The Narrows
4. Kepez
5. Eren Keui Bay
6. Kum Kale
7. Cape Helles
8. Anzac Cove
9. Suvla Bay
10. Morto Bay
11. *River Clyde* ashore
12. V Beach
13. Old Castle
14. W Beach
15. X Beach
16. Y Beach
17. Krithia
18. Achi Baba

ZEEBRUGGE

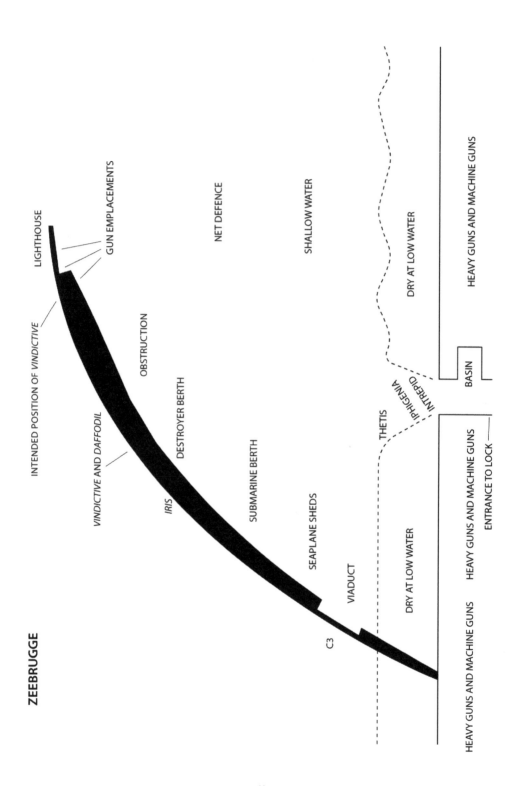

LIGHTHOUSE

GUN EMPLACEMENTS

INTENDED POSITION OF *VINDICTIVE*

VINDICTIVE AND DAFFODIL

OBSTRUCTION

NET DEFENCE

DESTROYER BERTH

IRIS

SUBMARINE BERTH

SHALLOW WATER

SEAPLANE SHEDS

THETIS

IPHIGENIA

INTREPID

VIADUCT

C3

DRY AT LOW WATER

DRY AT LOW WATER

BASIN

HEAVY GUNS AND MACHINE GUNS

ENTRANCE TO LOCK

HEAVY GUNS AND MACHINE GUNS

HEAVY GUNS AND MACHINE GUNS

Chapter 1

A Soldier's Son

Roger John Brownlow Keyes. The name Brownlow, with its Irish connections, gives a clue to his origins. It was the name of his father's great friend General Brownlow whose roots, like those of the Keyes's, stemmed from a seventeenth century English plantation family in Donegal. Roger's father, Charles Keyes, was a distinguished soldier. He was commander of the Punjab Frontier Force, keeping order among the unruly tribes of the North West Frontier between India and Afghanistan. He was no stranger to action and had won the admiration of the Indian military establishment by saving a desperate situation in which he led a charge into the Barrera Pass, putting to flight a strong band of ferocious Waziri warriors. On another occasion he, together with a single junior subaltern and a handful of men, stormed up a steep escarpment to recapture a vital hill feature, scattering a large force of tribesmen before him. For both exploits he was recommended for the Victoria Cross but it was not awarded.

It is seldom remembered today what a significant institution the Indian Army was in those far off Imperial days. Much more numerous than the British regular army, it defended the British interest and supported the civil power in much of the sub-continent. It provided an excellent career opportunity for an ambitious young British soldier of slender means, provided he managed to survive the Indian climate. The pay was better and living cheaper than for an officer in the home country and there was plenty of opportunity for fighting. British officers in the Indian service evolved a kind of coterie of fighting men who all knew each other, at least by reputation, and mostly maintained extremely high standards of loyalty, honour and behaviour.

In 1870 Charles Keyes, then a lieutenant colonel, had married Kate Norman, the much younger sister of Major General Norman, a hero of the Indian Mutiny. In doing so he took on 'Quite a girl'. One of his junior officers, actually Ian Hamilton, who will feature later in this narrative, described her 'as high spirited fascinating, clever creature as I ever saw.

1

Camel riding, hawking, dancing; she was the idol of the Punjab Frontier Force'. Kate rapidly presented her husband with a family of four sons and a daughter. Roger, the second son, was born on 4 October 1872 at Tundiani Fort in the Punjab. 1878 found this family embarked on a ship bound for England. (Eventually three more daughters and another son were to arrive, making a total of nine offspring.) The object of the long trek to England was to find a reliable carer for the older children in the home country so that they could be brought up in relative safety, away from the perils of Indian food and climate. The parents probably assumed at this stage that their sons would follow their father into the Army or into the Indian Civil Service, but young Roger, the second son, had already developed other ideas. Though he was a small and rather sickly child he had already decided that he wished to join the Royal Navy. Neither he nor anyone else knew what prompted this resolution. Perhaps he had heard something of the wonderful achievements of the naval artillery during the Indian Mutiny. Perhaps he had spotted and admired a naval officer's uniform at one of his parents' social gatherings – certainly he himself and his older brother had sailor suits to wear when he was only four years old. Maybe even something about the prospect of his long sea voyage impressed him. For whatever reason, his resolve was strong and unshakeable.

The Keyes family spent three years in England, then returned to India leaving the five eldest children in the care of 'Uncle Edward' – not in fact any relation at all but a country parson with a living in Norfolk, who made extra money by taking in families as paying holiday guests. Edward had two daughters who were put in charge of the Keyes children's education and welfare. It appears that the children were very harshly treated in fact and had a miserable time at the vicarage, the establishment providing few of the good things which had been promised and paid for by their parents. The redeeming feature was that the vicar was a great sportsman and took the older boys on fishing and shooting expeditions, teaching them the rudiments of English country sports. He was a friend of the Earl of Leicester who allowed him to fish in the ponds and rivers around the Holkham estate – very much the same territory, as it happens, on which the young Nelson had learnt to shoot and fish roughly a hundred years earlier. In term time the two eldest boys, Norman and Roger, were sent off to Albion House, a boarding school near Margate. Norman showed himself a bright and promising youth and achieved a scholarship to Wellington - a public school with strong army connections. Just before he was to start his first term at Wellington disaster struck. He suffered severe internal pain which was not recognised as appendicitis. After a few days agony he was dead. Roger, considered rather weak and a poor scholar, remained at Albion House in spite of the school being probably to blame for his brother's early death. He became a moderately capable cricketer and his letters to his parents, carefully preserved by his mother, show some signs of a robust and determined nature, but also betray painfully poor writing and spelling skills, typical of the dyslexia which was an entirely unrecognised disability in the nineteenth century.

A letter written to his mother in India demonstrates a tenderness which was typical of Roger's good nature.

Sunday 23rd Sept 1883

Dearest Mother

I went to dear Norman's funeral. I saw his face. It was so lovely. I wish you could have seen it.

His death was so sudden, it seems strange that only the day before he died he was talking to me so happily. But it is not exactly death. Aunt Alice told me you know we shall see him again in Heaven. Aunt Alice has been very kind, she sent me some of dear Norman's hair. Has she sent you any yet?

Do you think I can have a watch this berthday (sic)? We plyd cricket yesterday. I am in the first twenty now.

Poor Mother, when you come home we can go to dear Norman's grave.

Your ever loving son.

R.J.B.K.

In 1884, to their offspring's relief, the General and his lady returned from India to set up a permanent home in the UK. The General wanted initially to live on the family lands at Croaghan in County Donegal close to Lough Swilly, in what is now the Irish Republic. He had inherited a house there from his mother which he intended to modernise and where he could live as a country gentleman. Donegal, however, was one of the most inaccessible parts of the United Kingdom and Lady Keyes quickly realised that it would be no place to bring up her eight remaining children. She was able to quash the General's plan and the family eventually bought Shorncliffe Lodge, at Sandgate, near Folkestone in Kent – a much more suitable location. Lough Swilly, however, did not cease to exert its influence. While visiting the family properties near Croaghan, the Keyes were excited to see the great warships of the Channel Squadron anchor in the safety of the lough. General Sir Charles decided to pay a call on the flagship, *Agincourt*, and brought his rather unsatisfactory eldest son with him. *Agincourt* was a magnificent looking five-masted sailing frigate with an auxiliary steam engine. She had served in the Baltic during the Crimean War and had been very nearly wrecked recently off the coast near Gibraltar due to a navigational error, so there was plenty for the Captain to talk to the General about. Eventually the conversation turned to Roger and his determination to join the Navy. 'Don't let him.' said the Captain. 'Look at my watch-keepers, they are all elderly lieutenants. There is no future for them and small prospect of promotion. When the next generation of sub-lieutenants are promoted they will probably be ashore on half pay for a couple of years or more. There is no future in the Navy'.

The General and his little son, now twelve years old, had it out that day. Roger's determination was unshaken and the General at last wisely gave way.

For a boy to join the Royal Navy in those days there were some formidable hurdles to cross. The entrance exam was not too taxing; some elementary maths and writing basic English would see you through, but first you had to obtain a recommendation from a senior naval or political figure. The Keyes's family friend, Sir Henry Norman, happened to know Lord George Hamilton, who was First Lord of the Admiralty at the time, so with some exchange of letters, sponsorship was arranged; but the next hurdle was more difficult. The applicant's family had to settle an income on their offspring to pay for his training as a cadet. The sum, typically £50 per year (equivalent to £5,000 today), was unaffordable to any except the upper echelons of society. It followed that naval officers were predominantly drawn from a very narrow strata of the population – aristocratic folk who mostly knew each other and had wealth to spare. The result of these entrance requirements was, as the performance of the Royal Navy was to show, unfavourable. The magnificent feats of the navy in the Napoleonic Wars had attracted a degree of glamour to the profession which resulted in it being dominated by an aristocratic officer class, mostly ultra-conservative, wealthy, and resistant to social or technical change. Similar backgrounds and education resulted in lack of initiative and an inability to 'think outside the box'. There was no place in its ranks for the rising technically-educated middle classes. Indeed, although there were engineer officers to look after engines, they were regarded with, at best, tolerance and, at worst, contempt by regular naval officers. They were debarred from the higher ranks of the service. It has often been observed that Nelson himself, son of an impecunious clergyman, would have been unable to join the navy as it existed in the late nineteenth century. His father would never have found the money. Most senior officers in the 1880s' Royal Navy were fine seamen and would have been competent commanders of one of Nelson's battleships or even one of Drake's but, in the conflicts that were to come, dominated by mines, torpedoes, submarines, destroyers and dreadnought battleships, skills and disciplines of an entirely new order were going to be required. Young Roger was joining a force with a glorious past but an uncertain future. He was to live through a change in culture and in technology such as had never been seen before.

The Keyes family were not poor, but they had seven other children to cater for and finding the money for young Roger was not easy. The next step was to remove him from Albion House and send him to Mr Littlejohn's, a specialist 'crammer' at Greenwich which brought backward boys such as Roger up to the modest standard required by *Britannia,* the naval training establishment. At Littlejohn's establishment a high standard of cleanliness and general behaviour was enforced by the formidable Mrs Littlejohn, the boys being required to dress for dinner and wash diligently behind their ears. Lessons were taught in the mornings by a young under-master who took his pupils through endless past examination papers so that they knew the answers to most of the likely questions. Tougher were Mr Littlejohn's dictation sessions after dinner. Dictation is always a nightmare for bad spellers and Roger found them especially difficult. Often, he was kept back after the others had been sent off to bed and made to go on and on struggling with difficult words, being rewarded with a smack across the shoulders with a cane or parallel rulers every time he made a mistake. Roger does not seem to have resented this treatment; indeed it was considered perfectly normal at the time and he seems to have liked and respected Littlejohn. The teaching method was also successful. He passed the dictation exam with a few marks to spare, and came twenty-fourth out of thirty-nine candidates passing into *Britannia* in his term. Roger had to face one more hurdle, a medical examination. For most boys this was no problem but, besides being small and skinny, he had an arm which had been broken and badly set, which proved a handicap to him throughout his life. This would almost certainly have caused him to be rejected by the naval doctors at Greenwich but, perhaps not for the first time in his life, he was to employ his natural charm and guile to outwit authority. The doctor examining him recognised his name and told him that he had known his father in India. This gave Roger an opening and he started a long conversation about India and the various family friends there. By the time this had finished the time allotted for the examination was over and the doctor, unwilling to keep his colleagues waiting, didn't even measure Roger or test his eyesight, he simply scribbled '4 foot 10 inches' on the examination sheet and wished Roger well. He joined *Britannia* in autumn 1885 at the age of thirteen.

Britannia consisted of two old wooden ships, *Britannia* herself and *Hindustan,* moored together on the river Dart. Boys were taught some very basic maths related to navigation, a little naval history, some elementary French and had to endure the dreaded dictation in English. Also, of course, there was basic seamanship, knots and lashings, handling a ship under sail, etc. Afternoons were given up to games and to sailing boats on the Dart. Discipline was almost entirely enforced by the senior cadet term and this resulted in some appalling instances of bullying. Small and weedy, with one weak arm, Roger was a perfect target for bullies but, luckily, he had a formidable protector, a cousin on his mother's side, Walter Norman, whose parents lived abroad and who had spent summer holidays with the Keyes family. He and his friends kept a good eye on his little cousin and made sure he was left alone. Roger was too small and his arm too weak to be much of a rugger or football player but he had a good eye and quick reactions and played racquets, hunted with the beagles, fenced in the winter, and excelled in sailing during the summer term. He had one more health scare in *Britannia* when a nasty bout of tonsillitis upset his hearing so that the surgeon reported him unfit for service. He had to go before a medical board, but luckily his father had taken him to a specialist in London who showed him how to swallow and blow his nose in such a way as to give short-term relief. He also certified that any hearing loss would be temporary. It seems that Sir Charles was now doing all he could to promote his son's naval career.

July 1887 saw the end of Roger's days in *Britannia.* He passed out twenty-fifth out of a term of thirty-seven and with nine other cadets was appointed to HMS *Raleigh.* He was still a skinny little youth, only 5 foot 2 inches tall, and almost childlike in appearance, looking much less than his fifteen years. Astonishingly boys of this age were expected to work on yards and topmasts, shortening and making sail in heavy weather, and occasionally to take up a cutlass and pistol and fight with ruthless pirates, slavers or even the Queen's enemies in South Africa, India or the China seas. *Raleigh* was an iron frigate clad on the outside with timber above the water line and copper-bottomed. She was armed with muzzle-loading guns and a few 6-inch quick firers. She was reputed to be an excellent sailer, able to make 15 knots under sail or power and she served as flagship to Admiral Hunt-Grubbe on the South Africa station. Roger joined her at Cape Town. Unfortunately, there was seldom much to do for the fleet at the Cape and the cadets had to make their own amusements. Roger had been given a twelve-bore shotgun by a kind uncle and managed to get some quail shooting ashore. He also clubbed together with some other cadets and bought a small sailing boat for use in False Bay. After months of idleness there was an expedition up the coast to Accra where some native troubles had to be handled and then to Lagos, returning via St Helena.

Roger seems to have survived the rough house which was a typical midshipman's mess. On *Raleigh* this appears to have been a reasonably happy establishment, dominated by a huge bearded midshipman who kept missing out on promotion. He was a heavy drinker but was kind by nature and exerted a civilising influence on his domain. All this time, of course, the young cadet was learning practical seamanship, how to shorten sail in heavy weather, how to man the tops and yardarms and what it was like to handle heavy, wet canvas in the dark, swaying violently with the motion of the ship. He loved it. He was promoted midshipman in November 1887.

There was one exciting episode while *Raleigh* was at Cape Town. An exercise was arranged to test the defences of the colony against a seaborne invasion. *Raleigh* covered the landing of marines and some mobile artillery, then disembarked most of her crew, including Roger, to join the invading force. The pretend attackers appear to have made rings around the regular troops defending Cape Town. They advanced rapidly towards the town for seven and a half hours, mostly at the double in the hot April weather. The authorities concluded that Cape Town was indeed poorly defended. This little amphibious exercise was the forerunner of the many and various amphibious operations which were to become Roger's speciality.

In August 1888 *Raleigh* made a cruise up the east coast, giving the young midshipman his first taste of real weather. The Cape of Good Hope is notorious for its sudden violent storms and, en route for Durban, the ship was caught by a sudden gale which struck her after dark. The fore topgallant and main topsail were torn to shreds and Roger, as midshipman of the foretop, had an exciting time taming the flogging canvas. Eventually the wind eased enough for the ship to put into Durban and most of the crew, including Roger, went ashore to look around. While they were thus engaged another, more violent, onshore wind blew up, threatening to drive *Raleigh* ashore. The commander took her to sea with the remaining skeleton crew, parting the anchor cable and losing the anchor in the process. Once at sea the ship was safe enough, but the shore party were marooned until, on the third day, the wind dropped enough for a tug to be able to take them out to their ship. At nightfall the wind increased again so they had to claw off the coast under double-reefed topsails. It must have been a life-changing experience for a young midshipman, whose station was up the foremast, encouraging a team of tough old seamen. Roger commented later that 'It was all very interesting and delighted me'. Of such stuff great sailormen are made.

Returning to Cape Town there was another mock invasion of the city by a party of bluejackets, including Keyes. The men took off their boots and marched in bare feet, easily outstripping the regular soldiers defending the city. Apart from this there was little to do and Roger spent a lot of time refurbishing the little cutter which he shared with some friends.

Chapter 2

'Little E' – A Strapping Youth

There was a 'flap' on the coast of Africa in December 1889 when Britain challenged a Portuguese claim on huge tracts of the African continent. The Royal Navy deployed a force, consisting of twelve square-rigged sailing ships and two gunboats, off the coast of what is now Mozambique, ready to defend British interests. Warships were also sent to threaten distant Portuguese outposts such as the Azores and the Cape Verde Islands and the Channel Fleet was ordered to stand off the coast of Portugal itself. This was a classic case of Britain asserting her undisputed 'Command of the Ocean' which made her such a dominant world power in the nineteenth and the earlier part of the twentieth centuries. If there were pirates rampant in the Malay States, cannibals at loose in the Pacific islands, rebels seizing ships in South America or even a European power stepping out of line in Africa, the Royal Navy would be there to sort the problem. Through it Britain exerted a degree of authority worldwide that no nation could match. As he learnt his trade, Roger absorbed the ethos of this astonishing institution and it was to become instilled into every aspect of his thinking. Britain was ubiquitous and invincible. For over a hundred years "command of the ocean" had ensured that British interests were protected even in far away china or in South America. There seemed to be no reason why this situation would ever change.

Before the East Africa Fleet could assemble, the crisis was over and Portugal succumbed to the threat posed by the British navy. Instead of returning to the Cape however, *Raleigh* was ordered north on special duties. Here Roger saw a chance for adventure. His ship briefly joined a small squadron based off the island of Zanzibar, tasked to enforce a ban on slaving, which had been a major and profitable activity for the local Arabs. On hearing all too soon that his ship was to return to the Cape rather than remaining on the more active Zanzibar station, he wangled a transfer to the little corvette *Turquoise*. She was a 2,000-ton sailing ship with a small steam engine and muzzle-loading main armament working on sliding carriages – an arrangement considered primitive even in those days and which would have been familiar to a sixteenth-century seaman. Roger was desperate to join her as she was to remain on anti-slaving duties on the East African coast. Her captain, John Brakenbury, had received good reports on 'Little E' as Roger was nicknamed. He himself was a most eccentric fellow with a great love of music. He had, however, proved himself a doughty fighter and was much loved by his men. He seems to have taken the new midshipman under his wing.

The slave trade was still active around Zanzibar at the time. Arab traders would go inland and capture unfortunate Africans, killing or chasing off the men and marching women and boys to riverbanks or inlets where they were crowded into dhows for transport to the clove plantations on Pemba Island. Those unfortunate enough to be good looking might be dragged off to face an even more horrible fate. Conditions on the dhows were abominable: people were crammed together, tightly bound, with no food, water or sanitation. The Navy's tactic for stopping this traffic was to send small boats, commanded by junior lieutenants or midshipmen, cruising among the coastal islands and inlets, armed to the teeth, to pounce on the dhows. Sometimes there were savage encounters. On one occasion a cutter made the mistake of approaching a dhow from the lee side. The cunning Arabs offered no resistance until the boat was alongside, then they let go their main halyard, allowing the dhow's great sail to crash down and smother the British crew. They slashed and stabbed at the struggling bodies under the sail. The officer and almost all the crew were lost. In spite of the danger, these cruises were extremely popular with young officers. They offered a chance of an independent command, there was the spice of danger and there was a bonus pay-out of about £200 for each dhow captured, to be shared out among the boat's crew. Roger was, of course, madly keen to get a chance to command a cutter and, after some disappointments, his chance came.

Constant patrolling by the British had forced the Arabs to stop landing slaves on the sheltered west coast of Pemba island, but the navy had discovered that instead they had found a way of running their dhows through openings in the reef which lay off the east coast. This was, of course, exposed to the full force of the monsoon, blowing strongly across the expanse of the Indian Ocean, from the south-east. The gaps in the reef were unmarked and encumbered by shallow sandbars which made entry very difficult. It would be impossibly dangerous for the Royal Navy's boats to cruise outside the reef looking for dhows slipping through the gaps, as they would be on a lee shore, so a new tactic was devised. Boats would pass through one of the gaps in the reef and lie hidden behind the rocks, waiting to pounce on any dhow which came in. Roger was to take command of the little cutter *Rose,* with a crew of a first class petty officer, five seamen, a native interpreter and a West African cook. *Rose* was already on station inside the reef and Roger and his crew were to relieve her complement. They first embarked on a small gunboat *Somali,* which pitched and rolled horribly in the heavy seas breaking on the eastern side of the reef as it took them to the gap close to *Rose's* hunting ground. Even the hardened sailors on board, including Roger, were sick, but the gunboat reached the gap and hove to, waiting for *Rose*, which had been on station inside the reef, to come out and exchange crews. Eventually she came out through the surf, only just making the channel under oars and sail with terrific seas breaking on each side of her. She came alongside and stores were transferred. *Rose* was towed to windward of the gap, then she set off, deep laden, to make her way in through the narrow channel. Luckily, Roger had had some precise sailing directions from a friend who had made the passage before, so *Rose* came through safely, although darkness was falling. Inside the lagoon they found a sheltered sandy beach where they ran the boat ashore close to a little hut built by an earlier patrol. What a relief it must have been to get away from the huge seas and terrifying surf and settle down to a meal and a night's sleep in a safe anchorage. In the morning a lookout was posted on a prominent rock. He was equipped with a rifle and was instructed to shoot at any fishing boat close to the reef to discourage locals from warning any slavers of their presence. The following few days saw a gale of wind from the south which made the passage through the reef impossible for any dhow or fishermen. The party occupied themselves making friends with the natives, bathing in the lagoon and catching fish. They would not have bathed so freely had they known about an incident which was soon to occur on that very spot. A large shark came into the lagoon and grabbed one of the bathers. A brave petty officer leaped onto the shark's back and punched it as hard as he could. The shark took fright and swam off. The petty officer was awarded the Albert Medal for his bravery. For meals the party were provided with standard naval rations, salt pork, salt beef and canned meat, supplemented by fresh fruit bought locally and delicacies which had been purchased from *Turquoise's* purser. Roger noticed that his men made great efforts to ensure that he had the best of everything, and the crew actually embarrassed their young officer by going without themselves when food was short. It says a lot for his leadership that he was so popular with these tough seamen.

During *Rose's* patrol, to everyone's disappointment, no slavers attempted to enter the lagoon even when the weather had moderated. There was, however, a frightening incident when *Somali* came to relieve them. This time, instead of *Rose* herself remaining on station, another cutter was to replace her and this was being towed by the gunboat. There was still a big sea coming in from the east and it was breaking heavily on the reef. The replacement cutter was released from its tow well to windward of the gap, but the combination of the swell and the wind drove her to leeward and she missed the gap and found herself being driven dangerously close to the terrific breakers on the reef. Roger had *Rose* under sail at once and stood down the inside of the reef to be able to pick up survivors if the replacement boat was dashed onto the rocks. After a desperate struggle the newcomer managed to tack and claw off the reef. *Somali* floated down a grass rope for her to pick up and towed her up to windward again to have another try. This time she made the gap and came surging in over the breakers frighteningly close to a group of rocks. *Rose* then lost no time in standing out through the gap and picking up a line from *Somali,* ready for an uncomfortable tow back to *Turquoise.*

Roger, 'Little E', was still midshipman of the foretop, a responsible position, on *Turquoise.* Returning from a trip to Mauritius, the first lieutenant noticed something amiss with his work in the rigging and shouted angrily at him. Roger then broke every rule by answering insolently back. Furious, the first lieutenant made him stand on deck stock-still in the blazing African sun with neither food nor water. The punishment started at 6.00am and by noon he was ready to drop when the captain came past. Roger seems to have been something of a favourite as the captain came up to him and said 'You really must not speak like that to the First Lieutenant, Little E'. Just then the officers went to dinner and, seeing them safely out of the way, the captain sent up a large glass of lemon juice and a plate of the most delicious chicken sandwiches to the delinquent. He had never enjoyed a meal more and when, a little later, the first lieutenant re-appeared on deck and released him from his punishment station he was just in time to sneak back to his own mess and enjoy a second dinner.

A few weeks later Roger was, for the first time, involved in some real fighting. Germany was trying to establish a commercial presence inland of Zanzibar and news came in that a party of Garman traders had been murdered in Witu, a town ruled by an Arab sultan, not far from the island. The sultan refused to attend an enquiry into the incident and the East India Squadron was ordered to mount a punitive expedition. As a result, 700 marines and bluejackets, including Keyes, and some local forces, were sent on a long, hot march inland during which they were rather ineffectively harassed by the sultan's soldiers. The small artillery pieces which had been dragged up by the invaders were altogether too much for the sultan and he and most of his people fled the city as soon as the British arrived, depriving Keyes of a chance to show his mettle in a fight, but there had been some casualties on both sides and he clearly enjoyed leading the handful of men allotted to him into the enemy city.

The time had now come for the young midshipman to return home as he had been stationed in Africa for three years. He embarked on a slow voyage to Britain by troopship. This is an appropriate point to take a look at Keyes, who arrived back in Portsmouth on 10 December 1890. He was now eighteen years old. He had left England three years earlier, a skinny youth 5 foot 2 inches tall. Now he was a fine, strong 5 foot 10-inch young man, expert at handling small boats, a useful topman in the rigging and clearly a natural and popular leader of men. He was also now a member of what was the finest club in the world – the Royal Navy. It was a club whose members were effortlessly aware of their duty, their right even, to assert their authority over all comers anywhere in the world. There was no question of another nation's navy challenging their superiority. If the French, for example, built a bigger battleship the Royal Navy would immediately demand, and get, a bigger one still. Sometimes this self-confidence transformed into arrogance. Occasionally its ambitions had to be curbed, but basically it could project British power to any point on the globe. Members of the club had all been brought up and trained in much the same way as Keyes. Mostly from 'good' families they had only the most basic general education and hence a very narrow world view. Almost all of them had seen some fighting – mostly on land but hardly any had experience of a serious sea fight. In three years at sea Roger Keyes had qualified to join this club and his mindset was typical of its members. He had proved to the service and to himself that he had the potential to be a good sea officer. It was a sound start to a career.

Keyes appeared unexpectedly at his parents' house and spent a prolonged period of leave, mostly on horseback, learning the skills necessary to cut a good figure on the hunting field. He attached himself informally to a locally stationed cavalry unit and proved so competent on horseback that the riding master complained that he was wasted in the Royal Navy. He did indeed become a fine horseman and almost wherever he went in his long naval career he seemed able to spend some time in the saddle, hunting, steeplechasing, or playing polo.

The Royal Navy was preparing for a significant expansion in the 1890s. There was a new long-term ship building programme predicated on the doctrine, ratified by parliament, that Britain's navy must, at all times, be bigger than the next two navies of the world combined. The ambitious shipbuilding programme was commenced, and funds were committed for this and for more personnel. Recruiting and training boys to join the expanding Service became an important activity. Quite astonishingly, the navy was still building pure sailing ships in 1889, and it was to one of these, the newly commissioned brig *Martin*, that Keyes was appointed, joining her in March 1891. The ship was to be used for giving new recruits their first taste of seafaring. *Martin* was a most beautiful little ship and an excellent sailer. She had a captain, a lieutenant, a doctor and two midshipmen. A boatswain and twenty-five seamen looked after the hundred trainees on board. Most of the time was spent in leisurely cruises about the Solent with frequent sail changes and practice with the little guns which the ship carried. The ship was often left in the charge of the midshipmen who must have gained a lot of experience in the strong tides and busy shipping lanes. On one occasion there was almost a disaster. *Martin* had run down to Plymouth and was on her way home. She had hoped to catch the east going tide up the Needles Channel but was too late and instead had to take the North Channel, passing close to Bournemouth and anchoring for the night close to Hurst Castle, waiting for the flood tide to take her through the narrows. Quite suddenly during the night it came on to blow a violent gale from the west. It was a dangerous situation. *Martin* was on a lee shore pitching violently and snatching at her anchor chain, it was pitch dark and they were in an area of very strong tides and numerous sandbanks. The crew tried to raise the anchor, but the load on the chain was such that the capstan was wrenched apart; the anchor party was just able to buoy the cable and let it go as reefed topsails were set. It was lucky *Martin* was such a fine sailer as most ships under this rig would sag off to leeward, but she drove ahead and clawed up into the main channel, then ran before the gale into Portsmouth. When the weather moderated they returned to try to recover the lost anchor and chain, but it remained too rough for boat work and a further gale confined *Martin* to an anchorage in Yarmouth roads. The anchor was never recovered. The boys on board *Martin* had had a taste of serious heavy weather ship handling.

After his very enjoyable spell in *Martin* it was time for Keyes to go back to school. He had to get through his lieutenant's exams, which he found a struggle, emerging with second class results. No academic, he always found written work a problem and also seems to have much preferred a day out with the local hounds to revising for his exams. Eventually he scraped through with second-class passes, survived some pilotage exams at Greenwich and was promoted sub-lieutenant in November 1891.

The next ship was *Immortalite,* an armoured cruiser of the Channel Squadron, which sailed on a winter cruise to Vigo in northern Spain. Here he distinguished himself by re-rigging one of the ship's boats and racing her against all comers from the British fleet visiting the bay. His modifications produced a most extraordinary looking vessel and she required a crew of thirty in addition to as much iron ballast as they could lay hands on. She was difficult to beat in light airs, but an awful handful in a strong breeze. Roger seems to have had a lifelong passion for racing in small boats and he was a competent, if never brilliant, helmsman. The cruise continued to Madeira and the Canary Islands, returning in time for Roger to hear that he was appointed to the Royal Yacht *Victoria and Albert.* In those days an appointment to the royal yacht was a distinct mark of favour on the part of the Admiralty and shows that Keyes had attracted favourable attention. He must have made a very good impression on Brackenbury, the captain of *Turquoise* and on the training squadron while he was serving in *Martin.* His father's service in India would also have been an advantage. He was obviously considered to be a young gentleman with prospects.

Service in the royal yacht does not seem to have suited Keyes particularly well. He found Queen Victoria 'an alarming old lady' and he loathed her Indian servant (John Brown's successor, Abdul Karim). He was frequently tasked with taking parties of young princesses to watch the racing at Cowes in an ungainly barge. The little girls were quite undisciplined when away from the court and romped about the boat so that he was in an agony of worry that they would fall overboard. There were, however, compensations. He frequently lunched with the royal family at Osborne and made contacts which were to prove useful in later life. Prince George, later King George V, with whom he made friends, was a particularly important part of the network which was to dominate naval affairs in the future. Roger was able to watch *Britannia, Hohenzollern* and the other great yachts race on the Solent, which was thrilling, and, most important of all, he and the other young officers posted to *Victoria and Albert* all received promotion at the end of the season.

Keyes's next posting was to the South East America Squadron. His ship *Beagle,* with a selection of other foreign warships, was in Rio de Janeiro standing by to protect merchantmen who were constantly being threatened by a somewhat half-hearted civil war that was in progress ashore. It was boring work for the sailors, enlivened by some boat sailing competitions, in which British crews successfully beat all comers hands down. Roger made great friends with some German junior naval officers but it was in discussion with them that he began to realise that there was a real possibility of war with Germany one day. The Germans, he learnt, deeply resented what they considered British arrogance in naval affairs and the fact that the British Empire had left no 'place in the sun' for Germany. Like most other Britons, Keyes had previously thought the very idea of war between two countries, united by so many family and commercial ties, quite impossible. Eventually the conflict in Brazil fizzled out and the squadron made its way south to the river Plate.

It was there that Roger was to meet a turning point in his life. South America, at that time, was a paradise for a man such as he, horseman, adventurer and sportsman. The land was undeveloped, fertile and available cheaply. There were innumerable horses to ride, huge tracts of land to exploit and immense flocks of ducks and geese to shoot. Already, enterprising Englishmen had settled in the former Spanish colony and lived a life of Riley, herding beef cattle and growing crops. Living was easy. The government was ineffective, so a man had to look after himself. Keyes was in his element. It seems that the squadron had little to do while showing the flag in Buenos Aires and Montevideo, except to challenge local teams to the occasional game of cricket. Leave was readily granted and Keyes made the most of it. Attractive, amusing and so obviously a gentleman, he soon made friends with the English communities in Argentina and in Uruguay and had a wonderful time as a guest at various big estancias. He soon learnt to rope a horse or a steer and to ride with the toughest of the gauchos. His twelve-bore accounted for many a local duck and goose. He was welcomed in estates up and down the country. There is an account of an embarrassing occasion during which he was taking a bath in a guesthouse on a big estate owned by a family called Dickenson. After a hard day's riding, he indulged in a hip bath in the bathroom of the little annex in which he was to sleep. Over dinner he was ragged unmercifully by his fellow guests who had overheard the remarks passed by some local girls who had happened to be walking past the annex, and, finding a place commanding a good view into the bathroom, gazed excitedly in. 'Oh how thin he is, but oh how white!!' Further comments on his anatomy, not suitable for publication, followed as the pale, thin Englishman continued his ablutions.

The days in the saddle were certainly hard. There were cattle to round up, polo games to play and huge distances around the estates to cover. For example, Keyes wrote:

> When we had ridden our horses to a standstill Kenyon suggested that I should try my hand at lassoing, and he mounted me on his best horse and showed me how to do it. I used the lasso like a sailor's heaving line and threw it into the brown mass getting a winner every time ... after lassoing a beast one paid out the lasso gradually from the coil in one's hand then put spurs to one's horse and galloped for the gate ... it was something like playing a fish. .... The horse then spread its legs and stood like a rock with the result that the beast was brought up with a jerk and fell heavily.

Great fun for the young lieutenant, but a vigorous and dangerous game requiring good horsemanship, nerve and great dexterity.

There was, however, a serious side to this wonderful visit to South America which eventually lasted for almost two years. Keyes confronted a potentially life-changing decision. Having made a very favourable impression on the local British community, prosperous, carefree and vigorous as it seemed, the young naval officer was tempted to scrape together enough cash to leave the Royal Navy, start his own ranch and settle in this wonderful, unexploited land. He was encouraged in this by his new friends, the Kenyons and the Dickensons, both English families prospering on the great cattle ranches. There was a further tie which is not well documented. Roger had fallen in love. The actual identity of his lady friend is not revealed, but it was clearly a serious affair and he wangled extra leave, rode huge distances across country and attended numerous balls and parties in order to be with her. If his suit had been successful there seems to be little doubt that he would have settled down to life as a rancher and Britain would have lost one of the most celebrated admirals of the twentieth century. It was not to be. Before *Beagle* left the Rio de la Plata, in February 1896, to pay off in Portsmouth, he learnt that his love had given her heart to another. Typical of his time and class, Keyes says little about his personal feelings, but it must have been a sadder, wiser, young man who left his ship. To make matters worse he had learnt of his father's death when *Beagle* made a brief stop on her long voyage home.

By the late 1890s the programme of naval shipbuilding demanded by the Naval Defence Act of 1889 was coming to fruition and the many new ships demanded further efforts to increase recruitment. The days of the press gang were far in the past, but the idea came up that instead of recruiting very young boys for training at sea, older youths of eighteen- to twenty-years-old might be induced to join the service if some smart looking small ships were to visit small ports around the coast and lay on entertainments, lectures and generate local publicity. Young men would join the ship and go to sea at once. One of these small ships, the corvette *Curacoa*, was commanded by Commander Jerram, who was later to rise to admiral's rank and play an undistinguished part in the Battle of Jutland. He was, however, a fine sailor and Roger was glad to be appointed to *Curacoa*. He was to have a somewhat tough few months as Jerram was inclined to pick on this young lieutenant who, he probably thought, was inclined to get above himself. Roger's energy and charm, however, made him a natural for the job of recruiting and training young men. Life on land in those days was still tough, many young people being underfed and in poor shape. Regular meals, vigorous exercise and a sense of purpose could transform a sallow young landsman into a vigorous seaman in quick time. *Curacoa* soon picked up her complement of about 150 recruits, Roger made sure he knew each one by name and became a firm but popular instructor. The only criticism levelled at him in the job came from some of his aristocratic friends living near ports which the ship visited. They complained bitterly that he kept trying to recruit their house servants and garden boys.

After a successful summer of recruiting cruises, *Curacoa* sailed to Madeira and the Canary Isles for the winter. It was here that Keyes was really able to show his mettle. The ship was anchored in Funchal Bay when the island was hit by one of the hurricanes which occasionally stray across the Atlantic. Jerram decided that she would have to ride out the storm at sea. The youngsters were battened down below and the handful of regular crew and instructors had to handle the ship. She was a fine, powerful, sea boat but had very high bulwarks so that when a big wave came aboard it sloshed around the deck, waist deep, and took a long time to clear through the scuppers. To make matters worse many of the heavy items secured on deck, the sheep pen, the anvil, one of the ship's boats, several large pieces of timber and innumerable smaller items, broke loose and careered about the deck, threatening to break limbs or smash deck fittings. When Roger came on watch at midnight he found a chaotic situation. The captain was on the bridge, but most of the crew and petty officers were not used to small sailing vessels, having served only on steam-powered warships and were at a loss to know what to do. Many of them were also helpless with seasickness.

As Roger was appraising the situation there was a terrific crash and the fore trysail broke out from its gaskets and commenced to flog itself to pieces with a noise like thunder. This was a situation in which Keyes revelled. He rounded up the few men still able to work and soon had things under control, saving the errant ship's boat and preventing any further damage. By dawn *Curacoa* was in fine fettle, standing off the island and waiting for the tail of the hurricane to pass over. His actions that night totally vindicated him in the eyes of Jerram, leading to an excellent report on his conduct and a life-long friendship. He wrote home to his mother: 'We had a most entertaining night and I have seldom enjoyed myself more'.

Chapter 3

Destroyers and Adventures in China

In addition to the new generation of battleships and cruisers being built under the Naval Defence Act, the Royal Navy was at length allowing some new thinking to penetrate its upper ranks. As we shall see there was plenty of resistance to it but gradually, under the leadership of strong modernisers like Scott and the great Jacky Fisher, things were beginning to change. The principal catalyst was the invention of the Whitehead torpedo. The self-propelled, or 'locomotive', torpedo was originally developed in the late 1860s but it took some time before its true significance was realised. For the first time in history a small ship could carry a weapon that was a serious threat to a very large one. In the classic sea battles of the eighteenth and early nineteenth centuries, while battleships on both sides would fight each other, the smaller ships (frigates, corvettes and brigs for example) would pull away and concentrate on picking up survivors or perhaps towing away damaged battleships. There was no way that their main armament could do serious damage to a full-sized man of war. The torpedo changed this completely. A puny torpedo-carrying craft could now disable or sink even the most powerful battleship. Realisation of this alarming fact struck the Admiralty in the 1880s. The French, it was rumoured, were building a fleet of fast steam launches, equipped with torpedoes, which would wait for a misty night to sneak across the Channel and sink British battleships at their moorings. Something must be done.

After some experiment the concept of the 'torpedo boat destroyer' (TBD) evolved. TBDs should be fast enough to run down and sink enemy torpedo craft with their gun armament, and indeed their usefulness could be extended by giving them torpedo tubes so that they could act as aggressor as well as defender. These rapidly became known simply as 'destroyers'. To understand the next few years of Keyes's life it is necessary to have a good picture of the destroyers of the day and life on board them.

Destroyers were built under contract to the Admiralty by over a dozen privately-owned shipyards. The yards were given only an outline of what the little ships were to be like, and a performance specification. If the ships did not achieve the contract speed they would still be purchased but the price would be reduced; if they exceeded it the yard would get a bonus. Destroyers of a particular class might therefore look quite different and have very different handling characteristics. The first class to be built, the A Class, were known as the '27 knotters', this being their rated maximum speed. Forty-three A-Class vessels were built between 1893 and 1895 and many of them remained in service up to the end of the First World War. A brief look at their vital statistics gives an idea of what they must have been like to serve in. Typically of 260 tons displacement, they were 200 feet long and 19 wide, drawing 7 feet of water. There was normally one 12-pounder gun and five quick-firing 6-pounders, the main armament being either two or three 14-inch torpedo tubes. They were driven by two three-cylinder steam piston engines developing 4,000 horsepower and the bunkers contained sixty tons of coal. Imagine for a moment a ship ten times as long as it was broad, only a little wider than a modern shipping container, but ten times as long, with furnaces which, at full speed, would demand six tons of coal an hour to be shovelled into them by hand. The great engines would need constant attention as bearings overheated and steam pipes leaked. Somehow, stokers and engineers would have to tend these monsters while being flung about by rough seas, scalded by escaping steam and deafened by the roar of fans sucking air into the engine room. The crew on deck were not much better off. In anything except a calm sea, water was continually coming aboard and sluicing down the decks as the bows plunged into the waves. The helmsman was accommodated in a tiny conning tower which protruded a few feet above the deck and from which the view was minimal. There was no proper bridge structure, only a canvass breakwater behind which the officer of the watch would stand, completely soaked. Cooking and sleeping facilities were minimal; the crews lived ashore when in port and the bunks were sufficient only for one watch at a time to sleep. The little galley could manage little more than hot drinks or soup. Destroyer crews were compensated for their uncomfortable working conditions by a special 'hard-living allowance'.

Relationships and procedures in destroyers were inevitably entirely different to those which prevailed on the great ships of the fleet. With a complement of only fifty or so men and three officers, destroyers had no place for the formal, almost ritualistic practices which governed behaviour on big ships. A destroyer crew was a small closely-knit team, sharing uncomfortable and often dangerous conditions, with no time for anything getting in the way of rapid communication and swift action. Gradually, alongside the highly structured ranks of the Royal Navy, there emerged a quite distinct 'small ship navy' populated by young, often charismatic, officers and crews who enjoyed hardship and the opportunity to work in an informal environment. It is difficult to imagine a man better suited than Keyes for service in this branch of his profession. A born leader, fine seaman and somewhat irreverent in his attitude to his seniors, he was delighted to be posted to his first command, *Opossum,* an A-Class 27-knot destroyer, almost as soon as he left *Curacoa.* He was rather junior in the service to be given a command and he attributed his success to the good reports given him by Jerram. *Opossum* was one of a destroyer-training squadron consisting of six ships, five 27-knot A-Class and *Bat,* a C-Class 30-knotter. As the A-Class ships were all built by different yards, they had quite differing hull forms, Roger being considered especially lucky as *Opossum* had by far the best captain's cabin. There followed an idyllic year cruising about the south coast of England with the training squadron. Sometimes they would anchor for the night in a secluded creek, often they would return to their base at Devonport for a night ashore. Occasionally the flotilla would undertake quite exciting high-speed night exercises. Towards the end of his year in *Opossum* Keyes was selected to demonstrate his ship to a delegation from the Imperial Japanese Navy. The exercise must have been successful as Japan purchased a large batch of destroyers from British yards and indeed used them to deadly effect against the Russians in 1905.

Keyes, always keen for some sport, enjoyed beagling with the Dartmouth pack. His young brother, Adrian, was a cadet at Dartmouth and Roger made great friends with his commander, Craddock, also a great beagler. As we shall see, this friendship was to become very significant a little later, in China. Craddock was to lose his life in 1914 at the Battle of Coronel. Two more of Roger's brothers were in his thoughts at this time, both serving in the family's old stomping ground on the North West Frontier. Charles, a subaltern in the Guides, was injured by a sword cut at Chakdara and Terence, in the King's Own Scottish Borderers, was also wounded attacking Dargai. Roger's reaction to the news tells us a great deal about him. He was madly jealous. Why should his younger siblings get all the fun of a real fight? It wasn't fair. He wrote excitedly to his mother then, remembering that she must be worried, slipped in a thoughtful sentence: 'I hope it will soon be over. It must be awfully anxious work for you, poor mother'.

Training course over, Keyes was clearly deemed fit to command a destroyer on a foreign station. November 1898 saw him posted to the

China station to take command of *Hart,* another A-Class destroyer built by Fairfields in 1894.

Chinese affairs were in a sorry state at the end of the nineteenth century. Japan and Russia were both attempting territorial expansion in Korea and Manchuria and were in contention for the strategically important port of Port Arthur on the northern side of the entrance to the Gulf of Bohai. Japanese forces invariably proved far superior to any rivals, but Japan wished to stay on good terms with western nations and abandoned, for the time being, claims on the Chinese and Korean mainland. Russia was therefore able to occupy Port Arthur. Germany, France and Britain were impressed by the ease with which Chinese defence forces had been pushed aside and determined to seize territory, or at least commercial concessions, for themselves. Germany, partly under the pretence of protecting missionaries, procured a large concession in Tsing-tao and Britain expanded her territory of Hong Kong by negotiating the long-term lease of the 'New Territories'. At the same time the port of Wei-hai-wei, at the southern entrance to the Gulf of Bohai, was leased to her for as long as the Russians occupied Port Arthur. France obtained Kwang-chou-wan. China's situation resembled that of a dying whale at the mercy of hungry sharks.

Almost as soon as he arrived in Hong Kong, the two old destroyers on station, Roger's *Hart* and her sister ship *Handy,* were withdrawn from service, being in need of complete overhaul. Their respective captains, Keyes and Lieutenant Kelly, were transferred to two more modern destroyers, *Fame* and *Whiting. Fame,* Roger's ship, had been built by Thorneycroft in 1896. She displaced 360 tons and was driven by 5,800 horsepower piston engines. She was unusual in that her structure was built of high-strength steel to save weight. Unlike *Whiting* she had a rather broad, shallow stern and two rudders, thus having a draft of only 7 feet 2 inches, as opposed to the 9 feet of her companion. This arrangement made the captain's cabin in the stern very low and cramped, but her shallow draft was to become vitally important in the role she was to play. Roger was fortunate in his choice of officers. Sub-Lieutenant Wilfred Tomkinson was first lieutenant and Lieutenant John Ham was chief engineer. Both became trusted messmates and firm friends. Not so welcome on board was a multitude of cockroaches who seem to have joined the ship when she was being held in reserve. She had to be shut down and fumigated for several days to get rid of them. After a general clean up, however, she became a smart, happy ship, under her young captain and her crew would face any danger under his leadership. As we shall see, there was to be no shortage of challenges.

For the first few months Hong Kong was fairly quiet as *Fame* was undergoing a refit: Roger was able to indulge his passion for polo three days a week, riding the miniscule Chinese ponies which abounded in Hong Kong. Among the friends he made while playing was Prince Henry of Prussia, who was in charge of the German naval squadron on the China station. He was a keen sportsman and a great asset to the social scene, as was the princess, his wife. As well as polo there were steeplechases to ride in at Shanghai, quail to shoot and a punishing round of parties and social events. Admiral Seymour, the senior British officer, seems to have encouraged socialising by his officers. His flag captain was no less a person than John Jellicoe who was to lead the Grand Fleet at Jutland in 1916. By March 1899 *Fame's* refit was complete and Roger was able to put her through her paces. Her twin-rudder arrangement made her exceptionally handy and her captain and crew delighted in frightening the locals almost to death by charging through the harbour at a terrific speed and stopping the ship almost in her own length as she came up to her mooring buoy. Keyes enjoyed a bit of showing off.

Very soon the first signs of trouble erupted around Hong Kong. Britain had acquired the lease of mainland territories adjoining the island, the New Territories, and teams of workmen were being employed building barracks and some rudimentary defences along the new frontier. The locals became incensed at the idea of 'foreign devils' occupying their country. They were spurred on by members of the 'Boxer' faction, fanatical Chinese nationalists who were, at that point, outlawed by the government in Peking but were nevertheless extremely active and apt to murder missionaries, foreigners and Chinese Christians. In an attempt to put a stop to these activities the British decided on a mission to the local viceroy in Canton, hoping to persuade him to send sufficient forces to the area to restore order and allow the works to proceed in safety. *Fame* was tasked to bring the Governor of Hong Kong and a large party of diplomats and officers to Canton to confront the viceroy. Canton was about five miles upriver from the sea and the approaches to the river mouth and the river itself were very shallow and tidal. Departure of the party was delayed over and over again, and Keyes was desperate to be off so as not to miss the tide in the river. Eventually they set off with a local pilot who proved to be utterly useless and was terrified when *Fame* charged out to sea at almost 30 knots. Speed had to be reduced in the river, due to heavy traffic, but the journey was accomplished without incident, *Fame's* propeller churning up yellow mud as she forced her way up to the town quay. The whole party, including Keyes, changed into full-dress uniform in the consulate and were then carried in chairs to the viceroy's palace.

After some comically formal negotiations, the meeting was concluded and the British re-embarked. It was getting dark and the pilot was distraught when Keyes refused to wait to 'catchee moon' but charged downriver in the dark and arrived back in Hong Kong at 9.55 that evening. The effect of this mission on the behaviour of the Chinese was minimal but it gave Keyes and his crew a lot of extra confidence and laid the foundation of his reputation as a fine, no nonsense, ship's captain.

It soon became clear that nothing was being done by the Chinese viceroy to settle things on the borders of the New Territories and this brought Keyes the opportunity to get involved in some of the fighting for which he was longing. In the small hours of the morning he was summoned with orders to coal ship immediately and sail into Mirs Bay in support of *Whiting* which had already departed carrying senior officers and 100 troops. The reason for all this activity was that the Chinese had besieged a newly-built police post in great numbers and the senior police officer had called for immediate armed assistance. As dawn broke *Fame* found herself in thick fog. While in *Opossum* Roger had developed a technique for navigating along a coast in fog by using his siren to create an echo off the high rocky cliffs. He put this unorthodox method of navigation into practice as he approached the entrance to the bay. All went well until the fog lifted and they saw *Whiting* dead ahead with her bows stove in, pumping hard. She had hit a cliff head on, but luckily only the bow compartment was flooded. She was towed off and repaired locally. The troops were landed but found that the Chinese had retreated and the police were safe. A few days later more serious trouble occurred when the British governor decided that there should be a ceremony of hauling up the British flag in the New Territories. The Chinese resistance got to know about this and a large force equipped with *jingals*, a primitive type of short-range artillery, attempted to drive a small contingent of British-Indian troops off the site selected for the ceremony. *Fame* was tasked to take some troops and signallers to support the defenders. Keyes and Major Long, in command of the soldiers, decided not to wait for promised reinforcements but to attack the Chinese at once with their small force. To their delight they were too far from Hong Kong for any superior officer to be able to intervene. Supported by effective covering fire from *Fame*'s 12-pounder, the British quickly had the enemy on the run, Roger leading one of the assaulting columns. Night fell and the next day a large British force arrived to observe the flag hoisting, not aware of the fact that Keyes and Long had renewed their advance and had driven the Chinese from all the surrounding villages. The ceremony was able to take place in peace but the next night a force of some thousands of Chinese assembled and attempted to storm across a causeway between the New Territories and Hong Kong to attack the city itself. This was easily repelled, and the situation stabilised. Some hundreds of Chinese were killed, the British had fifteen men struck by musket balls, but all at too long range to do serious injury.

Keyes wrote home to his mother:

> It was awfully bad luck their making such a poor stand. If they had only given us a decent fight I might have got the DSO and early promotion probably, but of course they cannot take any notice of this – it was such a farce.

The incidents did indeed show that ill-armed, badly-led and poorly-trained Chinese forces were easy meat for properly trained and officered troops. The lesson was not lost on Keyes.

During the next few weeks, however, it was the sea, not the Chinese, which proved threatening. *Fame* and the now repaired *Whiting* were despatched to Wei-Hai-Wei where the main activity seems to have been arranging polo games and levelling a cricket pitch. While the latter operation was in progress a German squadron commanded by Prince Henry arrived. 'What strange people you are,' he declared. 'I find the Russians here building barracks and fortifications [he was doing the same thing himself in Kiaochow] and I find you building a cricket pitch!'

The squadron destroyers were joined by the main part of the China Squadron including the battleship *Barfleur* whose commander was no less than David Beatty, who was to become a lifetime friend. He had already won his spurs for his courageous conduct in Egypt and was clearly a coming man. Together the squadron steamed south east towards Port Hamilton, a natural harbour occupied by the British and formed by some small islands at the southern tip of the Korean peninsula. The passage was stormy and visibility bad. That sector of the China Sea had not been properly surveyed although it is encumbered by rocky islets. There were known to be strong tidal sets in the area making navigation at night extremely hazardous, especially when there was no moon and no way of taking a navigational fix. The squadron was spread out with *Fame* on the port flank and *Whiting* to starboard. Roger was on his bridge when a great black rock ringed by breaking waves reared up right ahead. *Fame* immediately turned hard to starboard, firing rockets and blowing her siren. She was just in time to prevent the flagship crashing into the rocks. The situation was saved, but it had been a near thing.

After a short stay the squadron moved up the Korean coast, stopping in several inlets. This allowed the officers to indulge in a little fishing. Both Keyes and Tomkinson landed some magnificent salmon, one of which was tactfully sent to the admiral. Soon enough, however, another maritime hazard reared its head. When entering the protected harbour at Korniloff Bay, the cruiser *Bonaventure* hit an uncharted rock. The ship was badly damaged and all her armament and stores had to be removed. The Royal Navy was brilliant at salvage at the time and she was eventually pulled off the rock and made her way slowly home to Hong Kong. *Fame* had been the first ship to reach her and to stand by to take off her crew if necessary. A more serious hazard threatened *Fame* on her return from Vladivostok where she had been sent to send telegrams home as wireless was not fitted to British warships at that time. Passing through a narrow passage between islands she ran into the tail end of a typhoon. The wind was not especially strong but an enormous following sea caused the little ship to yaw violently and made her almost impossible to steer. In Keyes's own words:

> As we were running at about twenty knots, yawing at least three points each way owing to the following swell we saw right ahead of us as we yawed to starboard a great pinnacle of rock. I put the helm hard a-starboard, and we went through two or three agonising seconds wondering if she would swing enough on the yaw to port to clear the rock. We tore past on the crest of the next great swell, as it broke with a roar on the rock, almost alongside us, and Tomkinson and I looked at each other speechless with relief.

Apart from these maritime adventures, Keyes seems to have taken away from Korea a few impressions which are typical of the man. He thought the children he met were astonishingly sweet and playful, but most of the women were ugly; perhaps the beauties were kept indoors. The fishing was good but local salmon would not rise to a fly; he had to use a spoon. The pheasants that had been introduced by the u.c. navy for sport many years ago seemed to have learnt not to get up, and it needed a good dog to get them to fly. He was cross that he had not brought one. The local rock pigeons, however, yielded good sport. It is difficult to imagine a more archetypical comment on a far country by a nineteenth-century English gentleman.

During the following winter, 1899-1900, Keyes was forced to eat his heart out in Hong Kong. He was furious because other naval officers were gaining glory fighting a serious enemy – the Boers in South Africa and he had had to deal with nothing but the pathetic Chinese. To rub salt into the wound, two cruisers just arrived on the China station, *Terrible* and *Powerful*, had been in the thick of the fighting. *Terrible* reached Hong Kong in April 1900, bringing with her a replacement crew for *Fame,* Roger, however, remained with her as captain. *Whiting's* captain was relieved by an old friend of Keyes, Colin Mackenzie.

On the Chinese mainland things had been moving apace during the winter. The Emperor Guangxu was horrified by the success the Japanese had had against Chinese forces and by the obvious superiority of Western arms and the methods of warfare which had been adopted by his enemies. He introduced a programme called 'the hundred days reform' which was intended modernise both the constitution and the armed forces. Unfortunately for him, the programme was very unpopular with many of the mandarin class and with the army, running totally against the strongly-held Confucian ethos embraced by a large proportion of the population. It was regarded as a capitulation to the principles of the 'foreign devils' who were tearing off great chunks of Chinese territory. Guangxu's domineering aunt, Cixi, the dowager empress, put herself at the head of the anti-modernisation movement. She quickly grabbed the reins of power and forced the Emperor into retirement, which he spent happily restoring clocks and watches and performing occasional ceremonial functions. The Boxers, fiercely anti-foreign, had at first been opposed by Guangxu and by Cixi, but eventually their nationalistic fervour weighed on the dowager empress and she connived at their ruthless slaughter of Christians and occasional forays against foreign outposts. Boxer fighters were sometimes fanatically brave and were brainwashed into thinking that bullets could not hurt them. Though ill-equipped they were formidable opponents. Matters came to a head when the Boxers appeared in Peking, murdered a German diplomat and besieged Western embassies and the Roman Catholic cathedral in the city. Chinese imperial forces joined with the Boxers and Cixi ordered that all foreigners should be killed. An international force from Russia, Japan, Britain, Germany, France, Italy, the USA and Austria-Hungary was assembled to rescue the embassies and put the Boxers to flight.

Rescue of the embassies was only one factor in the fighting which was to occur. Western powers had not given up on their scramble for Chinese territory and trade concessions. Particularly important was the contention between Japan and Russia for command of northern China. Both were determined to seize as much as possible for themselves and, even more important, to deny it to the other.

The only practical way in which a relief force could reach Peking was to enter the Gulf of Bohai, land troops at the mouth of the river Peiho, then advance on the capital by way of Tientsin (Maps 1 & 2). This was by no means easy as the gulf was very shallow, forcing large ships to anchor some twenty miles offshore. The entrance to the river was encumbered by mud and sandbanks so that only small ships could enter, and even they were restricted to a few hours each side of high tide. Once inside, however, there was normally enough water in the river for tugs and small vessels to get up to Tientsin. There were numerous fortifications along the river, the most formidable being the three Taku forts at the mouth of the estuary. These had recently been modernised and re-armed by Krupp and were believed to be strongly manned and very effective. There was a railway between Tonku, the garrison town near the mouth of the river, to the city of Tientsin, and from there on to Peking. (See Map 2) Tientsin was itself a considerable city with trading posts and consulates from many western countries and a significant number of international inhabitants.

Obviously sea power was to be a major factor in the landing and support of the rescue mission. The Royal Navy, being pre-eminent in Chinese waters, would have plenty of work to do. At the end of May 1900 the commander of the British Fleet, Admiral Sir Edward Seymour, was asked to send marines to Peking to protect the western diplomats. He ordered *Fame* and *Whiting* to the mouth of the Peiho to act as a communications link between the main fleet, anchored twenty miles offshore, and troops ashore as well as a few shallow draft gun vessels in the river. There was now quite a large international naval force in the offing, including ships from Germany, Russia and Japan as well as the UK. Close to the river mouth HMS *Algerine*, a sloop mounting a battery of 4-inch guns, was anchored. *Fame*, due to her shallow draft, was immediately busily engaged in running in and out of the river carrying personnel and messages since radio was not then fitted to ships on the China station. Keyes and Tomkinson at first used a river pilot for these journeys, but soon found out that the river pilots, who were mostly British, were very inconsistent in the courses they took. Over a glass of whiskey, Keyes wormed the truth out of one of them. They had no more clue than anyone else where the deepest water was but 'a man had to live'. From then on *Fame* did her work mainly without a pilot. In addition to carrying messages, she soon found herself carrying parties of marines ashore, landing them at Tongku so that they could take the train to Tientsin and protect the international community there.

Britain was not formally at war with China and at this stage there was no fighting. Keyes, however, had a good look at the forts and noticed that their guns frequently followed *Fame* on her comings and goings. He also noticed that the dockyard at Tongku was occupied by a large, fairly new cruiser in dry dock and four brand-new German-built Shichau destroyers alongside the wharf. These were exceptionally fine little ships, well-armed with guns and torpedoes and capable of at least 32 knots. They were specially designed for work in shallow water, drawing only 6 feet.

On 5 June *Fame* landed Seymour and a party of officers including his chief of staff, John Jellicoe, on a mission to inspect the situation at Tientsin, returning him to his flagship in the evening. No sooner had the admiral reached *Centurion* than an urgent message arrived from Peking to say that the diplomatic colony there was in grave danger and short of supplies. They had all moved into the British embassy building as this was the easiest to protect. Seymour called a conference of the senior officers of all the navies present and it was decided that he himself would put together an international force of soldiers, seamen and marines and move up to Peking by train to relieve the besieged diplomats. It is an astonishing, even bizarre, thought: a sixty-year-old British admiral advancing in a railway carriage with 2,000 troops, marines and bluejackets, British, German, Russian, French, Austrian, Japanese, Italian and American, on the capital city of the most populous nation in the world, with whose sovereign government Britain was not at war. Keyes and *Fame* were much too useful in the river for Keyes to be allowed to go with Seymour, a decision which made him furious. Once again, he was going to miss out on the fighting. He did, however, have the satisfaction of conveying Seymour himself to the quayside. This proved to be something of a drama. Keyes had warned Seymour that the tide was ebbing and there was no time to spare; nevertheless the admiral was not ready until long after the water was too low to enter the river safely and it was pitch dark. He insisted on going at once, however, and Keyes happened to find the only competent river pilot, so *Fame* was just able to make the quay, her propellers churning through the mud and her captain praying for her to keep moving.

We should briefly follow the progress of this extraordinary force on its way to Peking. For twenty-five miles the trains ran merrily along, crossing a key river bridge and ignoring a large Chinese force under General Nie Shicheng which made no attempt to interfere. The Boxers had, however, by this time, allied with the Chinese Imperial army. They tore up the railway lines and made a series of fearless but ineffective attacks, losing some hundreds of men in the process. The invaders could now advance only as fast as they could repair the railway track, giving another Imperial army under General Dong Fuxiang, which consisted mainly of Muslim soldiers, ample time to prepare to resist them. A large force, including 5,000 well-armed cavalry made an attack around the town of Langfang (See Map 2). The attack was easily repelled but Seymour's force was running short of food and ammunition and it was decided to abandon the advance and return to Tientsin. Unfortunately for them, however, Chinese forces in their rear had by this time received orders to fight and Boxers had infiltrated into the countryside around. To make matters worse the railway bridge over the Ha had been destroyed, forcing the retreating army to march along the riverbank where it was subject to constant skirmishing attacks. In one of these John Jellicoe was wounded, almost fatally. The force was starving and running out of ammunition to defend itself when it stumbled on a massive, almost undefended Chinese arms dump at Tsi-Ku, close to Pei -Tsung. Refreshed and re-provisioned, they continued towards Tientsin, meeting on their way a British relief force from the town's garrison, summoned by a Chinese runner sent by the admiral. They staggered, exhausted, into the city on 25 June. This was an ill-planned expedition and a humiliation for the Western forces. Seymour was lucky to escape with only sixty-two dead and 232 wounded. The Boxers showed incredible courage and commitment, charging at entrenched rifles with no regard whatever for danger. So confident were they of their invulnerability to rifle fire that it often took three or four shots at close range to stop a charging, fanatical swordsman.

We must now return to the activities of Keyes and the small ships in the river estuary. These had been joined by *Alacrity* under Captain Craddock who Roger knew to be spoiling for a fight just as much as he was. Together they cruised around the river mouth taking a good look at the Taku forts. They noted that the two on the north side of the river were linked by a massive stone wall and were mutually protective. They had to land to reconnoitre the south fort which stood by itself and seemed a quite formidable obstacle. There was a key weakness, however. They found the slope of the walls of the forts so gentle in places that it would be possible for attackers to run up them. The forts had 5- to 8-inch swivel-mounted guns which could command the whole of the estuary and the town of Tongku, but could not be depressed enough to cover the sloping sides of the fortifications. The two officers made a careful study of the topography, which would prove useful in the following days.

On 15 June Keyes was ordered to go up to Tientsin and report on the situation. At Tongku he learned from Captain Lans, commander of the German gunboat *Iltis*, moored alongside the quay, that the Chinese Army was trying to commandeer all rolling stock on the line. *Iitis*'s guns were preventing anything from moving except the regular trains to Tientsin. Arriving there himself Roger found general despair about the fate of Seymour and his force. Boxers were everywhere, the telegraph lines were destroyed and no relief column could get through. There was also a severe shortage of artillery and ammunition in the city itself. It was vital that this information should be taken to the fleet as soon as possible and so Roger commandeered a railway engine to take him back to Tongku. A troop train full of Chinese imperial soldiers, on their way to reinforce the garrison at the Taku forts, was on the line just in front of him. The Chinese soldiers paused on their way to jeer at the foreign officer scurrying about the station. The driver of the commandeered locomotive was very reluctant to take his passengers into the station at Tongku, Keyes encouraged him by drawing his pistol and crying 'Fightee Fightee!' which seemed to have the desired effect. There was a clear danger that not just Seymour, but Tientsin itself, with its Western inhabitants and its garrison would be cut off from the fleet.

Keyes had some difficulty in getting Admiral Bruce, in command of the British squadron in Seymour's absence, to understand the situation. Eventually, however, tugs were loaded with supplies and weapons for Tientsin. The major question was whether to attack the Taku Forts. It was extremely difficult for the senior naval officers present, representing as they did eight separate nations, to decide to take military action against a country with which none of them were at war. However, the situation was serious and immediate. The forts could close the river mouth at any time and destroy the city with their heavy guns. The Chinese had already started to mine the river mouth. The four destroyers alongside the quay, mounting a surprise attack, could make short work of the British, German and American ships in the estuary. Without relief from the forces at Tientsin, the embassies in Peking would certainly fall. It was eventually agreed that an ultimatum would be given to the commander of the forts. Either he surrendered them that night or the allies would open fire.

In the event of conflict the first essential would be to get rid of the four destroyers which were a very real threat to all the allied ships in the river and its estuary. This had to be done quietly so as not to alert the forts. Keyes had a plan. He had watched the four for several days and saw that they were loaded with equipment, had crews of about fifty each, but were very poorly guarded at night. His scheme was that both *Fame* and *Whiting* should take a tender in tow and fill it with a boarding party of about eight men. Other boarders would be assembled in *Fame* and *Whiting* themselves. The length of the tow would be the same as the gap between each of the Chinese destroyers, and *Whiting* would be the same distance astern of *Fame*'s tender. The four destroyers could thus be boarded at the same moment from *Fame, Whiting* and two tenders. The operation was scheduled for low tide – about 2.00am. It was strictly ordered that the ship's guns should not be used except in a dire emergency as this would certainly alert the forts. The main weapons used would be cutlasses and iron bars from the stokehold.

The ultimatum was delivered and was answered by heavy fire from the forts. Both *Fame* and *Whiting* were anchored close to Russian gunboats in the river and these were hit heavily but the destroyers were unharmed. They forged ahead to moor alongside the four Chinese destroyers. This was achieved and the Chinese crews, taken completely by surprise, were driven off without difficulty. Men escaping from the destroyers were allowed to get ashore without molestation and they vanished into the night. No one on the British ships was hurt. Some of the escapers turned round when they got into the dockyard and opened fire on the intruders but by this time Keyes's men had managed to get the main armament of the newly captured destroyers into action and the Chinese fled again. Keyes himself got together a party of seamen and cleared the dockyard completely. As they made ready to depart, the destroyers came under fire from a heavy gun somewhere ashore. *Whiting* was hit, with a shell fetching up unexploded in a coal bunker, but no serious damage was done. There were some difficulties in getting the four prizes safely moored and *Whiting* managed to get stuck on the mud so it was not until after 6.00am that Keyes had completed his mission. He was immediately hailed by the tug *Fawan* which was supposed to be delivering supplies upriver to Tientsin. The captain told him that his crew refused to go further upriver because of a fort, which was hitherto unknown to the Europeans, at Hsi-Cheng, several miles from Tongku. Keyes took *Fame* up to inspect this fort and it appeared to be strongly manned with several 6-inch guns commanding the river. He decided to leave this for another day and set off back downriver to the battle around the forts at the river mouth. He was too late.

Cradock had found himself in command of a force of British, Japanese, German, Italian and Russian sailors, tasked to capture the three formidable Taku forts which he had earlier reconnoitred with Roger. He himself was extremely fit and an able and vigorous commander. His first objective was the North-West fort. He led his men towards it but was met by concentrated heavy fire. He halted in a protected position and called on supporting fire from *Algerine* and the German gunboat *Iltis*. This rapidly silenced most of the enemy artillery and Cradock's party, consisting of British and Japanese seamen, charged towards the walls of the fort, ran clean up the sloping walls and clambered in through the gun-ports and over the parapet. Most of the defenders then fled so the gates were opened and the fortress was taken. The North fort then fell without too much resistance. Cradock simply ran at it, leading a force of British and Japanese who contended hotly to be first over the wall. They then stormed the gatehouse from inside the fort and allowed their comrades in. The Russians, who seemed to have held back from most of the fighting, then set to work bayonetting any wounded defenders. Japanese joined in this disgusting business until Cradock managed to get the situation under control. The North forts were then in a position to open fire on the South fort which was to be the final objective. Much more heavily armed than the other two, the South fort had been shelling ships in the river to some effect, seriously damaging a Russian gunboat. Lens, the captain of *Iltis,* who had helped Roger in the railway yard at Tongku, and Johnston Stewart, the captain of *Algerine*, had calculated that if they got close enough to the South fort its guns would not be able to depress enough to hit their hulls, so they moved downriver as soon as the North forts seemed to have fallen. At first they came under heavy fire and Lans himself was seriously wounded but, once in position, close to the fort, they opened rapid bombardment and were rewarded by a terrific explosion when the magazine blew up. This was a signal for the remaining Chinese to flee, so Cradock and a small party could be ferried across the river and take possession of the prize.

Altogether this was a brilliant victory by an international scratch force against a much more numerous enemy in well-prepared positions, with superb leadership by Cradock, Johnston Stewart and Lens. Allied losses were thirty-five killed and 137 wounded. Chinese casualties are unknown but were very heavy. Everyone present was impressed by the courage and fighting skills of the Japanese. The Russians, it was agreed, put up a pretty poor show.

In the early twentieth century it was still the custom for a captain and crew to be rewarded by the Admiralty for the value of ships captured in action. Roger had hoped for good prize money for the four state-of-the-art brand-new destroyers he had captured from the Chinese. He was to be bitterly disappointed. It was agreed that the prizes should be distributed among the nations involved in the action. One went to Russia, one to Japan, one, for some reason, to France and only one to Britain. She joined the fleet with the name of *Taku*. We shall meet her again in the course of this narrative. Even for her Keyes received only a minimal payment. It was ruled that as Britain was not formally at war with China at the time no prize money was payable and only a miniscule token payment could be made for the £50,000 ship. Before the distribution of the ships was agreed, Roger had had a violent quarrel with the Russians. One of the destroyers had gone onto the mud and Roger had put a small Japanese crew on board to keep her safe until he could pull her off. He was disgusted when he saw her flying a Russian flag. He stormed ashore in a fury and confronted the senior Russian officer in the dockyard, finding that this gentleman had also taken over command of the shore-side installations and of a Chinese warship which Roger himself had captured with no help whatever from the Russians. There were furious exchanges between the parties about who should fly what flag. Keyes eventually faced the Russians down and towed the destroyer off the mud, flying the British flag, then delivered her to the flagship to await disposal. The episode did not meet with Admiral Bruce's approval. He was terribly afraid that he would be held responsible for waging war without proper authorisation when he agreed to the attack on the destroyers and the forts and, also, worried that he might be criticised for upsetting the Russians whose friendship the British government was keen to cultivate. Worst of all, he was deeply concerned about what might be happening to Seymour, his chief, as a result of his attack on the forts. He knew that the admiral was blundering about on the way to Peking, out of communication and subject to numerous disturbing rumours. To an extent he was right to worry. The Chinese attack on Seymour's force at Langfang seems to have been prompted by the fighting at the Taku forts. Having such fire-eaters as Cradock and Keyes under his command must have cost Admiral Bruce a lot of sleep. Anyway from then on he decided that no more unauthorised activity should take place. He expressly ordered Keyes to stick to his task of acting as a high-speed ferry and not to even think of any further attacks on Chinese troops or installations.

The situation at Tientsin had now deteriorated to crisis levels. The Chinese controlled all access points to the city and supplies for the defenders were running very short. Messages were coming in by the occasional runner stressing the terrible conditions there; a typical one read as follows:

> Hard pressed, heavy fighting; losses 150 killed and wounded. Chinese Imperial artillery shelling the Settlement; women and children are all in cellars; fires all over Settlement; everyone worn out with incessant fighting.

A relief column was scraped together, consisting mainly of Russian and British troops and some bluejackets accompanied by naval guns – in fact the very guns that had been used for the relief of Ladysmith a year earlier. They fought their way through to reinforce the defenders but there was still a critical shortage of supplies, and especially of ammunition. The Tonku-Tientsin railway had been cut and there was no way of re-supplying the garrison by water as the Peiho river was closed by the fort which Keyes had reconnoitred at Hsi-cheng. In addition to this fort there was a large contingent of Tartar cavalry encamped a few miles away who would come to the aid of the fort if it was threatened. Keyes, however, was undeterred. He had seen the fort when he ventured up the river after capturing the four destroyers and was not convinced that it was as formidable as it looked. As for the cavalry, he believed that they would be in transit to join the besiegers of Tientsin and would move on after a short stay. In spite of strict orders not to make any move against the fort or to take *Fame* upriver towards it, he began to hatch a plan. At first he tried to persuade a Russian admiral whom he had befriended to co-operate with him in an attack, using the gunboats lying in the river. The Russian immediately pronounced the scheme ridiculous. Roger then worked on the local German commander with no more success. Captain Warrender, however, who was the senior British naval officer ashore, was a little more helpful. Under the influence of his forceful subordinate he wrote to Admiral Bruce:

> Dear Admiral
> I am very anxious to send the *Fame* up the river for a few miles to see whether there are any obstructions and whether the fort is occupied. Can I do this this afternoon? The river is very necessary for transport.
>
> > Yours sincerely
> > George Warrender

The reply came back:

> Under no circumstances is the Fame to risk being fired on by a fort, when other tugs and steamboats are available for this purpose. Eliminating this risk, you can employ *Fame* THIS AFTERNOON for the purpose of reconnoitring the river.

Roger had been given an inch. He would not be true to himself if he did not take at least a mile. When there was fighting in prospect he was determined to be in the middle of it. With Warrender on board, together with a pilot and Mr Baldwin, an English trader who knew the area and spoke Chinese, *Fame* stood innocently up the river. Baldwin was put ashore some way downstream of the fort and wandered about among the locals enquiring about the position in the fort. No, no one knew how many were inside. No, they had not seen much activity there recently. No, no one knew anything about the Tartar cavalry supposed to be camped a little way inland. Baldwin came aboard again that evening and reported to Keyes and Warrender. Roger then declared that unless they dropped down river immediately he could not be responsible for the safety of his ship, navigating the shallows in the dark. This was a complete red herring. The real reason was that he did not want Warrender to see the fort and its formidable armament. That evening he had a further meeting with Warrender, 'Surely,' he said:

> we would not be stretching the admiral's permission too far if *Fame* slipped quickly upstream first thing tomorrow morning to take a quick look at the fort? After all that's what we were instructed to do and we haven't seen it yet.

Warrender agreed and Keyes spent the rest of the evening rushing around his friends in nearby British warships to borrow men, explosives and Bickford's slow-burning fuse in sufficient quantities to carry out the total destruction of the fort. He also persuaded a young naval surgeon to join the party. The pilot and Mr Baldwin bravely remained on board for what seemed to be a suicide mission. That very night news arrived that Admiral Seymour had taken the arsenal at Xigu. He and his column were still short of food and were carrying hundreds of sick and wounded men. With help the party could probably fight their way to Tientsin, but then the shortage of ammunition and provisions there would become even more acute. Somehow, the supply route up the river must be opened.

At first light *Fame* steamed upriver and boldly moored in deep water right under the guns of the fort. Keyes, Duncan, the surgeon, Mascull, *Fame*'s gunner, and thirty-two men stormed ashore. Finding the gates open, they rushed into the fort which seemed to be crowded with Chinese soldiers. These soldiers put up no resistance at all but fled from the fort and melted away into the village and barracks. Sentries were posted to look out for the Tartar cavalry and the rest of the party ran to the gun emplacements where they found that ancient muzzle loaders had been removed and replaced with six brand new 5.9-inch Krupp guns commanding the river in both directions. These were immediately blown up. Meanwhile Baldwin had been questioning the locals about where the magazine was located and warning them to keep away as there was going to be a big explosion. The magazine was found to be full of ammunition, gunpowder, rockets and bits and pieces of artillery. They piled all this together and added all the explosive they had brought. Keyes lit the fuse himself and ran for shelter, arriving just too late. There was a massive explosion which shook all the shipping in the river and rattled the windows of the main fleet twenty miles away out to sea. A few seconds later a deluge of masonry came showering down onto the attackers. The sentries suffered some nasty cuts and bruises and Keyes himself was hurled to the ground, losing his helmet. When the dust settled he found it again, lying under a piece of rubble, squashed completely flat by the impact. Admiral Bruce, in his flagship, felt his cabin shaken by the explosion. 'I am sure,' he said to his secretary, 'that is Master Keyes. I only hope he is not on top of it'.

Keyes reported to the admiral, who, in spite of Roger's flagrant insubordination, congratulated him, warmly providing a precious bottle of iced champagne to celebrate.

The next day provisions started moving upriver to Tientsin in small boats and lighters. Keyes himself tried to take *Fame* as far as possible towards the city. It was almost a disaster. He left her at anchor while himself inspecting some loading operations on shore, and she swung across the river, broadside on to the current, firmly aground fore and aft. She might have broken her back. Somehow, however, by churning much mud with her propellers, she came off, heading upstream. They found a wider patch and ran her bows into the bank, letting the flood tide swing the stern round, then backing off the mud at the critical moment. She was then free to steam back downriver in safety.

Keyes now had his blood well up and could not be kept long from the fighting around Tientsin. He managed to arrange for *Fame*'s crew to be stood down for a few days and for her engines to be overhauled while he himself took a little convoy of tugs and barges upriver. He found the situation far from satisfactory. There was no unified command of the allied forces; as the Russians had the most men involved their general normally had the last word, but he was indecisive and unco-operative. Conditions for troops on the ground were horrible, with relentless shelling, poor food, little rest and many wounded. Morale was not high. David Beatty, who was to become Roger's stalwart friend and ally, was in charge of a naval contingent and refused to report himself sick although he had suffered several severe wounds. Roger attached himself to his contingent and together they led a successful charge, routing a large enemy formation while in support of a Japanese mounted force whose objective was to silence a large Chinese battery and capture a small arsenal. As ever, the Japanese fought with relentless dash and skill, achieving all their objectives. Keyes revelled in the chance to do some proper fighting, noting with interest that while the Chinese would stand shell-fire and small-arms quite well, a bayonet charge would invariably send them packing.

Roger's leave of absence from *Fame* was soon over and reluctantly he departed in his tug back downriver. In tow he had a large barge loaded with wounded men. Before leaving, he encountered Admiral Seymour who seemed to be unaware that he had orders to return to Taku and made some remarks which Keyes typically manipulated to mean that the admiral wanted him back in the fighting as soon as possible. He therefore reported to Admiral Bruce and suggested that *Whiting* could act as duty destroyer at Taku for a week while he took another barge up to Tientsin. He was desperate to be there as he believed that a joint assault on the main force of Chinese in the city's arsenal was imminent and he was damned if he would miss the fighting. The barge was loaded with artillery and set off up the river. On the way they were met by some firing from enemy forces on the banks which they silenced using machine guns mounted on the lighter. The tow was somewhat poorly attached to the barge with the result that it sheered about wildly, making steering difficult. A young midshipman, working on the stern of the tug to try to improve things, got caught in the hawser and was catapulted overboard. He seemed to be drowning until Keyes himself dived into the muddy water and grabbed him. The two were half an hour in the water before the tug could drop the barge, turn around and pick them up. Keys described the incident as 'rather unpleasant'. The midshipman turned out to be none the worse.

Arrived at Tientsin, Roger reported to Seymour, and suffered a rude awakening. He should not have left his ship and the admiral expected him and *Fame* to be on hand next day to take him back to his flagship, *Centurion*. His own role as commander of the allied land forces had been superseded and he expected to return in the same destroyer that took him out. Keyes was to command a convoy of barges back to Taku that evening, then return to Tongku to be ready to ferry the admiral back to his ship. There was nothing for it but to obey. *Fame*'s engines were rapidly re-assembled and she meekly returned an exhausted admiral to his flagship.

Keyes was then sent to report on the position at Newchwang, a concession on the north side of the Gulf of Bo-Hai, where there had been reports of Chinese incursions onto European concessions. It was immediately clear that the 'incursions' were entirely an invention of the Russians who wanted to get the coast clear to take control of the area themselves. He was then informed by his trader friend, Baldwin, that the powerful Chinese-held forts north of Taku might be ready to hand themselves over to British hands, but wanted at all costs to avoid take-over by the barbarous Russian forces arriving from Siberia. Nothing came of this as there were no spare British forces available. While all this was going on the events which Keyes feared most were in progress. Allied forces stormed the Chinese city and arsenal at Tientsin, Beatty and the Naval Brigade and naval artillery covering themselves with glory. The battle was won but he had not been a part of it.

The primary objective of the international force was still to be achieved. The diplomats in Peking were still under siege and messages kept turning up saying they were in grave danger of being overrun, starved to death, or both. Various European nations were sending reinforcements to Taku, the British sending a division under General Gaslee from India. Gaslee was a family friend of the Keyes and specifically asked for Roger to accompany him ashore and act as his naval staff officer. To do so Keyes would require specific instructions from Admiral Bruce and permission to leave his ship. Roger was not in Bruce's good books at the time as a result of *Fame* missing the tide that day into the river. This was not Roger's fault; he was delayed as his passenger had overslept. Nevertheless, the admiral was furious with him. Eventually he calmed down. He did not give permission for the young lieutenant to accompany Gaslee, but sent a message to Seymour, the senior admiral present, in his flagship, asking for a decision. Seizing the opportunity Keyes set off carrying the general upriver before any answer could be received from the admiral and rapidly attached himself to Gaslee's staff, leaving Tompkinson in charge of *Fame*. He took with him a Chinese servant and Able Seaman Brady, one of his ship's company who had distinguished himself in the cutting out of the Chinese destroyers and was to remain as his personal 'coxswain' throughout the rest of his career. To complete his entourage, he even bought a pony similar to the Indian animals brought over by the soldiers. 'The Torpedo' was a good-natured beast but had only two speeds, full gallop and stock-still.

The newly-formed relief column for Peking was an altogether more professional affair than Seymour's. Its main components were:

Japanese	8,500 + 50 guns
Russians	4,500 + 16 guns
British	3,000 + 12 guns
American	2,500 + 6 guns
French	800 + 12 guns

This force was opposed by about 70,000 ill-equipped Chinese troops and an indeterminate number of Boxers. As ever the departure of this force on its urgent mission was continually delayed by the Russians, who refused to move until they were certain that they had enough troops involved to prevent the Japanese from gaining too much advantage. Eventually, things got moving, but not before Roger had received a telegram from Seymour saying that he did NOT approve his transfer to Gaslee's staff. He should stay with *Fame*. The telegram was pocketed and 'lost'.

Finally the relief force moved off, accompanied by junks which were towed up the river by coolies, carrying heavy goods and the wounded. The weather was terribly hot and sultry, so tempers frayed easily and the advance was not pleasant. The dust raised by the marching army was terrible, choking noses and lungs and many men fell out of line with sunstroke. The heat was somewhat relieved each evening by a bathe in the river. Even this was not without its drawbacks. Keyes wrote to a friend: 'You know the colour of the river and the filth that floats down it. One often has to step aside to let a dead Chinaman or a dog pass … '. Everywhere the Chinese were routed when they encountered Japanese or British bayonets, but there were some lively cavalry actions and some artillery duels. On one occasion Keyes found himself among some American infantry under General Chaffee, who were being shelled mistakenly by British and Russian guns. Roger climbed up onto the parapet and waved his sword with a flag attached until the firing ceased. The force continued their steady advance, the Japanese leading the way and driving off all Chinese resistance. They had the advantage of much better transport than the other allies, but were also extremely well led and disciplined, proving themselves to be immensely tough soldiers.

The relief force arrived outside Peking on 12 August without suffering significant losses. General Gaslee had been informed by a British missionary that the best way to enter the city was through the Shawo-Men gate; it was a longer and more difficult approach than the Middle Gate or the North East gates, favoured by the other allied forces, but was more weakly defended (Map 3). There was clearly going to be a hot contest between the various national forces to reach the besieged diplomats first. The Russians declared, however, that their troops needed a rest before making their assault. This was a complete hoax. The Russians made their attack twelve hours before the agreed time, hoping to be first into the city and in the forefront of the looting which they knew would follow. Keyes, who had suspected some such mischief was afoot, was beside himself with worry that once again he would be too late for any fighting. He almost died when in the small hours of the morning he heard heavy gunfire announcing that his suspicions had been well founded. Eventually, at about 3.30am, the British moved forward, Keyes mounted on the faithful Torpedo and accompanied by a naval signaller, Yeoman of Signals J. Combs. They reached the Shawo-Men gate with little opposition, but it was closed. It was important that not only should it be seized as soon as possible, but also a British flag should fly over it to prevent it being bombarded by allied artillery. Keyes was in his element. He got Torpedo to stand against the wall and stood up on his back to be able to reach a part of the gatehouse where masonry was loose, allowing him to shin up the stonework and plant the flag over the gate. Peering into the city he saw that the defenders had fled, and soon the gates were opened and the troops burst in with Gaslee himself well to the fore. Regaining his pony, Roger rode into the town and tried to find a way to the wall which separated the legations from the little streets of the Chinese city. By this time no one thought that the besieged diplomats would still be there – surely they would have been overrun or taken hostage – but it was worth a try. He knew that the small embassy guard were Royal Marines and they might be able to communicate with flags to Combs. Eventually he found what seemed to be a dried-up canal bed running parallel to the wall. His first attempt to move along it was greeted by a volley of rifle fire, but he got closer under cover and was joined by the main body of the attackers.

To their delight they saw allied flags flying on the legation wall. At first they thought that these might be part of a Chinese trick, but soon the Marines inside replied to Combs's signals. There seemed to be a sluice running into the canal bed from the legation and an archway around it which would give some cover from the rifle fire. Keyes and a small party dashed into this, finding that the sluice was actually the main sewer and the position was far from pleasant. The entrance up the sewer into the legation was barred by an iron grating, but some American marines from the embassy guard were on the other side and loosened the barricade. Keyes, being very thin, was the first man through and stormed triumphantly into the building. The scene which greeted him could have come out of a comic opera. On the embassy lawn a tea party was in progress. The ladies, British, American, Russian, German, French, Austrian and Italian, were all nicely dressed and quite composed. Most of the gentlemen were in whites as befitted an embassy tea party but a few sauntered down from the walls, where they had been on guard duty, in combat uniform and armed to the teeth. Keyes and some other British officers who had broken in were politely invited to join the party. As they did so, Chinese gunners and riflemen opened a heavy fire on the embassy, but the high walls made direct fire impossible. The guests retired indoors quite elegantly 'As if', wrote Keyes to his mother, 'for a shower of rain'. British horse artillery and infantry patrols outside the building soon put a stop to the firing and the party-goers stepped outside again and resumed their polite chatter.

None of the other attacking forces got into the city until long after the British had succeeded. The Americans gave up their assault on Tungpien-men gate and eventually followed the British, about two hours behind. The Russians, in spite of their duplicity in advancing long before everyone else, got held up trying to enter the Tartar City where the Chinese defenders all concentrated, including those who were supposed to be manning the Shaow-men. The Russians actually asked for help from the Japanese who themselves were held up outside the city wall, being unable to blow open the Tungchi-men to which they were assigned. Neither got in until after dark.

Once the allied forces were inside the city there was some work to do releasing Christian Chinese who were being besieged around the Roman Catholic cathedral, but the main activity occupying Russian, French and some other foreign soldiers was looting and the most revolting rape and murder of defenceless Chinese. Siberian and Cossack soldiers were particularly brutal and their officers did nothing to stop them, being themselves busily absorbed in looting anything of value they could find. Japanese troops were told strictly that they must do nothing to discredit themselves in the eyes of the British and were highly disciplined on this occasion, behaving perfectly. There were a few unpleasant incidents involving British-Indian troops, the offenders being severely punished but, apart from this, the behaviour of Gaslee's forces was excellent. Keyes continued to act as ADC to the general. In late August he succumbed to a nasty infection brought on probably by exhaustion and filthy water. A doctor later concluded that he had suffered a bout of diphtheria. He made matters worse for himself by insisting on joining a triumphal procession of allied forces through the Forbidden City, returning to his quarters with a temperature of 103. After two weeks he felt well enough to go and watch some skirmishing about seven miles from the city, hoping to be able to assess the qualities of some newly-arrived German troops; he was so weak that he could hardly keep in the saddle. In the event the Germans were not engaged as the enemy were driven off by a British-Indian unit, the 26th Baluchistanis. He was then ordered down river to rejoin *Fame.* Typically, one of his concerns on leaving was the fate of his horses. He had bought a second pony while on the march to Peking, which he gave to a cavalry officer friend. He rode the faithful Torpedo most of the way back to Tientsin, having given up his place in an ambulance to a wounded customs official. The stalwart pony then had a spell as preferred conveyance for Roger's devoted coxswain, Brady, before being sold to another army officer.

On arrival at Taku, Roger was told he looked like an Indian famine victim. Admiral Bruce forbade him to return to *Fame* and insisted that he stayed on Bruce's flagship, *Barfleur,* as a guest, until he felt stronger. No sooner had Roger joined *Barfleur* than he learned that he was in serious trouble. Admiral Seymour was furious that he had bluffed his way into a shore appointment, leaving his ship in inexperienced hands. How dare he disobey a clear, written order? Bruce was partly to blame but the worst of the admiral's fury was reserved for Lieutenant Keyes. He was to leave *Fame* and go home at once. A new captain had been appointed for his ship and would be arriving shortly. No sooner had Roger absorbed this terrible news than the admiral himself came aboard *Barfleur.* He enquired briefly about Roger's health but treated him very coldly, leaving him close to tears on the quarterdeck. He was to lose his ship. The capture of four hostile destroyers, the storming of the fort at Hsi-cheng, the glory of being the first man to enter the legations, counted for nothing. He was in disgrace and his career prospects ruined.

Keyes now displayed courage of a kind not previously required of him. The admiral disembarked and went aboard *Alacrity.* Roger borrowed a barge and set off to beard him in his lair. It is not often that a lieutenant confronts an admiral and Seymour was a particularly imposing figure; he was of a large and powerful build and an imperious manner. He had a small trimmed beard and looked for all the world like a traditional Spanish conquistador. He was pacing the deck when the young offender approached him. 'What can I do for you, Mr Keyes?' He boomed. 'I think you have treated me very badly, Sir,' replied Keyes. The admiral looked astonished and coldly asked him what he meant. 'If you had been in my position, Sir, you would have done exactly as I did'. Keyes blurted the words out and they clearly touched a nerve. Seymour mused for a few seconds. 'Perhaps I would, it would certainly have been a great temptation – but you should have resisted the temptation'. The ice was broken. Keyes argued that the captains of other ships had been on the expedition to Peking; that he and his family were deeply respected in the Indian Army and were particularly close to General Gaslee and therefore he had been able to play a most important role as liaison officer between the Naval Brigade and the army. Tomkinson, who had been left in charge of *Fame*, was an excellent officer and had done every task demanded of him. The admiral softened before Keyes's pleading. He admitted that he had judged him too harshly and asked what he really wanted. Roger replied that his only wish was to return to *Fame*. Seymour consented but kindly said that that he was still too sick to be aboard a little destroyer at present. He should stay in *Barfleur* for a few weeks. She was to go to Nagasaki shortly and *Fame* could go with her. He could take her over when fully recovered. There were some difficulties about what would happen to the relief captain who was arriving shortly. Keyes suggested that he should take over *Taku,* the captured destroyer. He was roundly told to mind his own business, but in the event that was what happened. It was a relieved but totally exhausted lieutenant who was rowed back to *Barfleur* where he was thoroughly spoilt by Admiral Bruce and his wife.

Some pleasant days were spent in Nagasaki where *Fame* was slipped and had some damage repaired, many rivets being replaced in the process. Keyes eventually left *Barfleur* at Wei-hai-wei where he was briefly lodged in a naval hospital – actually a hotbed of infections of various kinds. By the beginning of November he was well enough to rejoin his ship as she sailed southward to Shanghai, then on to Hong Kong for the winter, sailing in company with *Taku*. It was on this last leg that he and his ship came within an ace of being lost.

Fame and *Taku* were just over 100 miles north of Hong Kong running before a moderate north-easterly monsoon which was kicking up a heavy following swell. Roger took the morning watch and was relieved by his gunnery officer with nothing significant to report. What both had missed was a sudden and dramatic fall in atmospheric pressure, announcing the onset of a typhoon. While *Fame*'s seakeeping qualities were well established – she could live with pretty poor weather as long as there was plenty of sea room to manoeuvre – *Taku*, with her shallow draft and strange hull form, was an unknown quantity. Furthermore, she only had coal left for a few hours steaming. Neither ship could be expected to survive a tropical typhoon driving her towards a lee shore. Ominously the monsoon wind died away, and great swells from the south-east began to collide with the monsoon induced north-easterly seas. Both ships battened everything down and prepared for the worst.

Roger expected the centre of the storm to pass well to the south, but typhoons are unpredictable and sometimes they tracked directly up the Formosa Strait – in which case the 'eye' would pass right over the two destroyers and they were probably done for. Sure enough, enormous seas came rampaging down on them from the south-east and the wind built up to hurricane force. At first both little ships stood out to seaward to clear the lee shore. Keyes could not help thinking what a fine sea boat *Fame* was. She would poise on the crest of a wave, propellers racing in the air and at least one third of her length airborne, then plunge downward, driving forward and ready for the next great wave. *Taku* seemed to be in a more precarious condition, her large diameter screws were whirling round in the air more than in the water, but she kept gamely on out to sea until an anchor on her foredeck broke loose and, together with three fathoms of chain, slid into the sea and thrashed about threatening to hole the ship. Luckily the anchor soon plunged down and sank quickly but the crew were unable to release it and it hung there throughout the rest of the storm. As conditions worsened it became clear that *Taku* was unable to make headway against the wind and both little ships were being driven relentlessly towards the shoals. *Fame*'s depth-sounding equipment had been carried away, but Roger had men sounding with old-fashioned lead and line and they announced that the bottom was shelving dangerously. Thirteen fathoms … twelve fathoms … eleven fathoms …. Both destroyers were in danger of being wrecked. On *Fame* another problem arose. The forward mess deck was found to be full of water, some rivets in the ship's side having pulled out. Luckily the bows were fairly buoyant as there was no coal in the forward bunkers, so the problem could just be contained using pumps and steam ejectors, but still the little ships were being driven relentlessly into shallow water.

Roger then took the only possible course open to him: signalling *Taku* to follow, he turned beam to sea. The danger was now that the effect of the howling wind and the big waves would roll the destroyers right over, but they had low freeboard and little windage, so they might possibly keep upright. With the wind on the beam they managed to forge unsteadily ahead, just skirting the shallows. Conditions in the stokeholds were unimaginable. Coal had to be shovelled from the bunkers along the ship and into the furnaces which had to be kept going. The gangways and openings were narrow and hot steam pipes were everywhere. Bearings constantly needed cooling with hosepipes. The engines had to be idled every time the propellers came out of the water to prevent damage. Filthy, sick, frightened and exhausted the 'Black Gang' kept on: lives depended on it. Soon after the change of course it seemed that the wind began to moderate. The typhoon had tracked inland and the danger passed. By 5.00pm the destroyers were ready to settle down on course to Hong Kong.

They found the harbour in some chaos due to the typhoon. There had been numerous wreckings and heavy loss of life. Their mooring had been obstructed by a sunken dredger, so *Fame* had to pick up a buoy in a somewhat obscure part of the harbour, off Kowloon, her crew utterly exhausted by their ordeal. The officers had hoped to get ashore that evening and have a hot bath and a proper meal, but that was impossible from their unaccustomed berth. Seemingly to make matters worse, a picket boat came alongside as soon as they were moored, Keyes suspected that it brought some irritating rebuke from a senior officer. The despatch it carried, however, was of a very different nature; Phillimore, the temporary captain of *Taku,* who had fought gallantly at Tientsin, learnt that he was awarded the DSO and Keyes learnt that he had been promoted to commander. His crew 'spliced the main brace' and it was a happy, contented ship that settled down for the night. Both destroyers had to be slipped after their ordeal. *Fame* had been leaking badly; she had sprung 1,300 rivets in her bow section, the area which had not been repaired at Nagasaki. *Taku*, often written off as being too lightly built for the open sea, was still tight as a drum and entirely undamaged. She continued to give good service in Hong Kong until 1916.

A commander at the age of only twenty-eight – at least four years ahead of almost all of his contemporaries, Keyes was now clearly marked out as an officer with a glowing future. It was thus with high hopes that he journeyed back to England after two years' service on the China station. This is a suitable juncture to take stock of his characteristics and achievements.

Pictures of him look wrong sometimes, the three broad gold rings on the sleeve seem too heavy for the fresh, youthful face. He's too slim, too boyish, too naïve for his seniority. 'Little E' dressing up. He had shown himself to be a doughty fighter, fearless and resourceful, but also he had displayed an almost childlike love of the process of fighting; he was jealous and depressed if he was not on hand when there was a good scrap, and resentful when the enemy melted away without putting up a fight. These are hardly the reactions of a responsible senior officer. Roger was clearly a fine seaman, able to take the correct decision in an emergency, expert at handling his small ship and able to inspire loyalty, even devotion, among his subordinates. His personal courage is unquestionable, as evidenced by his plunge into the river to rescue the unfortunate midshipman. He drove his men hard and took risks, but was seldom reckless. His ships were invariably smart ships as well as being happy ones. He was good at cultivating useful friends and making a name for himself with senior officers. How many humble lieutenants ever got cosseted by admirals as he did by Bruce? How many ever confronted a tough old admiral like Seymour? He knew, perhaps by instinct, how to make his way in Victorian society, making friends with influence at the Admiralty, at Court and within the fleet to which he was attached. His hobbies of polo and hunting, which almost amounted to an obsession, brought him into contact with the highest in the land and the smartest set in whatever society he found himself. This trait does not appear to have been deliberate or studied, it simply came naturally to him. He was clearly a very attractive personality, making friends easily and standing by them in time of trouble, with a wide acquaintance both inside and outside the Service. In spite of being unable to spell, or to write good English, he was a voluminous correspondent – his letters to his mother, especially after the death of his father, are thoughtful, frequent and unfailingly kind. His friend, General Aspinall-Oglander, wrote that he was inspired by a strong Christian faith; this is not apparent from his letters but it would be typical of his class and upbringing.

Unlike Jellicoe, he was no intellectual nor was he an innovator like Fisher. In fact even within the Royal Navy he was probably below average intelligence, as is evidenced by his struggles with his examinations. The fighting he had done in China and Africa had all been on land against inferior and badly-led opposition. He had no experience at all of fighting at sea or of facing up to a determined, well-organised, opponent. This was, of course, typical of the Royal Navy generally, which for the previous fifty years had fought magnificently on land but had faced no more than trivial opposition at sea and had hardly even considered the possibility of fighting at night. Keyes at twenty-eight embodied everything that was good about the Victorian Navy – balanced by a strong dose of all its shortcomings.

Chapter 4

A Rising Young Officer

By the early 1900s a curious change had begun to take place in the Royal Navy. Previously, service on a big ship had been the primary route to a successful career. Fleets manoeuvred with stately precision, one behind the other, looking to the senior admiral present for precise instructions as to what to do. Smartness and speed of response were valued above everything. Among personnel, too, the same rigid hierarchy prevailed. Advancement came to officers who performed their allotted tasks with speed and precision exactly as required by the captain and according to the established procedure. The various ranks were strictly segregated and respect for seniors was an essential requirement. Now there were changes afoot, however. This new entity, the 'Small Ship Navy', was evolving, thrust upon the service by the rapid development of minelayers and torpedo craft, especially the evolving destroyer fleets, soon to be augmented by submarines, and fast motor boats. On such little ships there was no room for formality or rigid class divisions. The crew had to work together as a close team, trusting each other to make good decisions and sharing the fearsome dangers posed by the enemy, the weather, and the sea itself. From being seen as a dumping ground for misfits or second-rate officers, the Small Ship Navy was to become an important adjunct to the battle fleet and eventually a breeding ground for the most senior and respected officers in the service.

In 1901, the year in which Keyes returned from China, the destroyer had still to establish its usefulness. Its detractors had a point. That very year *Cobra* broke in half and was lost off Cromer and *Viper* ran aground and was lost in a fog in the Channel Islands. *Salmon* sank in December after a collision. By the end of the First World War no fewer than eleven destroyers would be lost due to stress of weather and eighteen due to collision. Their frailty and perceived unsuitability for open-sea work caused many senior officers to regard them as unfit for any duties save guarding friendly shores and for river work. Certainly they could not endanger a battle fleet at sea, especially in heavy weather. They had no place whatever in deep-sea fleet manoeuvres.

It was thus to a rather marginalised unit of the navy, the Devonport Destroyer Flotilla, that Keyes found himself attached, after a few weeks' well-earned leave and a signals course. At first he was second in command of the flotilla and captain of *Bat,* a C-Class 30-knotter, but he soon took over as commodore, transferring to *Falcon* and later to *Sprightly.* His arrival certainly seems to have stirred up the organisation. He was disgusted by the condition of the little ships which had been allowed to become slack and dirty in spite of spending much of their time in harbour. The flotilla consisted of B- and C-Class ships, all similar to the familiar *Whiting.* They were 350-ton 30-knotters powered by 6,000hp coal-fired piston engines with one 12-pounder and five 6-pounder guns and two 18-inch torpedo tubes. As soon as he arrived he determined to show that the little ships could be effective in all weathers and all conditions and that slackness would in no circumstances be tolerated. The routine established by Keyes was to have the destroyers at sea on most weekdays, cruising in the western part of the English Channel and occasionally as far north as the Hebrides. He forced the crews to go through endless exercises at high speed; his favourite was the 'gridiron' in which the flotilla would split into two, then the two sections would charge each other at high speed, crossing at a closing speed of 40 to 60 knots in a flurry of foam and excitement. He was delighted when, on a trip to the Channel Islands, an elderly gentleman appeared on the quay and made some enquiries. He turned out to be Brackenbury, now a retired admiral, but previously captain of the old *Turquoise,* the very one who had sent up chicken sandwiches to 'Little E', a midshipman in disgrace. Roger insisted on taking the admiral and his family for a trip in his destroyer and gave him a demonstration of how modern high-speed craft could be handled at close quarters.

It took almost two years for Keyes to get his flotilla working as he wanted it, replacing deadwood among the officers with men in his own mould and getting them used to his relentless driving of his ships regardless of weather. In March 1903 he got a chance to show what his flotilla could do.

Admiral Noel was in command of the Home Fleet and was notoriously sceptical of the value of destroyers, especially in heavy weather. He had indeed given a lecture to the Royal United Services Institution in which he stated that the modern sailors were no seamen, being brought up in powered ships and not hardened by working aloft in heavy weather. He poured scorn on little torpedo boats. Three exercises were arranged to test his opinion. Keyes's destroyers were tasked with getting within torpedo range of the Home Fleet unobserved. The first exercise took place in a severe equinoctial gale. The destroyers failed to find their adversaries. First trick to the admiral. For the second exercise the weather had moderated, but a huge swell was rolling in from the Atlantic. The fleet was anchored at an undisclosed position and the destroyers had to find and attack it. The flotilla searched every creek and bay along the coast for seven hours without success. At last, just before dawn, when rounding Start Point, one of Keyes's lookouts spotted a suspicious light close under Bolt Tail. It was the Home Fleet at anchor close against the high cliffs of the South Devon headland. The attackers had to creep in very close to the shore, making use of their shallow draft, in order to approach without being seen, their silhouettes masked by the towering cliffs behind them. There was grave danger of being pushed onto the rocky headlands by the swell, but Keyes and one other ship managed to get within range and fired their torpedoes which found their mark. (The Navy used dummy torpedoes for these exercises. They had soft heads which showed when they had hit their target, they then floated to the surface and could be recovered.) The rest of the flotilla was seen before attacking and was deemed to have been sunk. One trick all.

The final exercise saw the battle fleet in Lough Swilly and the destroyers in the Isles of Scilly. The fleet would come south down the Irish Sea and the destroyers would try to intercept it unseen. It was now blowing a heavy south-westerly gale and the umpire wanted to abort the exercise as he thought conditions too dangerous with the little ships liable to be pooped by the huge following seas. Keyes would have none of it. He set off at 7.00pm and ran north-eastwards. Luckily, he got a sight of an outlying cruiser scouting ahead of the fleet at 1.00am. Unseen, he steered towards it and then spotted *Good Hope*, the flagship of the cruiser squadron, struggling south into the teeth of the gale. Determined to seek for bigger prey Keyes led his flotilla on to the north. From the top of a huge swell he saw the fleet's battleships, great seas breaking over their bridges as they steamed southward, head to sea. Their decks were awash and Keyes rightly guessed that the lookouts would be obscured by spray. The huge battleships were in single file and the destroyers steamed past them, undetected in the foul weather, then all turned towards the column together and attacked in unison. On this occasion torpedoes were not fired as they would have been lost in the heavy swell, but Very lights were fired from close aboard the targets so that the astonished watchkeepers suddenly realised that they had been entirely caught napping. Game, set and match to Keyes.

Admiral Noel was completely converted. He wrote in his report:

> The result is very creditable to the Commander of the Destroyers, and is a severe lesson as to the danger to which a Battle Fleet is exposed if the enemy's torpedo craft are not deprived of all their powers of attack ....

He also spoke to a colleague, Lord Roberts, who reported later:

> When off the Isles of Scilly he imagined his fleet was perfectly safe, as such a heavy gale was blowing he did not think torpedo boat destroyers would venture to sea. In this he was mistaken for several boats came up to his ship and would undoubtedly have inflicted most serious damage. I asked him who commanded the flotilla and he said 'A very rising young officer, Commander Keyes.'

In fact, as Keyes knew perfectly well, torpedoes would have been unlikely to achieve hits in such weather. Large waves and the violent movements of the destroyers would probably have sent them off course. His mission had been achieved, however, and accolades were received before Keyes was given notice of a new posting and had to leave his beloved destroyers in the hands of his second-in-command, Walter Cowan.

Chapter 5

Postings Ashore

Roger had expected that his next appointment would have been as second-in-command of a big ship. He had had no experience of serving on a battleship and he probably imagined himself as commander on a smart vessel, a flagship perhaps, in the Mediterranean Fleet, the crack formation in the Royal Navy. Such a posting would have been a normal development in a promising naval career. In fact, three of his comrades-in-arms from China, Jellicoe, Beatty and Craddock, were being made captains of major warships at the time and all three asked for him as their commander but, for various reasons, none of those opportunities came to fruition. He was reconciling himself to a period of unemployment on half-pay when, in July 1903, a totally unexpected opening arose within the Naval Intelligence Department. The department was headed at the time by Prince Louis of Battenberg. The prince was not without shortcomings, being inclined to be rather easily swayed by his subordinates, but he had succeeded in enhancing the status of the department, laying the foundations for its astonishingly successful performance in the First World War. Keyes was fortunate enough to be given the role of monitoring the navies and coastal defences of Italy, now a rising naval power with highly innovative naval engineers; Russia, possessor of large navies in the Baltic, the Black Sea and the Far East and of some very modern battleships; and Japan, an important strategic ally of Britain, her navy trained on the British model, equipped mainly with modern British-built ships, with possibly the most highly-trained and motivated naval personnel in the world. Thus, although confined to a desk when he would have preferred to be standing on the bridge of a warship, there seemed to be interesting times ahead. Whilst working in London he was able to live with his mother who had a 'grace and favour' dwelling at Hampden Court – a welcome development for Lady Keyes who had hardly seen him for seventeen years. Whilst deskbound he did not allow himself to become idle; he ran around the park most mornings and got up a naval polo team, which unsuccessfully challenged the Royal Horse Guards.

True to form, he never missed a party or an invitation to a grand house, his delight in socialising increased by the growing attractions of a very special young lady who was frequently to be found at the same events.

Tension between Japan and Russia rapidly increased in 1903 and open war broke out the next year. This provided an early chance for Keyes to exert his influence. The Navy was resolved to keep clear of the conflict as both combatants were potentially valuable allies; it therefore planned to withdraw its ships from Wei-Hai-Wei as they might be thought by the Russians to be a threat to their base at Port Arthur. Keyes knew a fair bit about the Japanese, their fine fighting qualities and their contempt for any sign of weakness. He was certain that they would regard the planned British withdrawal as a cowardly act and that it would ruin future relationships. What happened next is a good example of how early-twentieth-century politics worked. Keyes had been invited by Mrs Joseph Chamberlain, wife of the prominent politician and mother of the future prime minister, Neville, to spend a weekend at Highbury, the Chamberlain family mansion. Joseph was Colonial Secretary at the time and highly esteemed within the cabinet. The conversation in the smoking room after dinner turned to the Russo-Japanese War and Roger made his concern about the order withdrawing the British squadron very clear. Neville, who was a friend of his, came up to him later in the evening and said that he ought to know that his father had 'taken note' of what he had said. Twenty-four hours later the order was given for the withdrawal to be reversed.

After an indecisive start, with both sides suffering losses, the Russo-Japanese War turned into a disaster for Russia. To replace losses in the Far East, the Russian Navy sent its Baltic fleet on an ill-advised mission to Chinese waters. While steaming down the North Sea their flagship *Knyaz Suvarov* sighted some British fishing boats at about 1.00am and opened fire, on the assumption that they were in fact Japanese destroyers. Other ships joined the action and in the end one trawler was sunk and several others damaged. Immediately there were calls for the Royal Navy to intercept and punish the Russians and Parliament demanded an official response to the affair. This fell right into Keyes's area of responsibility. Naval Intelligence had been monitoring Russian signals ever since the fleet set sail. This was easily done because the east coast monitoring stations, recently established, were forerunners of the superb radio intelligence network which served Britain so well in two world wars. Russian signals procedure had been very slack so that their signallers talked to each other *en clair* and anyone speaking Russian could find out exactly what they were thinking. To make conversations doubly insecure, their radios were British Marconi sets and some Marconi operators were still aboard the Russian warships providing assistance. This allowed Keyes and his colleagues to get a clear picture of what had been happening and to understand that the Russians had not intended to be hostile to the UK, but that panic on the part of officers in their ill-trained fleet had led to a terrible error. Newspapers had in fact been reporting mysterious destroyers in Scottish lochs and the Japanese were known to be buying destroyers from British yards, so the suspicion was not entirely unreasonable. Keyes's report enabled Lord Lansdowne, the Foreign Secretary, to defuse the situation. The Russians landed a party of officers in France to take part in an international enquiry.

What had actually happened was that two Russian cruisers had been ordered to accompany the armed supply ship *Kamchatka* which had fallen behind the fleet as a result of a breakdown. *Kamchatka*'s inexperienced and panicky crew somehow thought she had been attacked by torpedo craft in the darkness and had fired on a German trawler and a Swedish steamer mistakenly, doing no damage. Meanwhile, the two escorting cruisers had blundered about in the darkness searching for their charge and been seen by watchkeepers on the flagship *Knyaz Suvarov*. As they were long and low and didn't seem to be part of the Russian fleet, they were mistaken for hostile destroyers and immediately fired on. Fire was then switched onto some British trawlers who happened to be between the flagship and the cruisers just as the cruisers disappeared into the darkness. Other ships in the division joined in the general firing. The Russians scored several hits on their own cruisers, causing casualties, in addition to the damage to the trawlers. Unfortunately, the Russians never admitted that this version of events was correct and persisted in the story that they had been attacked by destroyers.

The Baltic Fleet steamed on to meet its terrible fate at Tsushima.

Keyes was called as an expert witness at an international enquiry held in Paris into the incident. His evidence and experience as a destroyer officer seems to have carried much weight with the judges. It was concluded that there had been no torpedo boats in the North Sea at the time but that the Russians had made a genuine mistake and should pay compensation. An outright confrontation between the UK and Russia was avoided.

Early in 1905 Keyes took up another desk job, this time in a diplomatic capacity. It is a little curious that a born seafarer like him should have been so employed but in fact the job suited him very well. He was stationed in Rome as naval attaché, with responsibility for Italy, Austria (which was extremely hostile to Italy), Turkey and Greece (which was bitterly hostile to Turkey). It was a strange posting, but one in which he could indulge his passion for horses, as the Italian aristocracy were becoming keen on foxhunting at the time. He was able to borrow hunters from friends and was reputed to be the bravest of riders across country. He also managed to attach himself to the army's cavalry school where he was able to introduce some British cavalry practices to his hosts. He also made an unsuccessful attempt to introduce them to polo. Such was his reputation as a horseman that, on one occasion, he was lent a much-fancied horse to take part in a timed jumping competition. Unfortunately, his steed went too fast at the first fence then swerved, throwing its unfortunate rider to the ground. The crowd erupted in delight and the newspapers commented that they hoped 'Il marinaio' was better at the helm of a ship than on a horse. He timed a visit to Vienna very well to be there for the racing season and to participate in numerous parties and balls. He had much to celebrate as in July 1905 he was promoted captain. Returning briefly to naval intelligence affairs, he tried to make an assessment of the Austrian navy but found that security was tight and he does not seem to have learnt much. For security reasons an Austrian naval officer accompanied him on a visit to naval facilities on the Dalmatian coast, where the only intelligence he gathered was that it would be a marvellous spot for a honeymoon.

Indeed a honeymoon was due. In November he was enjoying a day with the Bicester Hunt, during a brief spell of home leave, when he eventually persuaded his long-term love, Eva Bowlby, riding side-saddle alongside him, to marry him. She was to prove a wonderful wife and mother. The following day it was hunting again and she celebrated the engagement by clearing a most challenging water jump, gleefully watching her fiancé fetching up on his back in the stream.

The young couple were incredibly lucky to be able to spend the next eighteen months based in Rome, able to travel freely to the sophisticated court at Vienna, the take in the delights of Dalmatia and even to accompany King Edward VII on a visit to the royal court at Athens. While he enjoyed the lifestyle immensely, there was a nagging doubt in Roger's mind. He needed a ship. With the rank of captain he should at least have been offered command of an armoured cruiser, but the Admiralty seemed to keep fending off his requests for a seagoing appointment. He noticed that several captains junior to him in the Navy List were commanding ships while he was stuck with a shore job, albeit a delightful one. He had his career to think of. Eventually the reasons for the problem became clear. The Navy in the early twentieth century was rent by a quarrel between supporters of Admiral Jacky Fisher, a maverick and compulsive moderniser of ships and of procedures, and Admiral Lord Charles Beresford, a conservative grandee with strong political and popular support. Although a fine seaman, Beresford did nothing whatever to bring the Navy or the units he commanded into a condition to fight a twentieth-century war. Keyes knew both protagonists, having met Fisher once in 1905, when he was quite pleasant, and again a year later when he was distinctly cold. Beresford he had met briefly in Rome. He does not seem to have had any deep involvement in the great controversy between the two admirals. Fortunately for Britain, and indeed for Europe, Fisher triumphed, but in 1907 the affair was in full swing and Fisher was a ferocious and vengeful opponent, determined to smoke out any Beresford supporter. It so happened that Beresford's naval secretary had tried to get an article against Fisher published in *The Times*. Fisher had got wind of this and was furious: by chance it happened that the name of the offending naval secretary was Keys (not Keyes). Mistakenly, Fisher muddled the two names and harboured a grudge against Roger, who he assumed was the Keyes (or Keys) referred to. As First Sea Lord, he was in a position to ruin Roger's career. Luckily, Roger was a friend of Hugh Evans-Thomas who was Fisher's naval secretary and the situation was resolved quietly.

In 1908 he got command of the armoured cruiser *Venus*. His time in her seems to have been successful but uneventful; she certainly became a very happy and efficient ship, comprising a part of the Atlantic Squadron under command first of Admiral Curzon-Howe and then Prince Louis of Battenberg.

Chapter 6

Submarines

To understand the next step in Keyes's career we should look briefly at the development of British submarines in the early part of the twentieth century. Initially the Royal Navy adopted a contemptuous attitude to subs, considering them as sneaky, cowardly weapons. One senior admiral suggested that crews of enemy submarines should be tried and hanged as pirates. In spite of this an American-built Holland boat was purchased and used for trials, which suggested that an improved version might have some value for harbour defence. Jacky Fisher, with his usual prescience, quickly saw the importance of underwater vessels and commissioned the Vickers Company to acquire the Holland patents to design and produce a boat suitable for a role in the coastal defence of Britain. He had in mind a situation in which an enemy squadron would appear outside an anchorage and bombard the ships inside before they could organise any sort of defence. A patrolling submarine might be able to bag the intruders with its torpedoes. An exceptionally competent and intelligent officer, Reginald Bacon, was appointed to oversee the development of these little vessels and he was to achieve an incredibly rapid pace of progress. In an attempt to speed up production Fisher had given Vickers a virtual monopoly of submarine building. The first series of boats (submarines were always referred to as 'boats') were designated the A Class, built between 1902 and 1904. They consisted of a single pressure hull with no internal partitions and almost no crew comforts. There was a conning tower amidships, a low structure surrounded by a rather flimsy rail. The boats were 100-feet-long and 13-feet-8-inches-wide with 200 tons displacement and were driven by a 400 or, later, 600hp Wolseley petrol engine on the surface and by electric motors when dived. Maximum diving depth was about 50 feet. They were armed with two 18-inch torpedo tubes. The crew normally consisted of two officers and nine other ranks. The boats were difficult to control under water and were notoriously unreliable.

In October 1904 a much-improved boat emerged, known as the B Class. These were 142-feet-long and 12-feet- 8-inches-wide. Their controllability was greatly enhanced by fitting hydroplanes to regulate and stabilise the attitude of the boat under water. Originally a single pair was fitted but a second pair was installed while in service. A 600 hp petrol engine drove the boats on the surface and a 180 hp electric motor underwater. Like their predecessors they had no crew comforts. Maximum endurance was four days in summer and three in winter. With the stink of petrol mixed with battery acid everywhere, no privacy, no form of air purification, and violent movement when on the surface, crews must have been delighted when their patrols came to an end.

C Class subs, built between 1905 and 1910, were only a marginal improvement on the B Class but were built in much larger numbers, thirty-eight being launched before production was halted.

Bacon's approach to submarine development had been logical, careful and progressive, with great attention to detail. By the time he was moved to other duties in 1906 it had become apparent to him that subs could be used in roles far more ambitious than harbour defence. What was required was a seagoing 'overseas' class of submarine. Perhaps these could cross the North Sea and patrol enemy coasts, ambushing any unsuspecting warships or transports. Perhaps they could co-ordinate their movements with the battle fleet and partake in a major fleet action. Maybe they could even confine enemy warships to port. To do any of this, subs needed more endurance, better reliability and better living conditions for crews. The new D Class submarines were designed to fulfil these requirements. The key to achieving more endurance was the installation of diesels instead of petrol engines. Two 600 hp Vickers diesels were fitted, driving two propellers. A further departure from the boats evolved from the Holland design was the fitting of saddle tanks, which were outside the pressure hull and provided a much better reserve of buoyancy. Two pairs of hydroplanes provided good underwater stability. There were two forward torpedo tubes and one aft. Surface displacement was 620 tons and there was space inside the pressure hull for some basic comforts for the crew of twenty-five. Diesels were very new technology at the time and gave many problems, delaying development and it was not until 1907 that *D-1* was laid down. She was the only 'Overseas' submarine complete by the time Keyes came into office. The submarine service was on the point of moving from a purely defensive to an aggressive mode.

It is worth noting that there was no method of detecting a submarine underwater at the time. Hydrophones were being developed which could hear any sound made by a boat underwater, but these only worked if the sea was flat calm and the vessel using the device, and all others around, were stationary. Even if a submerged sub was detected there were no depth charges or similar ordinance to destroy it. Underwater a submarine was entirely safe and its torpedoes could be deadly to any warship then afloat.

In 1910, when Keyes assumed the office of Inspecting Captain of Submarines, a rather strange role invented by Fisher, the fleet consisted of one operational D Class boat, thirty-seven Cs, eleven Bs, and twelve As. Roger's new role allowed him to settle his family in a rented house in Fareham, near Portsmouth, where his command was based. The submarine service had become a rather remote branch of the Navy with its own hierarchy and customs. Roger's appointment was a surprising one as he knew nothing about subs, except what little his brother Adrian, who was a submariner, had told him. The office had previously been occupied by technically inclined officers dedicated to improving the design and performance of the boats. Possibly the Admiralty, when making the appointment, hoped that Roger would be able to help the submarine to earn respect from the main body of naval officers, in the same way as he had enhanced the reputation of destroyers when he led the Devonport Destroyer Flotilla. The offensive possibilities of the submarine had been brought forcibly to the attention of senior officers by the exploits of a venturesome commander who had taken his boat unaccompanied up from the Channel to the west coast of Scotland and 'torpedoed' two armoured cruisers during the 1910 fleet manoeuvres. Keyes airily admitted as soon as he took up his appointment: 'To me machinery and material detail was a closed book'. He therefore left most design and production matters in the hands of his subordinates and concentrated on personnel development and the tactical deployment of this strange new weapon. Fisher, the great protagonist of the submarine service, had retired (he was to be recalled later), depriving submarines of a powerful and effective supporter at the highest level and in consequence budgets for building new boats were often tight.

In his previous role as a diplomat, Keyes had been able to get some knowledge of submarine developments overseas, French and Italian designs being especially interesting and possibly superior to the D Class boats then under construction and to their planned successors, the E Class. The Vickers Company had owned the patents for the Holland design and had been guaranteed a monopoly of submarine construction, so they put every possible obstacle in the way of deviation from their designs and were extremely slow in implementing any new development. Luckily for Keyes, a strong new supporter of the submarine service came to the fore in 1911.

SUBMARINES

Winston Churchill became First Lord of the Admiralty and very soon visited the submarine service's headquarters at Gosport. He loved going to sea and getting close to 'hands on' operations of any kind. Keyes took him for a trip in a submarine and the two men rapidly developed a friendship and mutual respect which was to last for the rest of both their lives. Churchill became a submarine enthusiast and formed a secret 'Submarine Committee' which operated independently of normal Admiralty procedures and controls.

One of the early results of Keyes's appointment was the improvement of submarine telescopes. British subs originally had fixed telescopes sticking up a short distance above the conning tower so that, to see his target, the captain had to take his boat very close to the surface. This always led to the boat porpoising, and thus being in grave danger of being seen. Keyes had seen practical power-operated retractable telescopes in Italy and eventually goaded British manufacturers to make them and the Admiralty to pay for them.

Before he had taken office the general design of the E-Class submarine had been decided. This was to be the most effective and numerous British submarine in service during the First World War, thirty-eight of them being built. They differed from previous subs in having two broadside torpedo tubes, as well as one forward and one aft. This inevitably meant that they were rather broad in the beam and therefore slower than some of their foreign rivals. They had transverse internal bulkheads, giving much better survivability and improved living conditions. A deck gun was fitted, and this was to prove of the greatest importance in many spheres of operation. Altogether they were excellent boats. Keyes cannot be credited with the design of them but his friendship with Churchill did contribute to the fact that the Admiralty was able to break the Vickers monopoly of submarine building, E-Class boats being produced in a number of different yards.

The requirement for new submarines was so urgent by 1914 that Keyes's suggestion of adopting foreign designs was taken up and a large batch of American-designed boats was commissioned. They were initially assembled by Vickers in Canada to preserve U.S. neutrality. These H-Class boats actually had no novel features but were extremely robust and dependable, continuing to serve in a training role up to 1945.

One of Keyes's projects was an attempt to develop submarine types which would be fast enough to operate as units of the Grand Fleet. For this role a surface speed of at least 23 knots would be required and it very soon became clear that this could only be achieved by building very large boats. The first of these, the J Class, were diesel-powered and proved not nearly fast enough, achieving only 19 knots. Seven Js were built and one of these, *J-1*, was to achieve the distinction of hitting two German dreadnoughts with a single salvo. The next step was to abandon diesels and build even larger, steam-turbine-driven monsters. A steam engine with its requirements for a high-pressure boiler inside the boat, furnaces, a funnel and numerous openings in the hull, is inherently unsuitable for a submarine. Nevertheless, the project was persisted with and seventeen boats were ordered in spite of Fisher himself proclaiming that steam-driven submarines would prove disastrous. The proper principle of the submarine is to rely on stealth and cunning and the huge K and M Class boats, emerging from Keyes's ideas, were enormous and anything but stealthy: 339-feet-long, they achieved a surface speed of 24 knots but were terribly clumsy and difficult to control. They were also fraught with operational problems and prone to the most appalling accidents. They never did any damage whatever to the enemy, but killed some hundreds of their own crews. The time, money and effort spent on those monsters could have been far better employed on producing more and better conventional diesel boats. The K and M Classes represented a radical departure from mainstream Admiralty thinking, which saw only two types of submarine; A, B and C Classes to be used for harbour defence, while D-, E- and eventually H- and J-Class boats would act as 'blockading' or 'overseas' submarines whose role would be to make it dangerous for the enemy fleet to leave harbour. The idea of the 'Fleet Submarine' was quickly abandoned. Keyes had of course not been solely responsible for following this false trail, but he was certainly one of its ardent supporters.

Roger was catastrophically wrong about large submarines but his ideas about the correct deployment of his existing fleet were sound. Early in 1911 orders were issued giving the war stations of the submarine fleet. They were to be based in the Dover Strait and the Firth of Forth, operating alongside some flotillas of old destroyers in a purely coastal defensive role. Keyes protested at this and instead insisted that submarines could be used offensively; he particularly emphasised the possibility of their lurking behind a force of cruisers and destroyers, blockading an enemy harbour to pounce on any enemy force trying to get out and attack the blockaders. A series of exercises carried off the west coast of Ireland indicated that this could be an effective policy. During the next three years Keyes kept his boats continually occupied in training and made mock attacks on formations of large warships. Whenever possible soft-headed torpedoes were used and the number of those that found their mark astonished many of the target vessels. Whatever Keyes's weaknesses were in the technical sphere he was always brilliant at motivating teams allotted to him. The expertise of his small body of submarine commanders and technicians increased rapidly, in spite of the scepticism in some parts of the Admiralty. Soon his drive and enthusiasm infected the select team of officers who became the core of the astonishingly effective submarine service, which was to serve Britain so well. Gradually, even the most sceptical began to understand the risks posed to a battle fleet by submarines and the vital importance of having a destroyer screen protecting the fleet became understood. By 1915 it became axiomatic that the Grand Fleet required an escort of a hundred destroyers before it could put to sea safely. The destroyers would be unlikely to sink attacking subs, but they would force them to dive so that their blindness and low speed underwater would make it very unlikely that they would ever be in a position to make an attack. During this period Keyes was able to work closely with Admiral de Robeck, whose title was Admiral of Patrols and thus effectively Keyes's boss. Like Keyes he was a destroyer expert and a very keen foxhunter and the two became close friends, although the friendship was to be sorely tested a few years later.

Although Keyes spent as much time as he could at sea in one of his boats, he was never entirely comfortable in this administrative role. He wanted to go to sea and fight; with his record he expected command of a major warship when his appointment to submarines was due to terminate at the end of 1913. He had heard that his close friend David Beatty had been given command of the Battle Cruiser Squadron, the crack unit of the Grand Fleet, and asked him for a command. Beatty was delighted that his erstwhile comrade in arms and companion on the hunting field wanted to join him and agreed to appoint him first to *Queen Mary* then to *Tiger*, the most powerful and fastest ship in the fleet. The probable onset of war, however, persuaded the Admiralty to keep its submarine force in the hands of an experienced officer. Keyes was promoted commodore and ordered to remain as commander of the submarine force. He was bitterly disappointed because, like almost all naval officers, he expected a Trafalgar-like battle between the rival battle fleets early in the war and was determined to be involved in it. As it happened, his role in charge of the submarine operation brought him much more activity than he would have experienced with the Grand Fleet in 1914. Commodore is a strange rank in the Royal Navy. Normally a commodore acts as captain of a ship and at the same time has a small squadron of (frequently similar) ships under his command. Although superior in rank to a captain, he cannot give orders to the captain of any ship that is not within his own squadron.

Fisher had retired in 1910 but was still highly regarded in the Admiralty and in the nation. He paid the submarine headquarters a visit in July 1914, shortly before he returned to office, and was shown the latest developments in submarines and telescopes. He was profoundly unimpressed and downright rude to his hosts. In particular, he blamed Keyes for the fact that so few overseas' submarines were at that time in service and that the Germans had more of them than the Royal Navy. Keyes, never very politic when riled, was stung by Fisher's attitude and replied that shipbuilding problems were Fisher's own fault for giving the monopoly of submarine building to Vickers, who were far too slow to build them. As they were faced by no competition, they were constantly placing obstacles in the way of producing any new type of submarine and wanted to keep on building obsolescent designs which were much more profitable. His guest took this very badly and stalked off without a 'goodbye' or 'thank you'. Fisher was a ruthless and vindictive enemy and it was Keyes's misfortune that the old curmudgeon was to once again become First Sea Lord. Recalled to the Admiralty in October 1914, Fisher placed the highest priority on submarine building, taking control of the situation into his own hands and relieving Keyes of this area of responsibility.

Submarines at the time had very poor radios and, of course, could not communicate at all underwater. Nevertheless, the tactic adopted in 1914 was to deploy the larger overseas' boats in small groups, each group commanded by a senior officer who would be in a destroyer. This was a strange arrangement as there was no way the destroyer could talk to its charges when they were underwater. Keyes was allocated two destroyers, *Firedrake* and the more modern *Lurcher*. He determined that he himself would normally sail in *Lurcher*, which was commanded by his old friend from China days, Wilfred Tomkinson, and endeavour to direct a small squadron of his submarines. In the days leading up to the war Roger developed his plan for deployment of his small force of overseas submarines:

> four would patrol the southern part of the North Sea to protect the troopers carrying the BEF
> two would be sent into the Heligoland Bight
> four would be held in reserve at Harwich where *Lurcher* was also stationed and Keyes had an office.

Also stationed at Harwich was Commodore Reginald Tyrwhitt with two flotillas of modern destroyers which were soon to be supplemented by a handful of light cruisers. The role of this force, and of the submarines, was to keep the enemy out of the southern part of the North Sea. Tyrwhitt was an active and effective leader of his little force and he thought in the same way as Roger about aggressive action against the enemy. He had been taken to sea in a submarine and had been delighted when he was allowed to fire a torpedo, which struck its mark. The two men got on famously together. Also patrolling in the same area were five old Baccante-class cruisers, obsolete vessels manned by reservists and cadets drafted in from Dartmouth, some as young as fourteen. They had been allocated this role as it was thought in the Admiralty that destroyers would be unsuitable for sustained cruising in heavy weather. All the more modern cruisers were required elsewhere. Keyes was incandescent with indignation about this deployment and went so far as to put his objections on paper to Their Lordships – a most unusual act for such a junior officer. Nothing was done, so the 'Live Bait Squadron', as it was called, continued its patrols.

As soon as war was declared Keyes was determined to be 'at 'em' and went to sea in *Lurcher,* supporting the boats guarding the BEF's Channel crossing. Nothing happened and in fact not one troopship was lost during the whole of the war; nevertheless, Keyes was eager for action. He wrote to Admiral Leverson, the operations director at the Admiralty, on 26 August – less than a month into the war:

> When are we going to make war and make the Germans realise that whenever they come out be they destroyers, battleships, cruisers or all three they will be fallen on and attacked. These are the views I have heard you express – for heaven's sake preach them.

In the Heligoland Bight Overseas-type boats were actively patrolling but it was not until autumn brought rougher seas that they bagged a victim; the old light cruiser *Hela*, sunk by Max Horton, who was to become a legendary submarine commander. Quite a number of attacks were made, but these were unsuccessful probably because the torpedoes they were using ran too deep and passed under their targets if fired at close range. However, the patrolling subs did detect a clear pattern of enemy activity. A group of German destroyers would patrol the bight at high speed all day, then be relieved by another batch at dusk. At about 6.00 pm each day, the night-time patrol would take over, emerging from the Elbe led by light cruisers which would escort them to their patrol area. They would be relieved about dawn and return to port. In case of trouble the Germans always had the option of retreating to the cover of the heavy guns on Heligoland itself. Keyes and Tyrwhitt devised a scheme for using destroyers and submarines to ambush the light cruisers and destroyers on their way home from night-time duty. Keyes took up this plan enthusiastically, bypassing the official operational planning team by taking his scheme directly to Churchill. It was just the sort of aggressive operation on the enemy's doorstep which delighted the First Lord. The two commodores were called to a more formal planning meeting, during which they suggested that perhaps Commodore Goodenough, whose squadron of light cruisers was based on the Humber, might join in and that two of Beatty's battle-cruisers could stand by in case any of the enemy's heavy ships came out to join the fun. This gave the planning staff a chance to turn negative about the whole scheme. They probably resented the fact that they had not thought of it themselves and that Keyes had seen fit to take his plan directly to Churchill. They told the meeting that none of Goodenough's force and no battle-cruisers would be available. Churchill insisted, however, and the operation was authorised. The encounter would take place on the night of 27/28 August. Tyrwhitt would sail in the brand-new light cruiser *Arethusa*, in command of the destroyers, and Keyes in *Lurcher* would endeavour to keep some control of the submarines. Astonishingly, it seems that no one had thought to consult tide tables to see if the German heavy ships would have enough water to get out of harbour in the Jade estuary and join the fight.

The idea was that submarines should show themselves briefly to the enemy light cruisers and destroyers, then lure them on towards Tyrwhitt's ships and a second line of subs. The Harwich Force involved consisted of two light cruisers and thirty-two destroyers. Due to appalling staff work within the Admiralty, just one day before the battle was due to commence, Jellicoe, in command of the Grand Fleet, heard what was afoot. He had little regard for Admiralty planners and on his own responsibility ordered Goodenough's light cruisers to the bight to assist Tyrwhitt. At the same time he instructed Beatty, with his powerful battle-cruisers, to stand by close at hand in case they were needed. The Admiralty sent a radio message to Tyrwhitt and Keyes while they were on their way to the fight, telling them of this new plan, but it did not get through; thus neither had any idea that friendly ships might show up in the battle area. To make matters worse, neither Goodenough nor Beatty were told that British submarines would be operating in the bight.

At first the British plan seemed to be working, an enemy destroyer was sunk, whilst several torpedo boats and a light cruiser were badly damaged.

But then things started to go wrong. *Arethusa* was hit, causing her turrets to malfunction, and her speed was reduced to 10 knots. She had to be protected by destroyers, driving off attackers with their torpedoes. This led to a hiatus in proceedings and during it seven more German light cruisers came out of harbour to join the battle. German light cruisers typically had twelve 4-inch guns as opposed to the British two 6-inch and six 4-inch. In the poor visibility which prevailed, multiple small quick-firers proved more effective, especially when allied to the excellent German gunnery and rangefinders. Just as the situation was at its worst, visibility improved slightly and Keyes saw another force of four-funnelled light cruisers approaching. They could not be British as there should be no British ships in the area apart from the Harwich Force, none of which had four funnels. Greatly daring, he challenged one of them and she replied stating that she was *Southampton* – Goodenough's flagship. This discovery highlighted a terrible danger. The submarines operating in the area had been told that any light cruiser sighted, except *Arethusa* which had three funnels, must be German. Keyes, on board *Lurcher*, had no way of communicating the changed situation to the captains of his subs. Goodenough's force was thus in terrible danger. Keyes spent a fraught few hours expecting the worst, but luckily only two of the subs got into a position to make a successful attack. *E-6* was about to fire her weapon at close range at one of Goodenough's ships when her captain saw, through his periscope, the white ensign at the stern. Another attack, on *Southampton* herself, failed and nearly resulted in the sub being rammed.

As the battle raged on the German cruisers suddenly faced an even graver danger. Goodenough had signalled to the Battle Cruiser Force that things were not going well and, regardless of the risk of mines or enemy submarines, Beatty led his great ships into the midst of the fighting. There was nothing a light cruiser could do about a battle-cruiser travelling at speed and three of the Germans were sunk in short order before Beatty, now the senior officer present, gave the order for a general withdrawal. Unlike the Admiralty, he had consulted his tide tables and knew that the battleships of the High Seas Fleet were about to steam out of the Jade. The outcome of the battle was that three German light cruisers and one destroyer were lost and two other cruisers badly damaged; 712 Germans were killed. No British ships were lost although *Arethusa* had to be towed most of the way home. Thirty-five men were killed. At some points the action had degenerated almost into farce. Keyes, before he had identified Goodenough's cruisers, was himself fleeing from them in *Lurcher*, signalling desperately for support. He thought they were Germans and when eventually the situation became clear he had quite a sharp exchange of messages with Goodenough in which he almost told him he had no right to be there. The Royal Navy had achieved an undeserved success. It was disgraceful that the muddle over the deployment of the battle-cruisers and Goodenough's force had been allowed to happen, and the whole affair was badly planned from the first. If it had gone ahead as the Admiralty had planned it, the British force would have been overwhelmed. As it was, the British only escaped because of the tidal conditions which they had not even considered. The Germans performed even worse. Their ships fought bravely but there seems to have been no overall tactical command, and their cruisers entered the battle one at a time, not as a single, overpowering co-ordinated force. They were clearly taken aback by such a daring raid on the very doorstep of their fleet anchorage.

During the battle, Keyes himself performed an outstanding act of gallantry. The cruiser *Mainz* was badly damaged by gunfire and a torpedo and was in a sinking condition. Some wounded had been taken off her by a boat from the cruiser *Liverpool*, but *Liverpool*'s captain then withdrew, thinking *Mainz* was about to explode. Keyes brought *Lurcher* right alongside her and as he did so one of the German officers seemed about to fire a gun, pointing it directly at the bridge. 'Don't fire damn you, I am coming alongside to save life,' yelled Keyes through a megaphone, 'Get your fenders out at once'. Sixty wounded and 150 unwounded men were taken off, one officer politely refusing to be rescued, preferring to die with his ship. She rolled over and sank seconds after *Lurcher* withdrew. The gallant German, actually the son of Grand Admiral Tirpitz himself, was flung into the water and hauled into one of Keyes's boats.

On 23 September the Germans took their revenge. As Keyes had predicted, this fell on the ancient cruisers, *Cressy, Aboukir* and *Hogue*. All three were torpedoed in rapid succession by the small submarine *U-9*. Keyes was at sea at the time and charged towards the scene, but could do nothing. There was no way in which a destroyer could find or attack a U-boat underwater.

His own submarines remained active in the bight and were able to locate and report on enemy minefields and the activities of small ships. He kept pushing for further, more aggressive, patrolling off the enemy coast, frequently getting himself into trouble by exceeding his orders and venturing too far into hostile waters. Eventually he was forbidden to go to sea in his destroyer at all, being told to stick to his desk and administrative duties. He was able to visit Zeebrugge where a British division was being landed to try to check the German advance towards Dunkirk. This allowed him to spend some time with Admiral Hood, commander of the Dover Patrol, whose ships were bombarding the German right flank. The two of them inspected Zeebrugge harbour carefully, noting the strong tidal streams and the massive breakwaters. This was a harbinger of activities four years later.

During this period it was decided to send submarines to the Baltic to interrupt the German iron ore imports. This was in fact an elaboration of a plan submitted by Keyes which involved occupying the Kattegat for a limited period. Three E-class boats were selected, commanded by Nasmith, Horton and Laurence. Nasmith, later to become known as one of the greatest of all submarine commanders, had to withdraw due to mechanical problems but the other two were to show what well commanded submarines could achieve, even in waters infested by the enemy and obstructed by minefields.

At the end of October a whirlwind struck the Admiralty as Battenberg, the First Sea Lord, was replaced by Fisher, recalled from retirement. For Keyes this spelt trouble. Fisher called a meeting, during which he railed about the way Keyes had failed to build enough boats and even goaded him with an accusation of cowardice as he was not at sea seeking out and destroying the enemy. Keyes stood his ground, depending on his relationship with Churchill to protect him. Sure enough, a few weeks later, he was at sea again in *Lurcher* and relations with Fisher began to improve. In December the Germans launched their raid on the north-east coast of England, during which their battle-cruisers shelled Whitby, Scarborough and Hartlepool. The British had wind of the attack before it took place and submarines were ordered to take station north of the Humber to ambush the German warships. Bad weather, poor visibility and signalling problems frustrated these attempts.

With the utmost difficulty Keyes managed to rally most of his little force and received orders to take them to the channel to the westward of Heligoland, right in the Germans' backyard, to make an attack on the returning enemy fleet. In giving him this order, Churchill and Fisher believed that they were launching what was virtually a suicide mission; two small destroyers and eight submarines would be facing the whole of the High Seas Fleet on its very front door. In the end the ambush did not work. Keyes's force arrived half an hour after the enemy had passed and returned home empty-handed. Only *E-11* got amongst the ships of the High Seas Fleet but a high sea was running and both her torpedoes missed. No criticism was made of Keyes who had done everything possible in the circumstances, and the truth was that if he had been given his orders earlier he would have been on station in good time. The orders had taken far too long to get through because the

Admiralty had insisted on using an overcrowded radio channel instead of the readily available one which Keyes had specifically asked them to use. What was inexcusable was the negligence of the Navy in not activating the defences of Hartlepool when they had ample warning of the attack. This was precisely the sort of action for which the old coastal submarines were intended. One was lying in Hartlepool, but failed to make ready and could not put to sea as the tide was too low. It thus lost a chance of making a devastating attack on the slow-moving battle-cruisers, travelling up and down, bombarding the city. Coastal submarines came under the control of the admiral responsible for coastal defence, not Keyes; if they had been under his authority things might have been different.

At this period of the war Keyes was exposing himself deliberately to mortal danger, especially from enemy minefields when entering the bight. A rare glimpse of his personality and thoughts is given by a letter written to his wife on 10 December.

> I don't quite know why I am writing this: but one never knows one's luck and one can't say that one is certain to come back from an enterprise such as the one I hope to take part in on Sunday morning. And so, if we are to part company for a bit I want to tell you before I go on my long journey, how blissfully happy I have been with you … .
>
> It is hard to believe that this will be the end of our partnership, and I will go in the hope that we will meet again in another world. I know mine is the easier part, but I know you will show a gallant front.
>
> It is proper and right to be ready to die at such a time, and I know you will give me credit for going out very confidently and buoyantly to meet my fate. May the God I believe in be with you … .

Although relationships with Fisher had improved, Keyes had no doubt that the First Sea Lord was determined to be rid of him. He was therefore not greatly surprised when he was summoned to Churchill's office and told to prepare to leave the next day to join a naval force which was ordered to force a passage through the Dardanelles, thus pushing Turkey out of the war. The mission was still top secret, and there was no time to say goodbye to his family, still at Fareham, or to his command at Harwich and Portsmouth. On 8 February he was off to the Eastern Mediterranean.

SUBMARINES

What had Keyes achieved as commodore of the submarine force? He was essentially a fighting sailor, not an administrator and apart from improved periscopes and the experiments leading up to the spectacularly unsuccessful 'fleet submarines', he introduced little in the way of new technology. There was probably also some justification for Fisher's criticism of the rate at which submarines were being built. A more focused administrator would have been able to make much more rapid progress. As they were a totally new class of weapon, no one knew how overseas submarines could be employed most successfully in 1914. Keyes's hands-on approach of trying to lead a flotilla of submarines from a destroyer suited his personality perfectly but was not effective due to poor communications. A submarine is best used as a solitary hunter, not part of a mixed taskforce and neither Britain nor her enemies were successful in co-ordinating submarines with fleet actions at any stage of the war. The astonishing achievements of British boats in the Baltic illustrates what could be achieved by submarines acting alone and unsupported. In one vital sphere, however, he was most effective. His inspirational leadership developed the skills and dedication of his commanders and crews to the very highest pitch. As the war progressed they achieved astonishing success in the Baltic, the Eastern Mediterranean, the North Sea and the Channel. Unlike the enemy U-boats, whose mission was to strangle Britain by sinking merchant ships, British commanders were primarily concerned with sinking warships. When, as in the Baltic and the Sea of Marmora, they were tasked with sinking civilian ships, this was performed with the utmost regard for the safety of the crews. These were men of which their commodore and their nation could be proud.

Chapter 7

Disaster in the Dardanelles

The Dardanelles campaign was to occupy Keyes for a year and its outcome would haunt him for the rest of his life. Turkey's traditional enemy was Russia, against whom it had fought alongside Britain and France during the Crimean war. In 1914 these two previous allies were allied to Russia, causing the Turks to think again. Another cause of friction between Turkey and the Allies was British and French ambitions in the Middle East. The whole area, including Egypt, had been a part of the crumbling Turkish Empire, but now the European powers were busily carving out spheres of influence for themselves, goaded on by the promise of the newly discovered oil fields. Turkey, considered the 'Sick Man of Europe,' was not in a position to halt European imperial and commercial ambitions. A more immediate threat to Turkey was her other traditional enemy, Greece. The Allies had hoped that Greece might be cajoled into leading an expedition against European Turkey, including the Gallipoli peninsula, but unfortunately for them the Greeks were afraid to confront Turkey without the support of Bulgaria, which was not forthcoming. Germany, seeing the Allies' frustration, made every effort to befriend Turkey, supplying arms, advice and industrial goods, but the Turks were too nervous of the might of the British and French fleets in the Mediterranean to make any firm commitment.

The situation changed when the German battlecruiser *Goeben* and her escort *Breslau* arrived off Constantinople, having cocked a snook at the British forces trying to intercept them. They and their crews were transferred to the Turkish navy. The Turks looked on them as replacements for two Dreadnoughts which were being completed for them in Britain but were seized by the British as soon as the war broke out. On 5 November 1914 Britain and France declared war on Turkey. Two months later the Russians found themselves attacked by the Turks in the Caucasus and begged their Western allies to mount a diversion. At the same time the British War Cabinet was in a quandary. The great German advance had been checked on the Marne in France and on the Yser in Belgium, with the help of the ships of the Dover Patrol. It seemed that instead of 'being over by Christmas', the war in the west was going to be a long slogging match and that any contribution Britain could make to it would be small compared to that of the massive armies of France. Would it not be better for the British army to find some way of setting up a second front elsewhere? Fisher and Churchill both at first favoured an attack somewhere on the north German coast. Others suggested Salonika or a landing on the Belgian sand dunes. Nothing was agreed and the French strongly objected to any scheme which would draw significant British forces away from the main battle in northern France. Eventually it dawned on Churchill and on the French politician Aristide Briand that the perfect solution both militarily and politically was an attack on Turkey, mounted not by the armies, who were too occupied in France, but by the Royal Navy, with the French navy in support, using mainly old ships which were too slow and vulnerable to serve with the Grand Fleet. This would please the Russians, placate the French and at the same time perhaps allow a telling strike to be made up through Bulgaria into the heart of the Austro-Hungarian Empire. It would also improve the prospects of extending British interests in the Middle East.

The commander of the British forces in the Mediterranean, Admiral Carden, was ordered to make ready a plan for forcing a passage through the Dardanelles and the Sea of Marmara to Constantinople. He already had some experience of the Dardanelles defences since in November, just before the final declaration of war with Turkey, a mixed British and French squadron had engaged the forts at Kum Kale, on the Asiatic shore (See Map 4). A lucky shot had exploded the magazine, killing a number of Turkish gunners and dismounting all the guns in the fort. Thus, in about twenty minutes, the outer defences were put totally out of action and the ships withdrew. This ill-considered action proved to be a blessing in disguise for the Turks and their German advisors. They learnt that the inner forts, which had not been engaged, must be strengthened and provided with better artillery and also that even heavy guns were not likely to sink allied battleships. A far better defence would be well-placed minefields.

Carden's plan was to employ twelve battleships, two battle-cruisers and a fleet of smaller supporting ships to fight their way into the Sea of Marmara. He thought that the process would take about a month and involve some losses among the old pre-dreadnought battleships. The only army involvement was to be some Australian and New Zealand troops, then being trained in Egypt, whose role would be to police Constantinople. Fisher at first disapproved of the plan, believing it to be a waste of time and resources which would be better spent on his pet project of landing a Russian army on the German Baltic coast. Eventually, under pressure from Churchill and Lord Kitchener, Britain's most famous soldier and Secretary of State for War, he gave in and actually insisted that the brand-new fast battleship *Queen Elizabeth* should be added to Carden's forces. His support, however, was grudging, needing frequent reassurances from Churchill.

Keyes's role was to be chief of staff to Carden, for whom he developed a deep affection. Second in command of the operation was his old friend Admiral de Robeck. He soon developed a network of friends both among the senior Royal Navy officers present and among the French who were acting under Carden's command. His position as chief of staff was not an easy one as he had no direct authority over the captains of the capital ships and was sometimes subject to the usual opprobrium attached to 'the man from head office'. His record was, however, well respected and he impressed everyone with his hard work and vigour. He had the initial advantage of knowing the area of operations quite well, having studied the forts carefully when on a diplomatic mission in 1906-07. He was convinced that they could easily be overrun by a landing party taking them in the rear. On 19 February Carden and his ADC embarked on the battlecruiser *Inflexible* and the bombardment of the outer forts on Kum Kale began.

At first long-range shelling seemed to have little effect. Even *Queen Elizabeth*'s one-ton 15-inch rounds only raised huge clouds of dust. Gradually the bombarders moved closer, but the enemy had learned not to waste ammunition and made no reply. Eventually, de Robeck was ordered to move right in and inspect the damage. He was greeted with a hail of close-range fire, which was not very effective and was soon silenced by the guns of the fleet. It became clear, however, that the coastal artillery was intact and remained a threat to any ship within its range. Darkness was by now falling, so the British and French warships withdrew to Mudros Island, which was to become their base. They were dissatisfied with their day's work. Clearly the enemy gunners were now well schooled and resilient. Keyes was able to press his case for taking the forts in the rear. Bad weather then hampered operations. On the 25th the attack was resumed. This time the Turks seemed to abandon their positions entirely; two ships moved further into the strait and shelled the intermediate forts while parties of bluejackets and marines stormed ashore and destroyed the gun mountings, facing almost no opposition. So far so good, but Keyes was worried chiefly on three counts:

The process was taking too long and Carden was so risk averse that he would not press on when favourable conditions arose.

There had been almost no progress in sweeping the minefields which would be essential for the next stage of the operation. The minesweeping trawlers were manned by civilian crews and they simply refused to sweep mines when they were under fire from the shore. The strong currents in the Dardanelles made their work doubly difficult.

The condition of the Admiral himself was disturbing. He worried about everything, he could not eat or sleep properly – he seemed to be heading for a breakdown.

By this time it was also becoming clear that, while a passage into the Marmara might be forced, the heights of the Gallipoli peninsula would have to be held by ground troops if any lasting progress was to be made. Mobile artillery fire from the hillsides was a constant worry for unarmoured ships, especially slow-moving minesweepers. It was also rumoured that static torpedo tubes were mounted on the shore. In truth there were none. Preparations were set in hand to convey more army units from Egypt for this and General Sir Ian Hamilton, the same Hamilton who had been so impressed by Roger's mother while serving in the Punjab, was despatched to take charge of the land forces.

Churchill and Fisher were also worrying about the slow rate of progress. Carden was sent a telegram instructing him to press on and move faster, even if making progress resulted in the loss of a ship or two. The telegram was actually delivered to Keyes as Carden was taking a day's rest. It was music to Roger's ears and he immediately charged off in a destroyer to find his chief. A long series of meetings ensued and eventually a plan emerged to take the battleships and the battle cruiser *Inflexible* into the strait and bombard the fortresses at Chanak at close range. While this was going on the trawlers would make a determined effort to sweep the mines which beset the strait. The fleet would then be clear to tackle the defences further up the strait and steam into the Sea of Marmara (See Map 4).

It was expected that this campaign would take two days. No sooner had the plan been formulated than Carden finally broke down and had to return home in a hospital ship. De Robeck was appointed in his place. He naturally asked Keyes to continue as chief of staff; in truth Roger had made himself indispensable. He was almost hyperactive, dashing from meeting to meeting, involved in everything, drafting orders, writing telegrams, and trying to inspire the trawlermen who were still refusing to sweep under fire. Their chief bugbears were the many mobile artillery pieces which the Turks concealed in the woods on shore.

By 18 March all seemed ready for the assault on the inner forts. The idea was that the British battleships would fire on them at about eight miles range, then the French would pass through the British line and engage at close quarters for four hours, after which they would be relieved by the remaining British ships, who would finally smash the gun emplacements at close range.

It all began well, by 1.45 the forts were almost silenced and de Robeck gave the signal for the sweepers to begin their work in the strait. Only one ship, the French battleship *Gaulois*, had suffered any material damage and there were few casualties. Then, suddenly, all went awry. First, the French battleship *Bouvet* struck a mine and rolled over and sank, taking 639 of her crew with her. She had been in the process of turning out of the firing line in Eren Keui Bay, just where most of the ships in the bombarding force made their turn after firing. Next the old battleship *Irresistible* was mined; then the dreadnought battle-cruiser *Inflexible* heeled over drunkenly. *Ocean* was ordered to take *Irresistible* in tow, and a destroyer was despatched to assist. She returned loaded with *Irresistible*'s crew but *Ocean* showed no sign of obeying the order. Two French battleships, *Gaulois* and *Suffren*, were then severely damaged by shellfire and had to struggle to Mudros for temporary repair. De Robeck realised that he was in an impossible situation and ordered a general withdrawal.

Keyes accepted that withdrawal was the only course open to the admiral but set off himself in the destroyer *Wear* to try to help save the damaged ships. *Irresistible* was under a withering fire from 6-inch guns ashore and her captain had decided that there was nothing for it but to abandon her. This Keyes could not tolerate. A battleship abandoned to be salvaged and captured by the enemy! He could not issue orders to *Ocean* on his own authority but he signalled her saying that the admiral had ordered her to take *Irresistible* in tow. She eventually replied saying that the water was too shallow for her to approach. Keyes ordered *Wear* to close the stricken ship to take soundings, and found there was plenty of water to allow *Ocean* to approach. During this operation *Wear*, an entirely unarmoured destroyer, was attracting the fire of numerous 6-inch guns ashore and it is astonishing that she was not hit. *Ocean* ignored Keyes's signal and continued to fire on the coastal guns, then suddenly she herself struck a mine and began to sink. Meantime, it appeared that *Irresistible* had resumed an even keel and was drifting out of the strait on the current so that there was no further danger of her running aground and being captured. Keyes sped back to report to the admiral who, seeing that he was overwrought and exhausted, insisted that he had a proper meal before entering the strait again. De Robeck seems at first to have been unshaken by the terrible events of the day. As soon as he had finished his meal, Keyes was off again, looking for *Ocean* and *Inflexible* with orders to torpedo *Irresistible* if she seemed likely to run ashore. In spite of a thorough search, the ships could not be found. In the end *Ocean* and *Irresistible* both sank in deep water. *Inflexible* was picked up at sea the next day and towed to Malta to be repaired.

The cause of these disastrous events was a single, small, Turkish steamer, *Nousret*, under command of Lieutenant Colonel Geehl, a noted expert in mining. The Turks had anticipated that the allied ships would turn in Eren Keui Bay, and laid a string of mines parallel to the shore in exactly the right spot. Keyes wrote that 'The devil did his work well that day. He prolonged the war for two years'. He himself was not disheartened by the day's events. He could see that the forts were severely damaged and that shellfire from them seemed to do very little damage to armoured ships. Now all that remained to be done was to find a way to sweep the minefields. He was also convinced that a landing by the army on Gallipoli peninsula would be vital to ensure the enduring success of the campaign which could not succeed in the long term if the peninsula was held by the enemy. There was by now quite general agreement that a land operation of some sort would be essential to the success of the enterprise. A purely naval operation would be unlikely to achieve the objective of overthrowing the whole Turkish Empire and it was also hoped that ground troops would have little difficulty in occupying the shores of the strait and silencing the mobile guns which were so effectively harassing the minesweeping operation. Little by little 'mission creep' was beginning to turn the whole campaign into a costly affair in which the lion's share of the fighting and of casualties would be borne by the army. This was, of course, exactly opposite to the original concept.

Minesweeping now became the prime task of the Royal Navy in the strait. The minesweeping effort which had accompanied the attack on the forts that day had been no better than previous attempts, the trawlers running out of the strait as soon as they came under fire. Some mines were swept but in truth it was almost impossible to sweep properly against the strong current. The trawlers, which could only make about 5 knots when towing a sweep, were almost stationary when sweeping against the 4-knot current running out of the strait, so they became excellent targets for artillery. They had even tried steaming upstream with their sweeps stowed, then turning and deploying them to sweep downstream, but this did not work well and the crews of the little ships were terrified of deploying their gear, working on deck under fire from artillery and machine guns. Keyes himself had accompanied this venture on 10 March in the old battleship *Canopus* which was tasked with giving covering fire to the trawlers. He wrote:

> One saw stabs of light from the hills in the direction of the six-inch batteries covering the minefields on both sides of the Straits followed by the whine of shells, the bursting of shrapnel and the scream of heavy projectiles which threw up fountains of water. The fire was very wild and *Canopus* was not hit but for all the good we did towards dowsing the searchlights we might as well have been firing at the moon.

Parties of midshipmen and sailors were sent into the strait with improvised sweeping gear mounted in ships' boats. They were told to do what they could to find and disable any floating mines and sweep moored mines near the surface. (Floating mines were assumed to have been launched by the enemy to drift down on the current and strike ships in the strait. In fact the floaters that were found must have been moored mines which had come adrift. The Turks had no floating type mines.) This dangerous job was performed with great courage and some success, but it was nowhere near enough to sweep the strait clear. At Keyes's suggestion, the trawler crews were thickened with bluejackets, including men from the sunken battleships but this did not solve the problem. Officers from the Fleet and indeed voices from the Admiralty at home began to accuse the trawlermen of 'cowardice'. This was hardly the way to inspire them to greater efforts.

Keyes had been extremely active in trying to get the mine problem dealt with and it seems that he rather thrust himself into the front row of this task, although he was not an expert in mine clearance. Also, his relationship with the trawlermen became sour. You do not get the best out of a tough old fisherman by calling him a coward. Keyes had not an ounce of tolerance for anything he believed to be weak or 'unmanly' and this made constructive discussion impossible. There was by this time plenty of experience within the Royal Navy in minesweeping in the North Sea and surely it would have made sense to have asked for the assistance of an expert from there. Quite simple methods of sweeping like using the River-class destroyers, of which there were fifteen on the station, to tow sweeps, were not exploited until later in the campaign, although back in home waters old destroyers were used extensively to sweep mines to clear a pathway for the Grand Fleet. There had also been a proposal to use 'mine bumpers' – merchant ships with their bows filled with concrete – to blast a path through the fields, exploding the mines as they went. This tactic was widely used by the Germans, calling the ships *Sperrbrecher*. They were never employed in the Gallipoli campaign.

This is a suitable point in the narrative to look at the Keyes who has so far emerged. His extraordinary energy, courage and superb seamanship had enabled him to climb the ladder of the naval hierarchy unusually quickly. He had also chosen his friends well, numbering among them Churchill, Beatty, Jellicoe and de Robeck. He was happily married and had successfully carried out a diplomatic role, so he knew the Italian, French, Greek and even Austrian navies well. He had every prospect of further success, but perhaps there is a hint of some weakness of judgement or some intellectual failing. He was not a clever man, nor a tolerant one. He was inclined to 'blow his top' and thus make enemies of senior figures who could damage him – Fisher being a prime example. Straightforward and sometimes short-tempered, he lacked the skills of a politician. His crews and close associates almost always liked and respected him, but his treatment of the trawler crews does show some lack of judgement. In action he always wanted to be in the front row, contemptuous of danger and always pushing forward. This attitude had served him very well as a junior officer fighting untrained and badly-led Chinese, but against a capable and determined opponent it was not always the best attitude for a chief of staff with flag rank. He was convinced, and remained convinced for the rest of his life, that forcing a passage to Constantinople was perfectly feasible with an acceptable level of losses. It irked him that the Navy seemed so loss averse while the army in France was losing huge numbers of men in every action and this point was reinforced by telegrams received from Churchill himself. This made the remainder of 1915 a particularly bitter experience for Keyes.

His first task after returning from his attempted salvage operation was to re-energise his chief. De Robeck was devastated by the losses resulting from the action, blaming himself. Three battleships *Ocean*, *Irresistible*, and *Bouvet* were lost; two more, *Suffren* and *Gaulois*, and the dreadnought battle-cruiser *Inflexible* were rendered out of action due to battle damage. Never, in more than a hundred years, had a British fleet suffered such a defeat. The admiral's self-blame was hardly fair as the plan had been made by Carden, agreed by his staff and approved by the Admiralty who had specifically told him that it was prepared to accept losses. De Robeck expected to be removed from his post, but Roger managed to cheer him up and struggled to encourage him to resume the attack very soon. Roger begged to be relieved of his chief of staff duties and to be put in direct command of the minesweeping force. De Robeck replied that he could not be spared, but could work on a planned re-organisation of the minesweepers.

Had anyone known the real state of the Turkish defences they would surely have attacked again the very next day. Almost all the ammunition for the coastal guns had been expended, half their guns were out of action and the minefields in the strait were actually in very poor condition. The Turkish government in Constantinople was panicked and expected to see the British Fleet in the Golden Horn in two days' time. Now was the time for the British to strike – but they missed it.

It is worth considering at this point whether the whole Gallipoli expedition was worthwhile. How much difference to the war being fought in France and in Eastern Europe would the fall of the Turkish capital make? The theory held by supporters of the campaign, such as Keyes and Churchill, was that it would enable the Allies to strike up through Bulgaria into the heart of the Austro-Hungarian Empire, causing undecided nations such as Greece and Bulgaria to throw in their lot with the Allies and strike at 'the soft underbelly of Europe'. At the same time the Turkish Empire in the Levant would crumble, giving Britain and France free rein to colonise virtually the whole Arab world. It is not easy to accept this scenario. Even if their capital had fallen the Turks would have been left with a large army which was to show itself to be a formidable opponent. Turkish troops were poorly trained and equipped but they would fight to the death for their country and for their faith. The British had greatly undervalued the fighting qualities of 'Johnny Turk'. The handful of British and French soldiers available in the Middle East would have been hard pressed to keep order in Constantinople, let alone strike up through Bulgaria. Another factor, often forgotten, is that the Allies had agreed that if Constantinople fell the Russians would be given possession of it. Given the crumbling state of the Russian army and government, it is difficult to see this creating anything but trouble for the Allies. Even if Constantinople had fallen, France would never have consented to weakening the Western Front to release sufficient forces to thrust up into central Europe, and would have objected strongly to any withdrawal of the BEF to join what they still considered as a sideshow. In their enthusiasm to achieve a naval victory Keyes, Churchill and their allies seem to have lost that grip on hard reality which is essential to sound strategic thinking.

Chapter 8

Frustration and Evacuation

After the debacle of 18 March Keyes spent much of his time busily and belatedly trying to fit improvised sweeps to destroyers and seems to have missed out on conferences being held between his admiral, General Hamilton and their various subordinates on the liner *Franconia*. He was eventually told that de Robeck had insisted that no more attacks would be made by the fleet until the minesweeping force was fully effective and, most significantly, that the army was in position on the Gallipoli peninsula. Furthermore, Hamilton had stated that his original plan to land at Bulair on the neck of the peninsula was no longer a possibility: he would land his men at its tip and fight his way north-east to Bulair (See Map 4). Keyes thought this absurd. It would give the Turks time to regroup, replenish their ammunition, lay more mines and occupy the peninsula in force. Hamilton wrote of him then: 'He is sick as a she bear robbed of her cubs, that his pets, battleships, T.Bs, destroyers, submarines etc. should have to wait for the Army. Well we are not to blame … '.

Back in London Churchill was fighting a battle of which Keyes knew nothing. He was appalled at the idea of abandoning the quite simple mission set for the fleet and foresaw the possibility of a landing by the army turning into a prolonged and wasteful struggle. He noted that the loss of life in the naval operations so far had been paltry and stated that only one valuable ship, *Inflexible*, had been damaged and she could readily be repaired. He wrote in a draft telegram to de Robeck:

> The entry of a Fleet into the Marmara strong enough to beat the Turkish Fleet would produce decisive results on the whole situation … we know the forts are short of ammunition and the supply of mines is limited. We do not think that the time has come yet to give up the plan of forcing the Dardanelles by a purely naval operation.

It was no good. Fisher and the Board of the Admiralty had accepted de Robeck's pessimistic view and would not budge. The telegram was not sent. Had it been, of course Keyes would have been delighted as it coincided with his view, although he would have preferred a situation in which the army occupied the high ground dominating the strait. Churchill, in spite of his strongly-held opinion, could not risk a total breach with his Admiralty Board. He and Roger were downright embarrassed that the army in France was suffering thousands of deaths every week, and it seemed that the Royal Navy had been scared by the loss of fewer than a hundred men.

The initial date set for the army to invade the peninsula was 14 April, by which time Keyes had undertaken to get a better-organised minesweeping force ready to work. It was expected that the troops would easily chase the Turks off to Bulair, or beyond, so that his sweepers would be able to work without hindrance from the mobile artillery which was infesting the shore. An amphibious landing on an enemy-held shore, however, is a notoriously difficult operation, requiring meticulous planning, preparation and training. It is best carried out in the strictest secrecy. In this case the military transports which carried all the equipment, ammunition, supplies and weapons needed for the invasion had not been loaded correctly. The ships all had to go to Egypt to be repacked, and there prying eyes were able to see exactly what was going on, what units and officers were involved, and what they were bringing with them. Furthermore, the Turks had plenty of time to rush reinforcements onto the peninsula. General Hamilton's plan was to land at several points on the peninsula to outflank the main Turkish defending forces which were mostly deployed on the extreme southern tip. At the same time the Fleet would make its assault on the strait. This plan was subject to many changes and modifications, the most important being that de Robeck and Keyes decided that it would be impossible to land the troops and give them the naval artillery support they needed whilst retaining enough ships for the simultaneous attack on the strait. The army would have to be landed and supported before there was another seaborne venture. Next the weather took a hand. A succession of southerly gales in mid-April made landing impossible and it was not until the 23rd that it was calm enough to go ahead, so the landing was scheduled for the 25th. Every day's delay was one more chance for the German general, Liman von Sanders, to improve his positions and critically to prepare a system of trenches and machine-gun nests which would be the key to the defence. For the first time, Keyes was going to witness an opposed landing on an enemy shore, just the type of operation in which he would specialise in later years. It was decided that the General Staff, including Hamilton, de Robeck and Keyes, would observe the whole landing operation from the comfort and safety of the fast battleship *Queen Elizabeth*, cruising from one landing place to another. Keyes was heard to mutter, 'How much better to be landing with those chaps ashore than to be waiting for news of them here'.

At first all went well. The Australian troops stormed ashore on their designated beach almost unopposed and chased a small body of the enemy up into the hills inland. Y Beach was also weakly held and the watchers on the battleship could see troops on the cliff tops drinking tea. V and W Beaches were a different proposition. They were known to be strongly held and the idea was that the ships in the offing would smother the defences with fire, then, when the troops were landing, switch their bombardment further inland. The troops would land from ships' boats and fight their way forward. An old collier, *River Clyde,* would carry 2,000 men close up to the shore and run herself aground, allowing the infantry to storm ashore via a bridge of boats between her and the land and overrun the fortifications. It soon became clear, however, that the Turks had not been driven off by the naval guns, nor had the wire entanglements on the beaches been much damaged. Turkish infantry waited until the troops were scrambling ashore, then opened a murderous fire with rifles and well-concealed machine guns. The slaughter was awful. It was clear to the watchers that the right decision would be to reinforce the landings on S and Y Beaches and order the forces landing there unopposed to attack the Turkish flanks to relieve their colleagues. Keyes also begged that the Royal Naval Division, which was carrying out a feint attack at Bulair, should be immediately diverted to join the landings at S and Y. Unfortunately, however, the commanders of the forces ashore showed total lack of initiative and nothing was done. Major General Hunter-Watson was supposed to be supervising the whole operation but seems to have done nothing whatever. Hamilton, out of a misplaced desire not to interfere with the conduct of a battle which he had delegated to his subordinate, simply looked on in horror. Keyes pleaded with him to intervene but he would not. By the end of the day the situation on land was obviously dire: at the cost of 4,000 casualties the invaders had a foothold on just five beaches; on V Beach they continued to be harassed by machine-gun and rifle fire as they lay exposed on the sand. Worse was to come. The soldiers who had landed almost unopposed on Y Beach were attacked during the night; they drove the Turks off with heavy losses, then for some reason decided that they should evacuate their position and signalled to the warships offshore to come in and pick them up. When their commander saw what was happening, he furiously called for the evacuation to cease, but it was too late. Half his men had already gone, and he had no option but to follow them. The most creditable action in this episode was performed by a Keyes – not Roger this time but his younger brother Adrian, a destroyer captain. He took a last boat ashore and diligently searched the battle ground on his own for two hours, looking for any wounded left behind.

Roger himself went ashore and got involved in the fighting whenever there was a chance. For example, he landed on W Beach and wrote:

> We walked over the hill to Sedd el Bahr, only a mile away but a bloody mile if ever there was one … after three hours on shore we returned to *Queen Elizabeth* with much to reflect on. The appalling nature of military operations under modern conditions and the magnitude of the Army's task were all too apparent and I felt that the sooner we took a hand the better, an opinion fully shared by Godfrey (his assistant). We felt that a naval attack could not fail to turn the position for the Army …

There was little further progress in the following days and no naval attack. Both sides were dug in and fighting a bitter trench war. The casualty list increased to 19,000. Clearly the army had not the slightest hope of advancing up the peninsula to clear away the guns which were harassing the minesweepers. Unless strong reinforcements arrived the situation would remain a bloody stalemate. This impasse caused Keyes to express utter frustration. He had always thought that the Fleet could force the strait without help from the army but had felt compelled to support his admiral's view that the coastal guns must be cleared away first. He had also agreed with the admiral that the Navy could not steam into the strait at the same time as supporting the landings with its heavy guns. Now he felt that all his doubts about Hamilton and de Robeck's plans for a joint operation were fully justified. He was disgusted and ashamed that the army had suffered 19,000 casualties whereas the Navy had only a handful. If every sailor in the Fleet had been killed fewer men would have been lost than the army had suffered in a few days' fighting. Now was the time to put things right. He longed to put his new minesweeping force to the test and trust to the heavy guns and the determination of the fleet. If they now made their charge through the straits, surely the Turkish troops on the peninsula would be cowed into submission. De Robeck would have none of it. Though the two men were good personal friends and admired each other, on this

Cygnet: She was a sister ship to *Fame*. Long and narrow, these were very fast ships capable of over 30 knots, but it needed steady nerves and a strong stomach to handle them in a heavy sea. Note the 'turtle back' foredeck and the flimsy screen around the men on watch, who would normally be soaked after a few hours at sea. The helmsman stood in a 'conning tower' low down just aft of the foredeck. (*Author's collection*)

Harpy in a rough sea: Launched in 1909. *Harpy* was a G-class destroyer typical of those used by the Harwich Force. In rough weather the best tactic was to steam slowly ahead with the wind about 15 degrees off the bow. 8 destroyers were lost during the First World War due to weather, 22 were lost to mines, 10 sunk by U-boats, 2 rammed, 13 lost in surface actions and 14 in collisions. (*Author's collection*)

Soult: Keyes made extensive use of monitors in the Dardanelles and with the Dover Patrol. *Soult* had massive 15-inch guns with a range of over 18 miles but she was terribly slow and unhandy, making only about 6 knots in still water. Cheaply built using parts and guns left over from other projects, monitors were considered 'dispensable' but they did excellent service. (*Author's collection*)

A K Boat under way. These huge steam turbine driven submarines were designed to be able to keep up with the Grand Fleet. They proved a terrible failure, killing many of their own crews. (*Source IWM*)

Vindictive alongside the mole at Zeebrugge. *Daffodil* is forcing her against the mole as it has been impossible to moor her correctly. Note the steep gangway. (*Source IWM*)

Commandos training in Scotland. Keyes and his staff devised extremely tough training regimes for the commandos and their boats' crews on the west coast of Scotland. (*Source IWM*)

David Beatty (2nd from left) and Chatfield, his Flag Captain (3rd from left) on the bridge of *Lion* (?)
Beatty became a national hero although his handling of the Grand Fleet was just as cautious as hi
predecessor's. He was a close friend of Keyes. Chatfield and Keyes worked together to prevent th
RAF from getting further control of naval aviation. (*Source IWM*)

The Battle of Leyte Gulf. US forces storming towards the beach under cover of fire from the flee
Some landing craft doubled as rocket launchers. (*Source IWM*)

Keyes and Churchill inspecting an army unit in the South of England. Churchill valued his old friend's opinions and advice but had to reject many of his harebrained schemes for aggressive action. (*Source IWM*)

Admiral of the Fleet Lord Keyes of Zeebrugge and Dover KCVO GCB CMG DSO. Keynes retained his slim build and boyish features into his late 60s. (*Source IWM*)

question there was to be no agreement. It was a difficult and hurtful time for Keyes; he loathed being at odds with his boss and loathed even more sitting in comfort at meetings in big, invulnerable ships, eating civilised meals, when he knew the hell being suffered by officers and soldiers on shore. It was contrary to every sentiment and instinct that he had. At every opportunity he went ashore, often right into the firing line, but his duties precluded any prolonged stay with the weary, hard-pressed troops.

Eventually de Robeck called a meeting of the senior officers present and allowed Keyes to put his case to them. The conclusion of the meeting was unsatisfactory. A telegram was drafted to be sent to the Admiralty stating that the Fleet *might* be able to force the strait but if they failed the army would be left abandoned on the peninsula. De Robeck stated that he would renew the naval assault *if he was ordered to do so.* Not unnaturally the Admiralty issued no such order to de Robeck. Their reply brought three new factors into play which would make Roger's position even more difficult:

- A German U-boat had been seen passing Gibraltar presenting a new menace for the fleet.
- Italy had agreed to join the Allies provided that four British battleships and four cruisers were despatched to the Adriatic.
- The *Queen Elizabeth,* by far the most effective ship in the theatre, must return home at once. This was in fact prompted by the fact that the old battleship *Goliath*, which had been providing covering fire to forces ashore, had been unexpectedly attacked and sunk with all hands by a German-manned Turkish destroyer just off the peninsula. (Certainly the enemy regarded *Queen Elizabeth* as a prime target. The Navy actually took the precaution of building a full-sized wooden model of her to confuse the Turks and this was duly torpedoed soon after the real battleship had left for home.)

The chief opponent of the whole Dardanelles adventure was now Fisher. He and Churchill fought bitter battles about the campaign, with Churchill always taking the same aggressive line as Keyes. Eventually, Fisher could stand it no longer and resigned precipitating a Cabinet crisis which caused the government to fall. It was replaced by a new non-party administration in which Arthur Balfour replaced Churchill as First Lord of the Admiralty. For Keyes this was a disaster. He and Churchill had become firm friends and staunch allies, both imbued with the same aggressive spirit. Now that he was gone from the Admiralty, Roger's position seemed only likely to become more difficult.

There was no sign of the rumoured U-boat until the end of May when the battleship *Vengeance* reported a torpedo narrowly missing her. Keyes heard of this whilst at a shipboard meeting near Imbros. He leapt up, commandeered a destroyer lying alongside and ordered her to make full speed towards the reported position. Help was at hand as Adrian Keyes appeared in another destroyer and the two brothers carried out an intensive but fruitless search. As they were doing so, they noticed *Triumph*, another old battleship, taking on a list, then rolling clean over – the victim of another torpedo. The very next day yet another old battleship, *Majestic*, was riding at anchor off W Beach, supporting the army with her heavy guns. A seaman on deck happened to be looking out to sea. 'Look, Sir,' he said to a nearby officer, 'There is a submarine's conning tower'. 'Yes,' replied the officer, 'and here comes the torpedo'. The ship was sunk, luckily in shallow water, and there were few casualties. *U-21*, the source all the trouble, slipped away undamaged. She was a small sub of 600 tonnes with a crew of four officers and twenty-five men. The Turks on the hillside nearby cheered her heartily. Keyes reflected gloomily that the loss of three battleships was almost certainly more than they would have lost if they had stormed into the strait as he had unsuccessfully urged. The Navy's reaction was decisive. It withdrew all heavy ships from duties assisting the troops ashore, prompting the army to say, quite justifiably, that they had run away. Some old cruisers fitted with anti-torpedo bulges were drafted in to give some limited fire support and two small monitors appeared from Malta. These were designed for shore bombardment and their shallow draft and bulged hulls made them difficult to torpedo. More, larger, monitors were summoned from England to make up for the withdrawal of the main fleet, but they were a poor substitute for the massive battleships, now lying safely out of harm's way. Furious and humiliated, Keyes had to content himself with even more risky visits to the troops ashore, accompanied always by his coxswain from the China campaign, Chief Petty Officer Brady.

There was, however, one bright spot. Keyes still regarded submarines as his especial 'babies' and he knew and had trained most of the commanders of the subs in the Gallipoli sector. As early as December 1914, *B-11*, Lieutenant Commander Holbrook, had penetrated the Dardanelles and sunk an old Turkish battleship. *Massoudieh*. *B-11* was a tiny, primitive boat and navigating her against the current up through the strait and safely back was an astonishing achievement. Shortly after this the much more powerful

E-class submarines arrived on the scene. *E-14*, Lieutenant Commander Boyle, had a spectacularly successful cruise in the Marmara, sinking a large trooper, a minelayer and numerous smaller vessels; then Nasmith's *E-11* successfully penetrated the harbour at Constantinople, achieving an astonishing run of successful attacks. By then submarines were being fitted with deck guns, normally 6-pounders, making them much more effective against small ships. Successful submarine operations continued throughout the campaign, making any attempt by the Turks to supply the peninsula by sea so dangerous as to be impractical. Losses were heavy but the little force virtually halved the size of the Turkish merchant marine and destroyed a large part of the Ottoman Navy. Four Victoria Crosses were awarded. Keyes's heart must have swelled with pride.

By the summer of 1915, the Cabinet in London was frustrated with the course of the war; Russian armies were crumbling, Bulgaria was joining the Central Powers, Italy was suffering reverses on the Isonzo and, on the Western Front, the bloody stalemate continued. Desperate attempts were made to find some sphere in which a victory could be claimed and, inspired by over-confident reports from Hamilton, the new government decided to reinforce the Gallipoli campaign strongly and knock Turkey out of the war. This was in spite of the fact that a series of offensives on the peninsula had recently failed, the Turks holding grimly onto their defensive trenches and counter-attacking strongly after each reverse. Needless to say, the Admiralty continued to insist that the peninsula must be in British hands before any naval assault could be attempted. Reinforcements, guns and ammunition were diverted from France and sent to participate in what was hoped would be a final push to dislodge the Turks on the peninsula.

The idea was to mount the main attack at Anzac, from where the fresh troops would storm across the peninsula to the shores of the strait. There would be a feint at Cape Helles to draw the enemy away from the ANZAC landing, and a strong flank attack would be mounted at Suvla Bay, so far untouched by the fighting. The Suvla attack would be carried out by 20,000 men who would land at night and storm up the hillsides, eventually linking up with the ANZAC forces. The task of organising all this, providing water, supplies, landing craft and small boats, and co-ordinating the attack with movements of the Fleet, fell squarely on Keyes's shoulders. He worked day and night on plans for the invasion, probably forcing himself to believe that all would be well this time. It was not. The troops were put ashore as planned but made only little progress. Once again, even small numbers of determined defenders, well dug in, showed that they could hold off the most determined assault. Also leadership and co-ordination ashore was poor. For example, on one occasion Keyes, on a trip ashore, found the forces landed at Suvla Bay enjoying a sort of beach picnic and bathing while the heights above the beach were still unoccupied by the Turks. Those same heights were their first key objective. He desperately sought an army officer able to sort this ridiculous waste of an opportunity, but he found no one who felt it was his job to do anything. By the time matters were brought into line the heights were occupied by the enemy and were to be the scene of a savage and costly fight some weeks later.

Hamilton, seeing that this great effort had produced almost nothing, wrote urgently to London demanding another 95,000 men, fully equipped. His request was not granted. Back in London, Kitchener, the Minister of War, began asking if evacuation of the peninsula should be considered.

Recent events had once again convinced Keyes that only a decisive blow by the Fleet would save the situation. Now they had effective destroyer-minesweepers and trawlers manned by the Royal Navy instead of fishermen, so mines were no longer such a threat. The new 12- and 14-inch-gun monitors could work close in shore in relative safety, delivering their fearsome firepower at very close range. Submarines regularly plied their trade in the Marmara and had greatly weakened any Turkish naval forces. After a visit to General Birdwood's (Birdwood was in command of the troops on the peninsula) headquarters at Anzac he wrote:

> He told me of all his hopes and disappointments and cruel losses. How I hate it. I feel all the time we could stop it and win this great prize … I had a long talk with [Admiral] Wemyss tonight and I believe I have persuaded him … I am sure that the majority of us would get through … and a most glorious page would be added to Naval History.

Keyes now felt that the time had come for yet another confrontation with de Robeck. He had recruited Admiral Wemyss, commander of the Fleet at Mudros, to his way of thinking; next he wrote a very clear memorandum to his chief stating his views. At the very same time, in London, Balfour was becoming impatient with the situation. He wrote to de Robeck explaining that Hamilton's request for 95,000 more troops had been reduced to 25,000. He went on to say: 'If you still think your old battleships could make a really decisive or important contribution to success of land operations you will be supported in any use to which you may think it desirable to put them'.

To Keyes this was in fact permission to renew the attack, just as he wanted, but to de Robeck it meant nothing. He replied saying that the best way of using his ships was by supporting the army as he was currently doing; any attempt on the strait would be a bad mistake. Roger was devastated, he wrote to his wife:

> When he sent the telegram I felt inclined to resign my appointment as Chief of Staff. Staying on of course if he would have me in some minor capacity … but he was so charming to me that I hadn't the heart to say any of the things I was simply boiling to say a few minutes before. He is so very weary. A very lovable person – very difficult sometimes nowadays – I expect I am too …

That same day a concerted attempt was made to capture the heights behind Suvla Bay where he had visited during the landing and found troops happily bathing. The Turks now held the hilltop strongly and the attack failed, leaving 7,000 British casualties. Things then went from bad to worse. Hamilton was at first promised more reinforcements and the French resolved to send four divisions to land on the Asiatic side of the Dardanelles. However, these plans were reversed and the Allies decided to send 150,000 men to Salonika instead because Bulgaria had formally joined the Central Powers and Britain and France were committed to supporting Greece against a possible Bulgarian attack. Bulgaria's support of the Central Powers had another consequence which quickly became apparent to the Allied planners. It opened the route for men and materials to be shipped directly from Germany to Constantinople, thus greatly strengthening the Turkish position. Angry criticism of the whole Dardanelles campaign arose in Parliament and Kitchener was prompted to write to Hamilton asking how many men he would lose if the troops were withdrawn. He replied that it would probably be half his force. The government decided that Hamilton must be replaced and General Sir Charles Monro went out to relieve him. On exactly the same day that Monro arrived, 28 October, another traveller left the Dardanelles. Roger Keyes had so badgered his admiral and so persistently argued for a naval assault that he had decided to resign his post and go home to London to argue his case at the Admiralty. De Robeck, still his loyal friend, refused to accept his resignation and wrote to the First Sea Lord, Sir Henry Jackson, saying that, while he disagreed with Keyes's views, they deserved a hearing. He ordered Keyes to London to make his case. It was a bold and risky career move for Keyes. He prepared diligently.

The mood in London was sombre. Just before Keyes arrived General Birdwood, commanding the troops on the peninsula, had sent a situation report directly to Kitchener. He said that, given substantial reinforcement, he might be able to make some progress at Suvla Bay, but it would need a simultaneous landing on the Asiatic shore to make any real headway. At the same time as he received this report, Kitchener was being pressed hard by the French to send immediate reinforcements to Salonika, including all the troops at that time engaged at Gallipoli. It was therefore against a sombre background that Keyes put his case to the Sea Lords. Their response was hardly encouraging. Nothing, they said, could be decided until General Monro had prepared his report on the situation. He then was summoned to see Arthur Balfour. Balfour cut an elegant, almost foppish, figure but he had a razor-sharp mind and was always on top of his brief. He listened to Keyes for two hours, asking frequent and searching questions. He concluded the interview by making two very significant remarks. The first was, 'It is not often that when one examines a hazardous enterprise … the more one considers it the better one likes it'. The second was to ask Keyes who he would recommend to take over command if de Robeck resigned, as he certainly would if Keyes's advice was followed. Keyes immediately suggested Wemyss – at the same time stipulating that he himself should be charge of the fleet making the actual attack. The meeting concluded with Keyes being ordered to go home to Hampshire for a weekend with his family then come back and have another go at convincing the Sea Lords on Monday.

Not much more progress was made at the Admiralty. Monro's report had by then reached London recommending immediate evacuation of the whole force. As Churchill bitterly put it, 'He came, he saw, he capitulated'. Kitchener summoned Keyes and asked him what he thought about this. He was utterly devastated. Kitchener himself thought Monro's report ridiculous and told Keyes that he would go to Gallipoli himself immediately. He suggested several ways in which the army and the Fleet could work together. There then began a series of meetings – mostly after dinner in grand London houses – about what should happen. Jackson, the First Sea Lord, seemed to have agreed that the naval attack should take place and undertook to send four more battleships and four destroyers to Gallipoli from Britain, but only if the attack was co-ordinated with a land offensive. Keyes had further meetings with Balfour, with the Sea Lords and with Herbert Asquith, the Prime Minister.

Churchill, still in the Cabinet as Chancellor of the Duchy of Lancaster, also became involved, supporting Keyes strongly, but somehow unequivocal support from the Admiralty was not forthcoming. In those circumstances none of the politicians would override the professional opinion of the Sea Lords. Always the proviso remained: no naval attack unless the army was prepared to assist. Nevertheless, more naval assets might be despatched to the Aegean pending a final decision about future action. At the same time as Keyes was deep in his meetings, Kitchener, departing for Egypt on his way to Mudros, telegraphed Birdwood telling him to prepare for evacuation of the peninsula.

Long after these events, discussions about Keyes's conduct in London raised some interesting points. His contacts with Churchill, though suggested by Balfour and by the Prime Minister, may have been a mistake. At that time Churchill, as an ex-First Lord, was persona non grata to the Sea Lords and profoundly unpopular in most influential circles in London. By being identified closely with him, Keyes may well have prejudiced the Sea Lords and members of the government against his project. Also, their Lordships probably felt that he was throwing his weight about rather too much for his rank. A deeper understanding of politics and a little more humility might have produced a more favourable result.

Keyes left London for more meetings in Paris with the French Minister of Marine, Marie-Jean-Lucien Lacaze, who promised to support the naval action strongly. At this stage the various meetings in London had not reached a definitive conclusion, so Roger still had hopes that a purely naval offensive might be launched. More old battleships, he hoped, would be sent out from Britain and these would be fitted with anti-mine bulges, allowing them to force their way into the Narrows. Marines would then be landed to take the gun positions in the rear. More modern ships would then take over and steam into the Marmara and on to Constantinople. De Robeck would to be recalled 'for a rest' and command handed over to Wemyss.

As it happened, Kitchener had been in Paris just a few days before Keyes, on his way to Murdros via Egypt, and had gained the impression that the French also still thought that victory at Gallipoli was a possibility, promising two fresh divisions. Buoyed by this, he tried to arrange for Keyes to meet him in Marseilles so the two could discuss how to present a viable new plan to Monro and Birdwood. Poor communications prevented this meeting from taking place, resulting in Kitchener arriving at Mudros well ahead of Keyes. He was greeted by the two chief 'quitters' – Monro and de Robeck. To make matters worse, the Admiralty finally decided that, as the army's efforts were to be diverted to Salonika, there was no point in renewing the purely naval attack. When Roger arrived and reported to de Robeck's headquarters he found that Kitchener was distracted by problems in Salonika, so he took the opportunity of convincing Birdwood and some of Kitchener's staff of the difficulties of evacuating the peninsula in winter (it was then mid-November). There was no way of bringing troops off the beaches if any sort of sea was running. There was also, he said, some evidence that Turkish morale was failing, so, if the army could hold on for the winter, a spring offensive, co-ordinated with the Navy, reinforced by the 'bulged' battleships, had every chance of success. It was no good. Monro was a dominating personality and Kitchener could hardly go against the advice of both him and de Robeck, the senior Army and Naval officers on the spot. Besides, the Admiralty's final verdict was negative. Kitchener telegraphed London recommending complete evacuation and, on 23 November, the Prime Minister agreed. It only remained for the Cabinet to set its final stamp on the decision.

A committee had already been studying the best methods of arranging the evacuation of the 134,000 men, 400 guns and 14,000 animals on the peninsula. There were not nearly enough boats or landing places to evacuate them all at once, so it was decided to make an early start by taking off support troops and supplies. On 25 November, de Robeck left for home, leaving Wemyss in command of Naval forces. Keyes saw his chance and he and Wemyss went together to Monro to urge that it was too dangerous to evacuate with the winter gales coming on. To emphasise the point, the following three days were marked by savage storms which destroyed many small boats and almost all the landing stages. The temperature fell to below zero and in the opposing trenches an unofficial truce was observed because of the cold. On the British side there were 5,000 cases of frostbite and 200 men died from the freezing conditions. Keyes visited Birdwood's headquarters and the two of them began to revive their plans for a joint Naval and military initiative. Monro found out and was furious. He issued orders that no army officer was to speak to a naval officer on any subject except evacuation. During this time, London was curiously slow in sending out the final approval for withdrawal. Lord Curzon was arguing cogently against it and, to reinforce his point, a serious reverse suffered by British forces in Mesopotamia made it doubly undesirable to hand the Turks another success. However, on 7 December, the final order was given. There could be no turning back. All troops and equipment must be withdrawn, the only exception being a small force at Cape Helles who would remain for the time being.

FRUSTRATION AND EVACUATION

After its pathetic performance so far in the Gallipoli campaign, the Royal Navy was to show its true colours in the evacuation. Co-operation between Birdwood's staff and Wemyss's was excellent, with Keyes himself super-active, going from meeting to meeting, and frequently dashing ashore to keep the soldiers informed of everything which was being planned. A collier was sunk to make a breakwater, small boats were rounded up from all corners of the Fleet, beachmasters were appointed, and meticulous plans were laid. All preparations and assemblies of boats had to be completed out of sight, and all movement undertaken at night. Keyes was particularly concerned to evacuate the 1,900 faithful mules and donkeys at Anzac beach. It had been decided to shoot them, but he smuggled all but seventy of them away safely. The evacuation took place over three days and for once everything went according to plan: the weather was fine and calm until the very last day when a gale sprang up, wrecking some lighters and causing the only fatal casualty. By 20 December there was only a small garrison left on Cape Helles itself, and that was successfully evacuated a few weeks later. In the final stages of the evacuation, bad weather and the shortage of landing stages meant that further ships had to be sunk close to *River Clyde* to form a breakwater and destroyers came alongside them by night to take off men, 1,000 at a time. This was a bold and innovative approach devised by Keyes himself. The evacuation was carried out in the nick of time as once again savage storms struck just as the last small boats were pulling away. It was noted that when the Turks finally realised that the British were withdrawing and their troops were ordered to charge down on their trenches, they refused to budge. In spite of a heavy artillery barrage supporting them, they were so demoralised and exhausted that they defied their officers and stayed put. Hungry, poorly supplied, and perishing with cold, they had no fight left in them. A few days later, after they realised that the British had finally left, they advanced readily enough to gorge on the supplies left behind by their enemies. One unfortunate Turkish soldier died after stuffing himself with a surfeit of Cooper's Oxford marmalade.

It became clear after the war was over that the moment to strike would have been immediately after the disastrous bombardment of the forts on 18 March 1915. Far more damage had been done by the bombardment than de Robeck and his team seem to have realised and the Turks were not only demoralised but had almost completely exhausted their ammunition supply. There can be little doubt that the British and French warships could have reached Constantinople in a few days, but what they would have actually achieved by doing so is far less certain. Keyes wrote that it would have provided 'A victory decisive on the whole course of the war'. Grand strategy, however, was never his strong point.

Churchill summed up the campaign from the point of view of the aggressive party: 'Searching my heart I cannot regret the effort. It was good to go as far as we did. Not to persevere- that was a crime'.

A naval officer who was involved wrote in a review of John North's volume about the Gallipoli campaign:

> No one who had any share in the naval operations in the Dardanelles or off Gallipoli can be satisfied with the part we played; most of us feel that the work could and ought to have been done better, not only as regards the larger issues but in the details.

Keyes would have agreed with both verdicts. He believed to his dying day that the Fleet could have forced the Narrows and was ashamed to be a part of an operation which had gone so badly wrong, at least partly due to what seemed to be lack of courage on the part of his chief. However, no one in the Royal Navy or in Whitehall could have doubted his personal enthusiasm for action. He certainly used every contact he had and pulled every string he could to get a more aggressive policy adopted. So much contact with cabinet ministers and the Sea Lords was unusual for a relatively junior officer and they certainly constituted a risky career move, although, at least in the short term, it does not seem to have harmed his prospects. What is most remarkable is that his honesty, decency and capacity for hard work kept him held in the highest esteem by his chief, de Robeck, although the two men held diametrically opposed views. Undoubtedly, de Robeck found him difficult at times. He wrote to Jackson on 24 December saying that he had told Roger firmly that he had to act as his COS, not as 'Leader of the Opposition'. At the same time he reported that the soldiers called Keyes 'The lunatic sailor'. In spite of all this, their relationship and mutual affection endured. Notwithstanding his reputation for lunacy, Roger actually got on exceptionally well with most of the army officers he had to work with, earning their respect and trust. Of course the generals who recommended withdrawal were a different matter. He loathed Monro ('I find great difficulty in thinking or speaking temperately about Monro,' he wrote to his wife) and despised Birdwood for not putting his case strongly or effectively to Kitchener.

For the rest of his life Keyes was to consider himself an expert in amphibious warfare on the strength of his work at Gallipoli. In reality this expertise was rather thin, as was to become clear later in his career. One lesson which he conspicuously failed to learn was that for amphibious operations troops must be specially trained and a robust command structure put in place. The ridiculous situation which he witnessed at Suvla Bay should have taught him that half-trained troops simply cannot be entrusted with the complex tasks and rapid decision-taking required in amphibious warfare. In 1940, his proposals for a landing in Norway were to show that he had not fully appreciated the importance of proper planning, training and leadership.

In any event he emerged from the campaign with his reputation high and with an expanded circle of friends in the very highest places. Particularly significant was his excellent rapport with Wemyss, who was to become First Sea Lord in December 1917 and an ardent supporter of Keyes and his various projects. Interestingly, after the war, Roger was to meet with Balfour, who made it clear that he still believed that Roger had been right about the possibility of the naval assault in the Narrows but that it was constitutionally impossible for him to accept the judgement of a relatively junior officer against the advice of the Sea Lords. Keyes replied hotly that not one of those Sea Lords had ever visited the Dardanelles nor had seen a shot fired in war.

Churchill, who had been the main and unwavering advocate of the campaign, suffered terribly personally and politically from its abject failure. He was at one with Keyes in lamenting the dismal performance of the Admiralty. The two men had faced adversity together and this forged a bond between them which was to prove strong and lasting.

De Robeck returned to the Aegean after a short rest at home, leaving Wemyss free to take up a new appointment in the East Indies. Keyes remained with his admiral for five months, which included 31 May 1916, the day of the Battle of Jutland). His duties in Salonika were mainly concerned with the threat of U-boats which were active in the Mediterranean, sinking the battleship *Russell* close to Malta. He managed to get very close to the French forces engaged in the campaign, always letting them know how much he personally regretted that Salonika had been allowed to divert reinforcements which he thought would have turned the tables at Gallipoli. Early in June de Robeck released him from his duties, and he returned to England.

Chapter 9

The Grand Fleet

Like the vast majority of Naval officers, Keyes was aching to be with the Grand Fleet to be able to show Germany and the world what the Royal Navy was really made of. It was essential to his career that he got some time in as captain of a major warship, as this would allow him to qualify for promotion to rear admiral, so he put out feelers to Beatty and Jellicoe as well as to the Admiralty, hoping to get command of a battleship or battle-cruiser. His great friend Tyrwhitt suggested that he should take command of a squadron of light cruisers, a task for which he would have been ideally suited, but which he had to reject as he needed battleship experience on his naval CV. At first it seemed he might get a brand new Royal Oak-class battleship, but for various reasons these plans fell through. Then, Beatty told him that there was a vacancy in one of the old Invincible-class battle-cruisers, but this was hardly good enough for a commodore; he would do better to wait for one of the new super battle-cruisers then being built. A long wait was, however, unacceptable and eventually he accepted command of *Centurion*, a 23,000-ton battleship launched in 1911 with coal-burning furnaces fitted with oil injectors to give extra power. She carried ten 13.5-inch guns. She was attached to the 2nd Battle Squadron, based at Scapa Flow. As ever he was soon a popular captain, demanding yet humane in his treatment of all ranks. He placed great emphasis on gunnery practice and on the filthy business of coaling ship – a process in which all ranks took part. He boasted that he made *Centurion* the fastest coaler in the fleet (several other ships made the same claim). In stark contrast to Gallipoli, where he had been the kingpin of all operational and policy matters, at Scapa his workload was relatively light, enabling him to enjoy sailing off alone in one of the ship's small boats and undertaking long vigorous walks ashore.

The constant subject of conversations at Scapa was the Battle of Jutland and the Navy's failure to give the German fleet the drubbing that everyone expected. As a matter of fact the battle had been far more successful than many people understood. A large part of the German High Seas Fleet had been seriously damaged and it had failed totally to dislodge the Royal Navy from command of the North Sea. Maintenance of this dominating position was really all that mattered and Jellicoe, by his cautious handling of his fleet, had ensured that it was achieved. Keyes refused to accept this view. He felt strongly that wars are won by aggression, not by careful husbanding of resources and felt that more risks should have been taken. He was furious when his colleagues suggested that Jellocoe's cautious deployment of the Grand Fleet had in fact been the correct policy. He read up on naval history and on the wars of Fredrick the Great to prove his point. His arguments made little impression on Jellicoe, or indeed on his hero, Beatty, who succeeded Jellicoe in November 1916 and, in spite of a great deal of bluster, proved just as risk averse. On one occasion, in August 1916, the High Seas Fleet ventured out from the Jade to attempt to raid the English coast and, at the same time, lure the British over lines of submarines which were lying in wait in the North Sea. Naval Intelligence got wind of this and Jellicoe put to sea before the Germans had deployed their forces, steaming south to try to get to grips with the much-depleted German fleet. Shortly after the Germans sailed, the battleship *Westfalen* was torpedoed and damaged by the British submarine *E-23*. A U-boat then torpedoed a British light cruiser, causing Jellicoe to turn northward as he was afraid that he was running into a minefield. When it turned out that a submarine, not a mine, had been to blame, he turned south again, but had missed his chance to intercept the enemy. The German admiral, Scheer, was warned by a Zeppelin that strong British forces were converging on his fleet (actually the Zep mistook some light cruisers and destroyers for battleships) and turned tail without firing a shot. A second light cruiser, *Falmouth*, was torpedoed on the way home. A most unsatisfactory outcome for both sides, but even worse for Keyes. He had been at Invergordon where *Centurion* was in dockyard hands. As soon as he heard there was a chance of a fight Keyes took her out of dock and raised steam to join the Grand Fleet. He was clearly terribly excited and kept on sending signals to the flagship asking where he should meet the rest of his squadron. Eventually he was told to shut up and stay where he was. Jellicoe explained to him afterwards that he could not possibly let a battleship go to sea on its own without a destroyer escort to keep down submarines. To Keyes such caution was anathema.

Being stationed in Scotland had its advantages. It enabled Roger to see his family. During his absence in the Dardanelles he had corresponded copiously with his wife, Eva, writing to her on an almost daily basis. The correspondence itself is extraordinary. For an extremely busy man, who found writing difficult, the letters are often very long – six or more pages were not unusual – and writing them must have been a considerable effort. They are mostly detailed descriptions of what he had been doing, who he had met, and accounts of the fighting with occasional outpourings of frustration at the stupidity, as he saw it, and the timidity of his colleagues. There are comments on the various ships and army formations on the station, their captains and commanders and snippets of news about their families. In his letters he also discussed with her what he should do – whether to resign and how he should handle himself in particular situations. A short extract from a letter written on 31 December 1915 illustrates his style:

> I only got one letter from you dated 20th. Evidently one or two are missing between 14th and 20th as you mention Mother as if I knew that she had been seedy. I can't understand Reggie Hall (Captain R. Hall, chief of naval intelligence) treating you like that, not answering, but I am sorry Fred Oliver persuaded you to go and see him … there is a very strong party in the Navy who put half our troubles down to these d…d Cabinet Ministers' wives. … I think those craven hearted admirals at the Admiralty must be given a share in this wretched business … they tried to shift responsibility onto the War Office and shirk making a bold decision … it is ten minutes to two. Two is your midnight and I will think of you for all I am worth my sweetheart, and I am sure that if you are awake you will be thinking of me ….

Typically, this letter runs to over 800 words. Eva showed indomitable spirit. She seems to have been able to meet a number of senior Naval and army officers in London and elsewhere and reported on these encounters to Roger, also writing almost daily. As soon as Keyes joined the Grand Fleet she had got rid of the house in Fareham, including a ménage of cows, pigs and ponies, then, accompanied by three young daughters, twenty-four hens, seven servants and two tons of luggage, she established herself at Udale House, near Cromarty. Her train was held up by a Zeppelin attack during the journey and they arrived very late to find that all the drivers who had been sent to meet them were totally drunk, so she herself had to drive a heavily-loaded horse-drawn bus to her new home. Her move brought Keyes a welcome period of home life whenever his ship was in dock. During a spell of leave the two of them managed a journey to Loch Nevis, which had been Eva's family home. Holiday over, Keyes would not have been Keyes if he had not organised grouse shooting for himself and a party some of his likeminded officers, being careful to arrange to get back to his ship quickly if needed. Eva's house moves were not over, however. Beatty, who took over command from Jellicoe, determined to move the Grand Fleet to the Forth, so she organised another house at Aberdour, to which she moved with an even bigger retinue of animals and a Ford car, travelling, heavily pregnant, through the snowbound Scottish countryside. A few weeks later Keyes returned from a visit to London just in time for the arrival of his first son – Geoffrey. A massive naval party was assembled to celebrate. Roger's letters to Eva reveal how he had always longed for a son; eventually the family was blessed with two, Geoffrey and young Roger, born in March 1919. Dauntless and full of energy, it seems that Eva was a most loyal and inspiring wife, so Roger enjoyed the unsurpassed blessings of a happy family home. Life was far from easy for the family in Scotland that winter. There were the children to worry about and Roger was continually inviting naval friends to visit. This would have been taxing enough in normal circumstances but that winter the weather was appalling and the house bitterly cold. The youngest daughter, Elizabeth, remembered her mother sawing up firewood to keep a fire going in the baby's room and for weeks the house was cut off from the outside world by snow and ice.

During the winter Keyes was questioned by the Dardanelles Commission, a seemingly sorry affair which reached no useful conclusion. He wrote that the members looked bored by the whole process – which they probably were.

In April 1917, Keyes was promoted to rear admiral. He remained at first as captain of *Centurion*. As was the custom while remaining in his ship, he did not hoist his flag or change his uniform in spite of his promotion. It was not until June of that year that he took up a genuine rear admiral's appointment, as second in command of the 4th Battle Squadron, hoisting his flag in *Colossus,* a slightly older ship than *Centurion*. His flag captain was Dudley Pound – a future First Sea Lord, and the commander of the squadron was Sir Doveton Sturdee, victor of the Battle of the Falkland Islands. As ever, he longed for action in his new role and was confident that Beatty would lead his fleet to a crushing victory. That victory never came, however, and as the Grand Fleet grew ever stronger its opponents became more and more determined to remain inactive. Submarines, minelayers, minesweepers, destroyers, Q-ships, monitors and escorts of all kinds fought bitter actions. British sea communication with her allies and her empire was sorely threatened, but for the great battleships and battle-cruisers there was frustratingly little to do. The greatest excitement that *Colossus* got was testing the newly-invented paravanes used to protect ships from mines. The first of these to be issued placed a terrific strain on the towing cables, and one of them parted, severely wounding one of the ship's officers, Commander French, as it whipped across the deck. Keyes hurried to him to give comfort before the stretcher party arrived. Then, on the other side of the foredeck, there was a crack and the other paravane broke its tether. Luckily this time it was a chain that parted, not a cable, and the whole rig disappeared harmlessly into the sea. It had been typical of Keyes to be at the point of greatest danger. Shortly afterwards, he ventured up in a 'kite balloon', a gas-filled balloon towed behind a ship to enable an observer to see beyond an enemy smokescreen. While he was aloft the wind came on to blow unexpectedly and the balloon lost control. 'Now we're for it, Sir,' muttered the pilot as the kite surged from side to side over *Colossus,* almost crashing into the sea on each side. Luckily, a party of a hundred sailors assembled on the afterdeck managed to grab a mooring line attached to the basket, so the passengers got out safely. Keyes remarked as he went to his cabin that he had never felt so seasick in his life.

Chapter 10

The Dover Patrol

In the summer of 1917 the government decided to shake up the Admiralty and appointed a new First Lord – Sir Eric Geddes. Geddes was a businessman and a hard-nosed tough egg. He had organised the military railway system in France and shaken up the British shipbuilding industry in the face of the terrible losses suffered to U-boats. He found the Admiralty, under the First Sea Lord, Jellicoe, a pit of pessimism and despondency. The U-boats were unstoppable. Convoying of merchant shipping was impossible without depriving the Grand Fleet of the hundred destroyers it needed. Mined nets to confine the enemy to the North Sea would be beyond the resources of the Navy to arrange. All was doom and gloom. Geddes wouldn't stand for this. He paid a visit to Beatty in Scotland and found out for himself that not much new thinking could be expected from that quarter. Beatty was just as cautious as Jellicoe had been. During this visit he interviewed Keyes in Beatty's presence. The ostensible reason for the questions was to determine whether Wemyss would, in Roger's view, make a good First Sea Lord. Roger replied that although Wemyss was no great tactical genius he would choose good subordinates and deal with situations calmly and logically, as he had at Gallipoli. The appointment duly went ahead.

The next thing that Keyes heard was that he himself was to leave the Grand Fleet immediately and go to London as Director of Plans. He was horrified. He loved life in the Grand Fleet and had only recently hoisted his flag as a rear admiral. He wanted to be afloat, and was still naïve enough to think that his hero, Beatty, was about to lead the fleet into a crushing victory against the Hun. He soon discerned that he had no choice. Beatty released him and off he must go to London. He was given a great send off by the Grand Fleet and particularly by the crew of *Colossus* who, to his delight, had just won the fleet regatta. The only person who seemed to be pleased by the move was Tyrwhitt, still in command at Harwich. He wrote to say that with Keyes in the Admiralty at least there was a chance of some of his more enterprising suggestions for aggressive action getting approved. Significantly he ended with the words 'a place beginning with Z being always on my mind'.

Keyes was not cut out for office jobs, and Jellicoe, his chief when he arrived, knew it and much resented the appointment. However, Jellicoe himself was shortly to be succeeded by Wemyss, so his views carried little weight with Geddes. Reluctantly, the Keyes family moved from Aberdour to London, taking a house in Wyndham Place. Eva arrived there on a moonlit night in September to be greeted by an air raid on the West End. As she and Roger walked out to dine together bits of casing from anti-aircraft shells rained down on them, causing some serious injuries to people on the streets. Eva calmly said that she wished that she had brought an umbrella.

Roger started work in October 1917. Once again Dudley Pound, who had moved with him from the Grand Fleet, was under him, leading the Operations section. Roger had another department head, Captain Fuller, responsible for supply. This team found a number of knotty problems to consider. The most pressing at first was an urgent request from Kerensky's provisional government in Russia to send the Grand Fleet, or at least part of it, to the Baltic to reinforce Russian forces and encourage continued support for the war. For once, Keyes emerged on the side of caution, pointing out that if the Fleet was divided the Germans could use the Kiel Canal to shuttle their battle fleet between the Baltic and the North Sea, gaining temporary superiority in both. The idea was rejected. The chief concern in the Admiralty was the terrible toll which U-boats were taking on Britain's vital supply routes. As there was still no way of locating submarines underwater, the most effective way of combating them was by using minefields to hem them into their bases. This meant blocking off the North Sea between the Shetland Islands and Norway, as well as the English Channel. Plans were already afoot for the Northern Barrage, which would require at least 100,000 mines set at depths to deter submarines. Located well away from German territory, these minefields would be impossible for the enemy to sweep. Manufacturing, laying, organising and maintaining this enormous barrage was beyond the capability of British factories and the Royal Navy, so the mines were manufactured in America and US Navy ships were involved in the laying of them. This mining operation was under the control of a separate section of the Admiralty – Mines Division, under Captain Preston, and Keyes was not directly responsible for it; the English Channel was an entirely different proposition.

The Dover Patrol, whose many duties included the closing of the eastern part of the English Channel to enemy submarines, was the responsibility of

Admiral Reginald Bacon. Bacon was a man of the very highest intelligence, a fine seaman and had an excellent understanding of anything connected with engineering. He was something of an 'oddball' in the Royal Navy and not universally popular among his colleagues. His nickname 'The Streaky One' speaks volumes. He had laid a series of mine barriers and mined nets across the approaches to the Zeebrugge and Ostend, the main bases from which the U-boats operated, and had established a network of minefields in the southern North Sea and the eastern approaches to the English Channel. There were also constant patrols, day and night, by a range of surface vessels, trawlers, destroyers, monitors, sloops, drifters and many others, defending the nets and minefields and looking out for submarines on the surface. Bacon was convinced that these measures were effective, so that hardly any U-boats were getting to their hunting ground in the Western Approaches by way of the English Channel. Others were not so sure. An extraordinary event in August 1917 confirmed that the doubters had a point.

UC-44 was a large minelaying U-boat. The Germans maintained a minefield off the south coast of Ireland, which was regularly swept by sweepers working out of Queenstown (the port of Cork, now named Cobh). Over 400 mines were laid there in 1917, of which 330 were swept up. It was noticed by the sweepers that as soon as they removed a line of mines it was mysteriously replaced shortly afterwards and the officer in charge was convinced that this was being done by a submarine. This gave him an idea. On a fine day with good visibility he ordered all his sweepers to the minefield, telling them to steam through it as if sweeping but not actually to deploy their sweeps. As he had expected, *UC-44* watched this going on and naturally thought the field had been cleared so she entered it on 4 August to replace the mines she thought had been swept. But they had not been swept. Of course, she quickly hit one of her own mines and was lost, the captain, being rescued, complaining bitterly about the inefficiency of British minesweeping. *UC-44* was lying in quite shallow water and was salvaged by the British. Onboard they found instructions for boats leaving the southern North Sea U-boat bases:

> It is best to pass this [the Dover Barrage] on the surface. If forced to dive go down to 40 metres. As far as possible, pass through the area between Hoofden and Cherbourg without being observed and without stopping. On the other hand, boats which in exceptional circumstances go round the North of Scotland are to let themselves be seen as freely as possible in order to mislead the English.

This was rapidly communicated to Naval Intelligence and to Bacon himself. It proved without doubt that U-boats regularly used the Channel route and that the enemy wanted the British to believe otherwise. Bacon chose to ignore it and kept it away from his staff.

As soon as he took up his appointment, Keyes became involved in the business of closing the Channel to submarines. His friend 'Blinker' Hall, the legendary head of Naval Intelligence, convinced him, correctly, that at least thirty U-boats per month were getting safely through the Dover Strait. In this, as in most things, Hall's intelligence was extremely good. Not only was his team reading all German wireless traffic, he also had a spy network deployed in Belgium providing regular intelligence to his team who occupied an area known as "Room 40" in the Admiralty. Room 40 was of crucial importance to the Royal Navy's operations throughout the war.

Beatty had actually suggested that Captain Monro, who had successfully built the submarine defences of the Scottish fleet anchorages, should go to Dover and help. Monro had prepared a scheme for a huge anti-submarine net to be deployed from the Goodwin Sands to a point close to Calais. Bacon had refused even to see him, claiming that the net would not last a single tide in the Channel, although Monro's experience of constructing net defences in the strong tidal streams around the north of Scotland was second to none. Bacon remained deaf to any advice. When he had been appointed in April 1915 he had undertaken to prevent any submarine from passing through the Dover Strait and by 1917 he believed that he had achieved this and arrogantly persisted in his claim in spite of all the evidence.

Keyes got his teeth firmly into the matter. He obtained further nets and tried unsuccessfully to get Bacon to use them. Keyes showed that it was easy for German destroyers to sink the buoys supporting Bacon's defensive minefields overnight, opening a passage for submarines to pass through, but, critically, Roger insisted on the need to patrol the area strongly by night and day, using searchlights at night, to ensure that any U-boat on the surface would be destroyed or forced to dive, thus striking one of the deep mines. Searchlights became a sticking point. Bacon absolutely refused to employ them as he thought they endangered the ship using them too severely. Geddes soon became aware of the impasse. A high-level meeting of senior naval officers and civilian engineers was called and a host of suggestions put forward, including one from Roger's brother, Adrian, for a line of fixed concrete forts right across the Channel. It was then decided to form a 'Channel Barrage Committee' to consider all proposals in detail, including timescales, costs, and personnel and warship requirements. Bacon was not a member of this committee; he remained in Dover, furious that anyone should dare to try to tell him how to do his job. On 20 November the whole committee visited Dover and Bacon took them to sea in *Swift,* a large, fast destroyer. He showed them his nets and mines (actually *Swift* managed to run into a mined net and might easily have been lost, with all her distinguished passengers, if the mine's fuse had been more sensitive). Keyes pointed out yet again how easy it would be for the enemy to sink the nets by smashing the large supporting buoys. He suggested they had not done this to keep the British thinking that they were no longer using the Channel passage. They also looked at the location for Bacon's next project – a deep minefield between the Varne bank and Cap Gris Nez. Keyes suggested that it was useless unless patrolled by surface vessels fitted with searchlights to force U-boats down onto the mines. Bacon violently disagreed, citing once again the danger to the light vessels involved.

Another field of Bacon's responsibilities was a large force of naval artillery on land near Dunkirk. Bacon, a gunnery specialist, had procured old guns from redundant warships, shipped them across the Channel on the foredecks of monitors and installed massive batteries to counter-bombard German heavy artillery in Flanders. Unlike the anti-submarine systems, this unit was highly effective and much admired.

Bacon was then asked to draw up a scheme for using lighted surface vessels. These would force the submarines to dive down onto the mines beneath the surface. Reluctantly, he did this, but at the same time demanded a large increase in the ships available to him and various modifications to make them suitable for the job. This would take an unacceptably long time and demanded resources which the Navy simply didn't have. Britain was losing 350,000 tons of merchant shipping a month to U-boats and could not continue to sustain such losses. The country would be reduced to starvation, would no longer be able to sustain the army in France, and would have to sue for a dishonourable peace.

As December wore on, the correspondence between Keyes and Bacon became more and more contentious. Jellicoe, the First Sea Lord, generally supported Keyes's thinking but baulked at giving direct orders to Bacon who was a long-term friend and colleague. On 8 December, Keyes wrote a memo pointing out the slow progress being made on constructing minefields and particularly on arranging for aggressive patrolling of the Dover Strait by night and day. He emphasised the part which could be played by suitable pyrotechnics which had been designed by Wing Commander Brock of the RNAS (Royal Naval Air Service), whose family were leading firework manufacturers in peace time, and by improvised light vessels. Intelligence reports suggested that at least one U-boat per day was still safely passing down channel. This was in fact an underestimate. Particularly threatening were the large *UC-* type minelaying boats. These were tasked with laying mines off the French ports, especially Bordeaux, where American troopers were expected to arrive, and le Havre, where much of the war traffic was handled. It is easy to imagine the effect on public opinion in America of the sinking of a crowded trooper. Luckily this never happened. Once they had laid their mines these boats would operate in the Western Approaches in the same way as conventional U-boats. On the 14th Jellicoe sent a definite order to Bacon instructing him to concentrate all his efforts on closing the strait, regardless of danger to patrolling craft. By now Bacon was feeling defensive and vulnerable, deeply resenting the interference of a 'committee in London' which was trying to tell him how to do his job. He was convinced that he alone understood the complexity of the difficulties involved, the ferocity of the weather and the tides in the Channel. Once again he prevaricated. It became obvious that he could not continue in his role at Dover. Jellicoe was also under pressure from Geddes, who was now impatient for some definite results. During Christmas week, matters came to a head. Wemyss was appointed to replace Jellicoe and, on 28 December, he sent for Keyes and announced, 'Well, Roger you have talked a hell of a lot about what ought to be done in the Dover area, now you must go and do it'. Bacon was dismissed and never served again in an active role. He generously offered Roger to serve as his second in command, but this arrangement would have been very disruptive and impractical and was rejected. His parting words to his successor were, 'Now you are going to find out that I was right and you were wrong'. Roger took over as Acting Vice Admiral Dover on 1 January 1918.

He was not happy at the prospect. He desperately wanted to return to the Grand Fleet, perhaps to command a squadron of battle-cruisers under his friend and hero Beatty. He still had no doubt that a great sea battle would take place and hoped that he might play a heroic role. There were also important family reasons for wanting to move north. He had only recently moved his family to London where, despite the air raids, they were settled. However, Eva complained that food was very hard to get, especially meat for the children, and that fat for frying was unobtainable. This was in stark contrast to Scotland where food supplies were still plentiful. Dover, they believed, would be as bad as London in that respect. Much as he longed for a return to Beatty's command, Roger had no option and in Dover he had to be. The Admiral's accommodation was a large dockside building, known as Fleet House, which contained offices as well as the domestic quarters. Keyes and Eva chose to acquire a large bungalow on the cliff top at St Margaret's, where the children lived with their nanny whilst he and Eva flitted between it and the official residence.

Bacon had been thoroughly decent and helpful during the hand-over process, but had warned Keyes that some of his ideas would lead to disaster. His staff had developed a high regard for him, but complained that he worked so incredibly hard, doing almost everything himself, that he did not have time to communicate very fully. Nevertheless, he was liked and respected and this made his replacement's task doubly difficult. At his first staff meeting Roger found out how far Bacon's lack of communication went. No one at Dover had been told that submarines were still using the Dover Strait or about the information gleaned from *UC-44* in August. They were astonished and horrified when told the full story. As ever Keyes soon gained the respect and loyalty of his staff. He managed to lure his old friend from *Fame* days, Tomkinson, to take charge of the destroyers on the station. This was a daunting task as the destroyers were old Tribal-class ships built in 1907-9. They were the first oil-burning turbine-powered destroyers, very fast, but requiring a lot of maintenance and they were worked incredibly hard, patrolling night and day. This was extremely hard on their crews as they were quite small ships of less than 1,000 tons displacement and notoriously uncomfortable in bad weather. Somehow, Tomkinson had to find ways of getting them to redouble their efforts to satisfy their new chief.

In his new role Keyes had a frighteningly large range of responsibilities. He had to control merchant shipping in the Channel, inspecting them at a protected anchorage in The Downs and sending them on their way to the continent or to London. He had to convoy troopers in the Channel, he had to control his advanced base at Dunkirk, including a French force of destroyers and small ships placed under his command. He also had to control the Naval gun batteries in Flanders in co-operation with the army. He had to use his large complement, about ninety machines in all, of aircraft to mount bombing, reconnaissance and scouting operations over Belgium and Northern France, and to intercept enemy bombers. He had to deploy monitors and, sometimes, obsolete battleships to bombard the enemy-held Belgian coast and he had to use his force of trawlers and drifters to tend nets and maintain minefields and sweep mines which the enemy might lay. His forces also had to lay mines and all kinds of obstructions in the Channel and southern North Sea and, most important of all, hunt and destroy any U-boat trying to make its way up or down Channel. As well as submarines there were strong forces of powerful enemy destroyers and high-speed motor torpedo boats based in Belgium which had to be watched for and contained. Overall, it was a fearsome responsibility requiring the highest organisational skills. A constant worry to whoever commanded at Dover was the situation of Belgian citizens in territory occupied by the Germans. Any activity by aircraft, artillery or naval guns had to take the greatest care not to add to the sufferings of Belgian civilians.

One of the great difficulties of conducting a defensive operation with so many ships of different types is that everyone tends to assume that any ship encountered is friendly. Thus a determined enemy can very often make a lightning attack, damage or sink some patrolling craft, then get away before any counter action can be organised. This was particularly the case when German destroyers were the enemy, as they were superbly trained in night fighting and, on several occasions, had made successful raids on destroyer and minesweeper formations of the Dover Patrol. Keyes lost no time in re-organising the patrolling ships so that a far more aggressive attitude was adopted, using a system of rocket signals to give warning of approaching danger. Everyone was instructed to assume that any approaching vessel, unless definitely expected, was hostile. Some nasty surprises awaited, however, showing that there was some substance in Bacon's warnings. The first incident occurred after Keyes had been in post for only two weeks. Five destroyers had been despatched from Immingham to lay a small minefield just north of Zeebrugge to trap unwary enemy destroyers and U-boats. As they started on their voyage information was received that the enemy was at sea with a force of large destroyers, so Keyes immediately took command of a mixed force of destroyers, light cruisers and monitors to protect the minelayers and, if possible, trap the enemy. A south-westerly gale blew up and the whole operation fell apart in the reduced visibility. Time and resources had been wasted. A month later heavy firing was heard in Dover from the direction in which a U-boat was being hunted. Various light signals were seen but no meaningful news arrived from the scene of the action until an old destroyer, *Syren*, reported that she was picking up the crew of a sunken drifter. Keyes was astonished and sought desperately for information as to what was happening. This was not clear until late the next day. At least two U-boats had been making their way up-Channel and their progress was being covered by a half-flotilla of powerful German destroyers who also raided the anti-submarine nets and supporting vessels. The net patrol in the area was under the command of a small monitor, *M-26*, which had taken no action at all in spite of reports that enemy ships were in the area. Other ships had sighted the enemy destroyers but for various reasons had not engaged them. The British casualties were heavy: one trawler and seven drifters were sunk, a minesweeper and five more drifters were damaged and seventy-six officers and men were killed with thirteen wounded. Keyes was utterly furious, and his temper was not improved when a U-boat appeared off Dover and shelled the town, killing one small child. The next night a bombing raid on the town fortunately did little damage.

There could hardly have been a worse course of events. The Royal Naval Minesweeping Reserve men, who manned the sweepers, drifters and trawlers, had taken almost all the casualties and they were civilians. Why had the Navy done nothing to protect them? With all the destroyers available to him how had Keyes allowed a submarine to shell Dover itself? Perhaps the policy of lighting the guardships really was an invitation to the enemy to make a surface attack. Perhaps Bacon had been right after all. Keyes insisted on taking action against slackness. The captain of *M-26*, Commander Mellin, was dismissed from his command and the captains of two destroyers who had actually sighted the enemy but done nothing were court martialled but, to Roger's fury, were found not guilty of negligence.

Actually, although no one yet knew it, the new aggressive patrolling policy was beginning to yield some results. The following account of a voyage up-Channel by Werner Furbringer, a highly-experienced commander, in *U-58*, who had sailed up and down the Channel many times before, illustrates the difficulties caused by Keyes's policy of aggressive patrolling:

> By the time I judged it safe to surface it was dark, but what was this ahead? The boat was bathed in the glare of five or six huge searchlights trained on us from the direction in which the barrier lay. The obvious conclusion was that the British wanted us to run submerged to elude the light barrier because they had set some ghastly new trap below. In a heavy swell a breakthrough on the surface could usually be risked for the boat would rarely be visible, even in the searchlight beams, but tonight the sea was calm. I had no choice but to do what the English wanted and submerge, but I would not do them the favour of going deep as they obviously wished. I would trim the boat to run as close to the surface as I could and allow

nothing to force me deeper, navigating neatly between the patrol boats above and the minefield below.

We set off on the surface for the searchlight barrier, not diving until blinded by the glare. I trimmed the boat so the keel was thirteen metres below the surface, the highest point of the conning tower then being five metres below the water. I knew there were bound to be mines here moored below eight metres where they were harmless to steamers but lethal to U-boats.

Finally, by my reckoning we were directly before the barrier. Here the mines would definitely be set shallow and we would have to hang only inches below the surface. I trimmed the boat to eight metres so that the bridge was almost breaking through. Then came the ticklish part.

I raised the periscope half a metre above the surface. It was bathed in light and I could see nothing. After a while I got used to the glare and managed to pick out where the searchlight ships were. One was stationed on our starboard hand and we would have to pass him very close. For a few seconds the searchlight trained away and I could make out the lines of a large destroyer. He changed course and bore down on us suddenly, his beam shining directly into my periscope eye. In the light I could not see him, and I had been so cautious with the periscope I doubted he could have detected us, but he might have heard us. I retracted the tube and whispered for the revolutions of the motors to be put at minimum. The grinding of the destroyer's propellers grew louder but after listening for some time we decided that his engines were at slow ahead, and soon he turned away.

Nevertheless, the British concentration must have known we were about for no sooner had we left the first bag of tricks astern than another presented itself. Behind the line of searchlight destroyers the night was suddenly illuminated bright as day when another group of patrol vessels fired star-shell simultaneously. These vessels were probably blinded by their own pyrotechnics and were a matter of no concern to us. Our worry was the more distant warships which we suspected would be closely examining the backcloth of light for the outline of an enemy submarine. I remained submerged, if only just.

Once again we were in an abysmal situation. Below us the mines, astern a sea of light against which the silhouette of a submarine would be instantly visible should we be incautious enough to surface; ahead the impenetrable darkness in which more ugly surprises were undoubtedly lurking.

About twenty minutes after passing the searchlight battery a large destroyer crossed our wash on a course parallel to the brightness. This would be one of the distant observers waiting to pounce on any U-boat unwary enough to be surfaced after having emerged from the lit area. I blessed my lucky star that I had read the situation correctly and decided to remain submerged.

Furbringer was lucky on this occasion and was blessed with a highly-experienced crew, able to keep the boat trimmed accurately – no easy task in a submarine of that time. He was to prove less lucky a little later when he was rammed by an escort whilst stalking a convoy in the North Sea.

Other commanders were even less fortunate. At least five U-boats were sunk in the Dover Strait in January and February, a great improvement on previous scores. The Channel route was becoming too dangerous to use. This, combined with the improvement in anti-submarine weapons, more extensive minelaying and, most important of all, the introduction of an efficient convoy system, made it seem possible that the underwater menace could be beaten. There was no shortage of new ideas. Monro, the expert who had been curtly rejected by Bacon, had been called up by Keyes to act as an advisor. He pushed forward a scheme for a barrage of concrete forts to be built across the Channel. These would be well armed, equipped with powerful searchlights and impervious to enemy gunfire. They would be linked to acoustic and magnetic detectors which would warn of submarines and allow the towers to call up destroyers. Mines could also be detonated by remote control from the forts when U-boats were in the area. This was a massive engineering project and got under way at Newhaven. Only one tower was completed by the end of the war and it has survived to this day: the Nab Tower, east of the Isle of Wight. Monro also worked to perfect magnetic underwater detection systems, linked to controlled ground mines, which claimed their first victim, *U-109*, that summer. On a more mercenary note Keyes instituted a prize of £1,000 – an immense fortune at the time – to any trawler or drifter which forced a submarine to dive into a minefield.

A young Sub-Lieutenant, Bill Fell, left a good picture of what it was like to be patrolling the minefields at night:

> We were under Admiral Roger Keyes. I was on a P Boat [a shallow-draft sloop used as a submarine and mine-hunter], P 11, which had one low funnel cut off diagonally across the top, hopefully to resemble a U-boat. They were frightfully bad sea boats, low in the water but capable of 24 knots. We spent our nights sitting over the top of minefields with hundreds of trawlers milling around us. Every few minutes a 3,000,000-candle-power flare would be set off. Because of the mines, U-boats had to come up and it was hoped they would be illuminated then hunted by us. This method certainly kept the U-boats down though one or two got through. The others had to go round the minefield which meant a much longer journey for them. When occasional raids took place, and the Germans came down in their fast destroyers on a black south-westerly night our job was to shepherd the trawlers out of the way. We couldn't get mixed up in the action as we had only one miserable 4-inch gun and a couple of pom-pom guns.

As ever Keyes made the best use of his various contacts at the highest levels to get things done. He was desperate for more destroyers and took the opportunity of a voyage conveying Lloyd George, the Prime Minister, across the Channel to a conference, to make his case. The Grand Fleet, he argued had a hundred modern destroyers at its disposal. He had only his flotilla of the small Tribal-class ships and a sorry collection of ancient coal-burning 30-knotters. Frequently, he said, his trawlers detected subs on the surface but could not catch them as a U-boat could make over 15 knots on the surface and the trawlers only about eight. He also complained bitterly about the shortage of mines available to him and begged for more of the excellent new H-type contact mine. Lloyd George, who was well briefed on the submarine menace, had to agree and more fast ships were handed over to Keyes's command. Roger also used his close friendship with Tyrwhitt to borrow ships from Harwich from time to time. Personal relationships like this within the Royal Navy had been one of Bacon's weak points and were Keyes's particular strength. He was constantly corresponding with Beatty in Scotland and, most important of all, with 'Blinker' Hall, the head of Naval Intelligence. By this time Hall had a superb network of informants watching the German Navy so that he knew almost immediately when a major movement took place, and could trace enemy ships at sea using radio-direction-finding equipment. He could also read all their signals traffic. Bacon had been reluctant to trust Hall's intelligence, as is illustrated by the *UC-44* affair, but Roger made excellent use of it and corresponded voluminously with Hall.

As usual Eva was a wonderful hostess to the many visitors to Dover and somehow was able to keep the bungalow on the clifftop as a sanctuary from the busy goings on at Fleet House. She also had the none-too-easy role of keeping her hyperactive husband reasonably sane and happy in spite of the heavy workload and frequent emergencies. One typical incident illustrates the burdens under which the pair laboured.

Roger had been glad when his friend Commander Neston Diggle arrived at Dover with his new monitor *Glatton* in time to join the bombardment of the Belgian coast. The admiral invited his friend for tea with his family and they were walking on the cliffs together when a terrific explosion shook Dover and a black mushroom cloud erupted from somewhere near the harbour. The two men rushed back to the admiral's house where they were informed by telephone that *Glatton* had experienced an explosion in one of her magazines and was on fire. Jumping into Eva's old Ford they were driven by her at breakneck speed to the harbour to find an operation already in hand to evacuate many terribly burned people from *Glatton* and tugs alongside her pumping water into the fire. They also saw that in the next berth lay the ammunition ship *Gransha*. *Gransha* had enough ammunition aboard to devastate the whole of Dover. Diggle found that the only surviving officer on board his ship was a junior surgeon who was busy with the wounded, but a petty officer on shore leave came on board and joined the captain in a desperate search for the sea cocks and the flooding keys for the magazines. They managed to flood the forward part of the ship but the after part could not be reached through the still raging fire and it was only a question of time before the aft magazine blew up, probably taking *Gransha* and most of Dover with it. To make matters worse, there were many men below crying out for help and seamen from nearby ships had swarmed on board to try to save them. After about forty-five terrible minutes the cries from below ceased and the admiral ordered the ship to be abandoned and sunk to put out the fires.

Keyes at once went on board the nearest destroyer and ordered her to manoeuvre to torpedo the blazing hulk, but she did not have steam up. Disgusted, he transferred to another destroyer and told the captain to get close to *Glatton* and sink her. To do this the little propeller on the front of the torpedo, which was intended to prevent it from exploding too close to the ship firing it, had to be disabled. Although the captain ordered this to be done it was not, so the torpedo struck the side of the hull of *Glatton* but did not explode. Keyes was now in a 'fever of impatience', as he called it. Well he might be in the circumstances. Another torpedo was fired, this time successfully, and it blew a great hole in *Glatton*'s side. Keyes wanted the ship to sink on an even keel and ordered a third torpedo to be fired from the other side of her. When he got into the firing position, however, he realised that the missile might pass clean under the ship and hit other vessels in the harbour. He therefore returned to his original position and put the third torpedo through the hole made by the second. This did the trick and *Glatton* sunk safely to the bottom of the harbour. Sixty men had been killed and 124 seriously injured. Ninety of the injured died soon afterwards. The remains of *Glatton* still lie, buried in sand, just outside Dover. Poor Eva had parked the long-suffering Ford at the Admiral's office on the quay and climbed up onto a balcony to watch the gruesome process going on in the harbour. She was joined there by the general commanding the troops in the town who had ordered his men to clear all the quayside houses of their occupants in case of an explosion. He begged Eva to leave also because the whole quayside was in grave danger, but the admiral's spirited lady stayed on, ready to help if she could.

Glatton had been on her way to join another of the Dover Command's activities – the bombardment of the Belgian coast. This had been in progress by fits and starts since 1914 when three small monitors had been highly effective in halting the German advance along the coast towards la Panne and thence to Dunkirk. When the fighting in the coastal sector subsided into a stalemate the objective of the coastal bombardment changed and was now concentrated on smashing the harbour facilities and lock gates at Zeebrugge and Ostend and maybe damaging U-boats or destroyers in the harbours. The monitor force had been increased and now included three ships with massive 15-inch guns, *Soult, Erebus* and *Terror.* To oppose these, the enemy had constructed a string of heavy artillery batteries on the coast, well protected by sandbanks and almost impossible to destroy by fire from the sea. The monitors had managed to do some damage to ships in harbour and to dockside machinery but overall the effect had been little more than an irritation to the Germans. *Glatton* and her sister ship *Gorgon* had specially modified long-range guns which the Navy hoped would swing the advantage their way. Under Bacon's management each sortie by the monitors had been prepared carefully and planned in the finest detail, then frequently frustrated by a change of wind or fall in visibility. Random firing was out of the question due to the danger to Belgian civilians. Keyes introduced a much more opportunistic regime. A large monitor was constantly on standby at Dunkirk, waiting for suitable weather to allow it to make a hit-and-run raid. These raids were not very effective until the very last stages of the war, but they were important to Keyes and to the Navy generally as they were almost the only openly offensive action which the service was undertaking anywhere. There was real embarrassment in naval circles that the army was suffering so terribly in France while the many hundreds of ships of the Royal Navy did nothing except defend themselves and the trade routes. Roger, ever aggressive and rearing for a fight, set about to change this. He determined on something much more radical than a few monitor shells crashing into Belgian coastal defences. He was going to take the fight decisively to the enemy, and at the same time cripple their submarine offensive.

Ever since 1915 the Germans had been developing a U-boat and destroyer repair and maintenance facility at Bruges, well inland and out of reach of the Royal Navy. A canal connected Burges, a safe city, with extensive repair and engineering facilities some twenty miles from the coast, to Zeebrugge, with a branch which would allow smaller subs to get to Ostend as well. At the two seaports small ships could pass through massive sea-locks into the harbour where they could lie against the harbour wall, fairly safe from bombardments from the sea. Shelling from the monitors would occasionally damage a ship in harbour waiting to depart on a mission or for the tide to rise enough to allow it to enter the canal, but overall this problem was minimal.

Keyes and his friend Tyrwhitt determined to change this situation. They reasoned that if the harbours at Zeebrugge and Ostend could be damaged severely, access to the North Sea and the Channel would be denied to the destroyers which were making successful attacks on the Channel barrage and its defenders and to the submarines which were proving so devastating to British and Allied shipping. The two set about to devise a plan to achieve this.

They were by no means the first to consider a raid on the Belgian coast. Bacon had certainly not been short of suggestions for aggressive action. He had proposed three different schemes to be carried out in conjunction with the army. The first of these was a landing, supported by monitors and cruisers, at Ostend. The local civilians would be warned to clear the city, then 10,000 troops would storm ashore from trawlers and seize the town, supported by close-range fire from the vessels offshore. Armoured cars and tanks would be landed from shallow draft vessels. The perimeter would then be held, creating a thorn in the German right flank. British, French and Belgian troops on the left wing of the Allied armies in France would make an attack at the same time and, crossing the river Yser, advance to link up with Bacon's force at Ostend. This scheme was not proceeded with. Although Haig, in command of British forces in France, was interested, neither he nor the French and Belgian commanders was prepared to commit themselves to an advance in Flanders. They pointed out how easy it would be for the Germans to use their excellent railway system to rush reserve troops to Ostend and beat off the invaders.

Bacon's next scheme was even more ambitious. He was aware of the plans for an advance by the British armies around Ypres in autumn 1917 which would, if successful, cut the rail links between Germany and the Belgian coast. He proposed to land a strong force of infantry, armoured cars, tanks and artillery on a beach close to Ostend. These forces would then strike down into the interior and link up with the army advancing from Passchendaele. The plan involved over 13,000 men to be drawn from the reserve of 100,000 kept in Britain for home defence. The scheme was extremely ambitious and complex, involving gigantic rafts which would be chained to 12-inch monitors and pushed onto the beach. There were special ramps to enable tanks to cross the sea wall. It was expected that there would be about 30 per cent casualties, mostly from the heavy enemy coastal artillery, but this, as Bacon said, was nothing compared to the losses being suffered by the soldiers elsewhere on the Western Front. The rafts were built and tested and the troops briefed and trained for the job, but it never happened. There was no great advance from Ypres, the troops who were supposed to link up with Bacon's 'Great Landing' – as he called it – got bogged in the terrible Flanders mud so, to Bacon's deep disappointment, this enterprise was cancelled.

Nobody could accuse 'The Streaky One' of lack of aggression or diligence. No sooner had the Great Landing been abandoned than he came up with another, less ambitious scheme aimed at preventing U-boats from using the harbour at Zeebrugge. His scheme was to embark a force of soldiers and marines on two 12-inch monitors. The monitors would be specially modified with false bows, which they would ram into the breakwater, and huge gangways which would be lowered onto the parapet of the mole so that troops could swarm over them and destroy any ships secured alongside it (there were normally two or three destroyers there). In the meantime, other monitors would stand off the harbour entrance and use their great guns at very short range, about 2,000 yards, to blast the lock gates, destroying them to make the canal to Bruges unusable. In case the lock gates were not completely destroyed, two old cruisers would dash into the harbour and sink themselves close to the lock entrance to block it, while 15-inch monitors out to sea would mount a bombardment of the coastal batteries to prevent them firing on the troop-carrying monitors. This scheme was very weather dependent as it demanded an effective smokescreen to cover the approach of the attacking ships. This would be laid by coastal motor boats (CMBs). Bacon presented his scheme to the Admiralty and discussed it in detail with the Plans Department, of which Keyes, who considered himself an expert in amphibious warfare, was chief. Keyes presented a number of objections. He himself had been at Zeebrugge in 1914 and had stood on the mole, watching the tide sluice past. He was convinced that it ran too hard to allow the clumsy monitors to moor themselves 'bows on' to it. He also observed that the operation would have to take place at high water so that the blockships could enter the harbour and the monitors could approach the mole. At high water the lock gates would be withdrawn into their huge stone and concrete casements and would probably be impervious to shell fire. The argument got swamped by the issue of how to deal with submarines in the Channel and Bacon's scheme eventually evolved into Roger's own plan for the Zeebrugge Raid. It is impossible to know how successful it might have been. There was some substance in Keyes's objections, but Bacon, who was an excellent engineer and seaman, believed until the end of his life that his scheme would have worked.

Chapter 11

The Raids

It was natural for Keyes, determined as ever to carry the fight to the enemy, to embrace the idea of an attack on the Belgian ports. He had mulled over the possibility of this with Beatty and with Tyrwhitt long before he got involved with the Dover Patrol and Tyrwhitt had been developing the idea further. As soon as he was appointed to the Dover command Roger got to work in earnest. He described his objectives as, firstly, to deny the enemy the use of his advanced naval base at Bruges and, secondly, to immobilise the forty or fifty submarines and six to twelve destroyers which would be there resting and re-fitting. He might have added that the action could have a dramatic effect on Allied morale. This was sorely needed. Having been locked in a bloody stalemate since 1914 there were ominous signs of change on the Western Front. After the Treaty of Brest Litovsk in March 1918 one million German troops were released to reinforce the armies in France and Flanders. New tactics including more effective counter bombardment by artillery and the practice of so called 'storm-trooper' advances on the part of German infantry threatened to result in a breakthrough. The Germans were preparing to drive the Allied armies back in confusion, hoping to bring the war to an end before the arrival of fresh troops and equipment from America. In March 1918 the blow fell. German forces thrust forward on all fronts. An advance into Flanders threatened the critical seaport towns of Dunkirk and Calais, causing near panic in the Admiralty. Everywhere Allied morale seemed to be cracking. Politicians, generals and admirals alike longed for something which they could hail as a victory.

In Bacon and Tyrwhitt's plans Keyes at least had a useful starting point. He soon realised, however, that attacking Zeebrugge and Ostend would be a formidable task (See Map 5). The mole which formed the harbour at Zeebrugge was a massive structure consisting of four distinct sections. The section springing from the land was a stone pier 300-yards-long carrying a roadway, a railway and a footpath. On its seaward side there was a stone parapet. The next section was a steel viaduct, also 300-yards-long, with a raised footpath protected from the sea by a steel barrier. It rested on great steel pillars. This was built to allow the tidal stream to rush under a part of the mole, scouring the harbour. The next section was just over a mile long. It was a massive concrete-and-stone structure with a huge concrete wall twenty-feet high and twelve-feet thick on the seaward side. Along this wall, below its summit, was a walkway protected from the sea, with a steel handrail on the landward side. In places there were steps down from the walkway onto the main body of the mole. The parapet was thirty feet above high water. It was alongside this section of the mole that destroyers or submarines waiting in the harbour would moor. There were numerous buildings on the mole including a railway station, seaplane sheds and some warehouses and barracks. The fourth section was narrower than the third, but the same height. It was 360 yards long and had a lighthouse on its end as well as emplacements for eleven guns of various calibres and assorted military buildings, including a redoubt within which protected infantry were covered by heavy machine guns. The commander, known to U-boat men as the 'Pope of the Mole', had his headquarters there. The total length of the mole was just over 1.5 miles. In addition to the guns on the mole there were machine guns and heavy artillery pieces on shore covering the mole and harbour and the whole coastal area was protected by the massive coastal artillery pieces which were the main defenders of the German right flank. A further complication which particularly affected the blockships was a string of heavy barges and net defences moored across the harbour. There was only a small gap between these and shoal water allowing traffic to pass through, close under the guns on the end of the mole.

The formidable coastal defences meant that any assault on the harbour or the canal locks would have to take place in the dark, on a moonless night with a light wind blowing on shore to drive the smokescreen over the defending gun positions. Without a good smokescreen, attacking ships would be at the mercy of the numerous guns on the mole and on shore. The CMBs which would make the smoke could not operate in strong winds and rough seas and the smoke would be no good if it was blown in the wrong direction, exposing the attackers to fire from the shore. To enable blockships to approach the canal locks, the attack would have to be made close to high water in the harbour, with exactly the right conditions of wind and sea; thus the number of possible dates on which an assault could be mounted was very limited. The approach to the harbours was a further difficulty. The waters were shallow and navigation marks were often removed or changed by the enemy. The strong tides setting along the coast made the pinpoint accuracy of navigation required very difficult to achieve, but it was essential unless the whole expedition was to end in disaster.

Ostend was a less formidable proposition than Zeebrugge, having no protective mole, just two piers covered by coastal guns. It was, however, of little value as an objective because the canal linking the Bruges-Zeebrugge canal to Ostend was believed to have become so badly silted up that only the smallest U-boats could use it, and then only at high tide.

Keyes liked the principle of Bacon's plan to land forces on the mole to silence the guns and allow the blockships safe entry into the harbour, but devised an entirely different method of doing so. He wanted to land his men not from a monitor but from a faster, handier, ship, perhaps a civilian ferry fitted with special gangways allowing troops to swarm onto the mole and re-embark after silencing the guns. At the same time as this was happening he determined that the steel viaduct joining the mole to the mainland should be destroyed to make the mole useless to the enemy in future and prevent reinforcements from dashing down the mole to join in the fighting. This was to be achieved by an obsolete submarine which would be towed across from England, loaded with explosive. It would then start its engine and charge between the steel props under the mole where it would blow itself up. The crew would jump off into a motor dinghy before the explosion and be picked up by a picket boat to be taken home.

To distract the enemy from the invading force, which would amount overall to over a hundred vessels, the week before the attack would be devoted to constant bombardment of the coastal batteries by aircraft and by monitors. Tyrwhitt's destroyers and cruisers would patrol ostentatiously in the southern North Sea. At all costs the enemy must be prevented from seeing the blockships and guessing their purpose; otherwise the harbour would be closed with nets and mines before the attack could take place.

Keyes inserted another change in Bacon's plan which was typical and tells us a lot about his character and mentality. He knew the casualty rate would be high, so, conscious of the disparity of suffering in the war between the army and the Navy, he insisted that this operation would be conducted solely by naval personnel and Royal Marines. Every participant would be a given an option of withdrawing and it was made absolutely clear to all ranks that the chances of coming back alive were small. Married men were particularly encouraged to withdraw. Keyes personally selected all the key officers to participate in the action and made himself personally known to all ranks. One young Royal Marine wrote, after a delay in the attack:

Admiral Keyes came on board *Vindictive* and we all fell in on the quarterdeck. He mounted a bollard and explained that at the last moment the wind had changed but told us to have patience as we would go again. We gave him three hearty cheers as he left the ship.

Keyes was a rotten public speaker but, somehow, he managed to strike up a bond with the seamen under him and they recognised and respected his sincerity. They knew that he himself would be in the forefront of the fighting. There is, however, something naïve, even a little immature, about his worrying that the Navy were not suffering enough casualties and excluding experienced soldiers from the operation. Surely officers and men involved in a complex and dangerous task should be selected solely on their experience and suitability for the job, not on the colour of their uniform. An officer of flag rank such as Keyes might have been expected to take a less emotional view.

Roger's reputation and popularity in the Navy naturally ensured that there was no shortage of officers clamouring for a place in his team. Beatty allowed him to recruit officers and men from the Grand Fleet to take part in the enterprise; he considered this a great honour and a real gesture of friendship on the part of his revered friend. Seamen in the Grand Fleet had a boring time at Scapa, so many of them longed for action, even if it was extremely dangerous. One bored Grand Fleet seaman wrote:

> The Commander asked if I would go. Having served a miserable six months in that ship and my third year in that dismal theatre of war I informed him promptly that I would be glad of it. To get away from his tender care was an ambition of mine … .

The ships selected for the blocking operation were five old cruisers, *Thetis, Intrepid, Impigenia, Brilliant* and *Sirius*. The first three would go to Zeebrugge and the others to Ostend. These blockships retained some of their armament and were given additional protection by having their steering and control positions surrounded by concrete and duplicated. More concrete was used to ballast them so that they would be more difficult to raise when sunk. Another old cruiser, *Vindictive,* was to carry the bluejackets and marines who were tasked with storming the Zeebrugge mole to prevent the guns there from firing on the blockships and their associated small craft. She had been selected as no suitable civilian ferry could be found. She was modified by being given an upper deck on her port side, accessed by a companionway on the starboard. The upper deck would be about four feet below the parapet of the mole and was fitted with gangways to assist the storming party to get over it. On the landward side of the parapet of the mole there was a steep drop onto the walkway. To avoid this obstacle it was decided to bring *Vindictive* alongside just where the third section of the mole joined the outer section, because a large, low shed was located against the parapet there, making it easy for the attackers to drop down onto the roof of the shed and thence onto the mole itself, abreast of a 4-inch gun battery. To assist *Vindictive* in berthing alongside the mole two small river Mersey ferryboats, *Daffodil* and *Iris,* were pressed into service. They would also each carry a contingent of marines and bluejackets who would transfer onto *Vindictive* to join the landing party. The first blockship, *Thetis,* was intended to charge into the lock itself, smashing against the lock gates, then sink herself in the entrance. The other two would steam into the approach channel, where they would scuttle themselves to form a further obstruction. The crews of all three blockships would be picked up by motor launches and taken to destroyers which would be standing by near the harbour mouth. At Ostend *Sirius* and *Brilliant* would attempt to ram into each side of the approach channel and sink themselves there. Keyes himself at first intended to travel in *Vindictive,* but was persuaded to transfer to the powerful new destroyer *Warwick* on which he flew a huge silk flag which had been donated to him by the crew of *Centurion* to mark his promotion in 1917. Besides acting as command ship for the whole operation, *Warwick* would use her main armament of four 4-inch guns to shell the mole and try to silence the guns installed on it. She would also pick up survivors from the launches. She would thus be in the thick of the fighting.

Immediately after the blockships had done their work and while it was still dark, Keyes intended to send a squadron of Handley Page bombers to Bruges to bomb the destroyers and submarines stranded there by the closing of the lock. In practice it was very difficult to hit any small target like a ship in the dark with the equipment available at the time, so the proposed bombing raid was really little more than a gesture. Day bombing was potentially more accurate but would have exposed the aircraft unduly to anti-aircraft fire.

On 11 April the wind was a light westerly, the high tide just before 2.00am when there would be no moon. The sea was calm – ideal conditions for the raid. Special light buoys had been laid to help the lead ship, *Vindictive* navigate accurately. The mighty 15-inch monitors steamed out from Dunkirk, ready to launch their terrible bombardment of the coastal batteries. At a point about ninety minutes steaming from the objective the armada paused to transfer the temporary contingent of stokers and seamen who had operated the blockships so far into an attendant minesweeper. This was done to ensure that the small crews left onboard were as few and as fresh as possible for the final charge. Amazingly, quite a few of the men who were due to be evacuated could not be found – they didn't want to miss the fun and decided to remain hidden on board with the attackers, orders or no orders. As this transfer was taking place, however, experienced seamen noted a change in the sea conditions. The wind quietly fell away then came in from the south. If this persisted it would be fatal as the covering smokescreen would be useless. Keyes wrote:

> I went through a pretty difficult time during the next few moments. I knew that every man in the expedition felt as I did, keyed up for the ordeal … it would be so much easier to go on and trust in the God of Battles. An Admiral afloat has one great advantage over his brother the General who, of necessity in modern war, must remain in safety far behind the lines. At least I could share some of the risks I was asking others to take …. However, with a last thought of the shades of Nelson and Troubridge at Tenerife, I made the fatal signal – one word on the wireless – which cancelled the proceedings for the night.

Warwick lay stopped in the water to make sure the reversal of course was correctly made, when suddenly the comparative peace of the convoy was shattered by the arrival of a salvo of heavy shells from the coastal battery 32,000 yards away. It was an ominous reminder that eyes and ears on the enemy shore were alert. In fact the Germans were correctly suspected of having perfected a sound-detection gun-ranging apparatus. One of the subsidiary objects of the raid was to try to get a look at this. This task was entrusted to Brock, the pyrotechnics expert, who, unfortunately, was never to return from his mission. He had been a key member of Keyes's team, using his expertise as a firework manufacturer to develop the Navy's first really effective flares and smoke generators. He was a close friend of both Keyes and Fisher and appears to have been an exceptionally brave and resourceful officer.

Soon afterwards the peace of the night was shattered again by the roar of anti-aircraft guns as the planned bombing raid on Zeebrugge which was intended to accompany the naval assault went ahead.

There was one unfortunate outcome of this first, aborted, expedition. *CMB-33*, a motor boat assigned to the Ostend force, got lost, ran aground and was captured. From charts and documents recovered the Germans got some warning that an attack was to come.

The day after the expedition Wemyss arrived at Dover. He announced that the Admiralty now believed that the raid must be cancelled. The element of surprise had been lost. It would be three weeks before the next favourable conjunction of moon and tidal conditions and by then the Germans would have learnt all about the plan and have defences in place.

'Three weeks? replied Roger, 'I want to go again in nine or ten days'.

'But it will be full moon', said the First Sea Lord.

'Yes, that's what I always wanted, I just couldn't wait for it'.

'Roger, What a damned liar you are, but I'll do my best for you'.

The order was duly revoked, and the expedition cleared to go ahead, moon or no moon. All eyes were on weather forecasts and tidal predictions.

The first possible day for the venture proved a non-starter due to high winds, then 22 April seemed to offer a ray of hope: the tide was right and, although the moon was full and the weather looked doubtful, the order to sail was again given. Eva Keyes walked down to the harbour with her husband to see him off. He was still in some doubt about the wind direction but she was resolved. She had noted that the next day was Saint George's day. 'Saint George for England,' she said (in spite of her Scottish roots), 'It is sure to be the best day for our enterprise. Saint George is sure to bring good fortune to England'. Her husband, re-invigorated, hauled up the signal 'Saint George for England' alongside his enormous battle ensign and the armada put to sea. Once again the force moved in three columns; *Vindictive,* with *Iris* and *Daffodil* in tow led the centre and acted as fleet guide. Behind her were the five blockships, three for Zeebrugge and two for Ostend, followed by a minesweeper to take off surplus crewmen. The starboard column was headed by the admiral in *Warwick*, followed by three destroyers, two to protect *Vindictive* as she went alongside the mole and one towing the two submarines. The port column consisted entirely of destroyers. Distributed among these larger ships were twenty-four CMBs and sixty motor launches.

The CMBs were tasked with torpedoing any destroyers found in harbour and rescuing the crews of the blockships. One was to dash into the harbour and burn a flare to mark the canal entrance. The launches were intended to make smoke, essential to the whole operation, and pick up survivors of sunken vessels.

As the armada drew near to the coast a steady drizzle veiled the moon. Once again there was a mysterious disappearance of the men supposed to be leaving the blockships – in fact in the case of one ship, *Intrepid,* they had no option as the launch that was supposed to collect them broke down. The Ostend contingent parted from the main force as planned. They were to have a disappointing night. They reached their starting point on schedule to find that the buoy marking it was not there, the Germans had moved it the day before, possibly because of the charts captured from *CMB33*. Certain of his position, however, Commander Godsal, in charge of the two blockships, made for where he knew the harbour entrance should be. The missing buoy was then spotted and, thinking that perhaps his navigation was at fault after all, Godsal changed course to the one indicated by the buoy and almost immediately ran hard aground. There was nothing for it but to blow the bottoms out of the ships and evacuate the crews into launches. They escaped with no serious casualties.

The main force continued towards Zeebrugge. Rain was falling and there was little wind. Far out to sea the monitors opened up their bombardment of heavy shells as the CMBs approached the harbour, still unseen, and the launches made a thick fog of smoke. The Germans were alert and efficient, however. The sound of engines alerted the gunners and soon their starshell illuminated the scene. At first the fog hid the warships, then, as *Vindictive* approached the mole, a puff of wind carried away the smoke revealing the intruder to the gunners on the mole. They opened a withering fire at point-blank range. Crammed with men on deck, the old cruiser suffered terrible casualties, including one of her captains. Most unusually, *Vindictive* had two captains, Halahan and Carpenter; Halahan was to take charge of her landing party and was killed at this point, Carpenter continued to handle the ship. *Vindictive* sped up to get close to the mole where the enemy guns would not bear, but then was unable to stop in the correct position. Instead she scraped on alongside of the mole, smashing many of her storming gangways and rather than fetching up alongside the sheds in a position to storm the gun position on shore, she stopped almost 400 yards farther inland. She could not secure herself to the mole and would have drifted away had not *Daffodil's* captain had the presence of mind to use his ship as

CHURCHILL'S ADMIRAL IN TWO WORLD WARS

a tug, forcing *Vindictive* against the wall. The unfortunate storming party, who had trained exhaustively on a model of one section of the mole, found themselves scrambling ashore in quite unfamiliar territory. What happened next is best described by a Sergeant Harry Wright of the Royal Marines Light Infantry:

We were crowded together, shoulder to shoulder as thick as bees, when the silence was broken by a terrific bang followed by a crash as fragments of shellfire fell among us, killing and maiming many as they stood to their arms. The mole was in sight – we could see it off our port quarter, but too late. Our gunners replied to their fire, but they could not silence the terrible battery of 5-inch guns, now firing into the ship at a range of only 100 yards and from behind concrete walls. A very powerful searchlight was turned on us from Zeebrugge and their batteries also opened fire on us. The slaughter was terrible, Col Elliot and Major Cordner were killed by the same shell whilst on the bridge waiting to give the order to advance. The shells came on board thick and fast but our brave fellows stuck to their post … .

Captain Carpenter stood on the forebridge calmly and steadily giving orders to the engine room staff as if he was taking it alongside the mole in peacetime. The gun crews of the *Vindictive* fired away. The pom-pom in the crow's nest had three crews wiped out but luckily Sgt Finch, in charge, was only wounded and remained at his post and kept going all the time. At last we came alongside and were only 30 yards from the muzzles of the German guns. The grappling irons were dropped and officers tried to get ashore to make them fast, but as each one attempted it he was killed by machine-gun fire. The *Iris* came up on our starboard side and rammed *Vindictive* against the mole, and gangways, only two left out of fourteen, were lowered onto the parapet.

… The officer in charge of my platoon, Lt Stanton, had been killed so I, as Platoon Sergeant, led 10 Platoon on shore. Up the ramp we dashed carrying ladders and ropes. We passed over dead bodies lying everywhere, finally crossing the two remaining gangways which were only just hanging together. Our casualties were so great that out of a platoon of 45 only 12 of us landed ... everyone was anxious to get down as machine guns were mowing our lads down. As some of us were getting down the ladders and ropes a few Germans rushed across the mole with bombs, but we made sure not one of them got halfway across.

The desperate battle for the mole continued but the Germans were well-entrenched and the invaders never got up to the guns which had been their first objective. They dropped bombs on a destroyer they found alongside them:

> The submarine *C-3* went under the bridge and blew herself up. The explosion was so great that the whole concrete mole shook from end to end. A shell struck *Vindictive*'s siren so that she could not make the retire signal, but another ship was ordered to make it, but instead of making short blasts she made a succession of long and short blasts. We took it, however, as the order to retire and commenced doing so when, as an order was passed that it was not the signal to retire, we were ordered back to our position. We obeyed the order and very shortly afterwards had the nightmare of seeing our only means of escape move away. The *Vindictive* had left, the officers thinking that everyone was aboard. We were 200 yards from the ship and still had a 20 foot wall to climb.

Two hours later Harry Wright and a few others gave up the fight and were made prisoners of war.

The great explosion which Harry and his colleagues had heard was, of course, the submarine *C-3*. She had come under machine-gun fire as she approached her destination and then drew the attention of a battery of 4-inch guns, but she pressed bravely on, speeding up to 9 knots to reduce the duration of her ordeal. She crashed into the steel underpinnings of the metal section of the mole and wedged herself firmly. Her captain, Sandford, set the fuses while his crew got out the motorboat which was to carry them to safety. Unfortunately, they found that the propeller had been damaged by gunfire and they had to resort to the oars. The tide was running strongly past the mole and they made little progress, so were in some danger of being caught up in their own explosion. To make matters worse, soon they were picked out by a searchlight and became the target for a heavy machine gun which riddled the little boat and wounded Sandford twice. The brave submariners were saved when their charges exploded, apparently destroying the machine gun and the searchlight along with a large section of the mole. Their boat was rocked but remained afloat. They were, however, in a sinking condition and it was only by a stroke of luck that they were found by the launch designated to pick them up. Its commander was another Sandford, the elder brother of the sub's captain.

Apart from *C-3*'s activities, the assault on the mole had been a desperate and bloody failure. However, it did at least attract the attention of the defenders for long enough to allow the CMBs and blockships to approach the mole unmolested, and the light on the end of it was left burning so they had no difficulty in finding their mark. The blockships were intended to enter the harbour twenty minutes after *Vindictive* had got alongside. They would be preceded by a CMB marking out the channel into the harbour with a series of calcium flares. At first all went well, a motorboat came alongside *Thetis* and gave her the course to the lighthouse exactly on time, and she steamed towards it through clouds of smoke from the screen-layers. The motor launch designated to lead her to the lock gates, however, did not appear. In fact, it had been seen as it entered the harbour and was hit by two heavy shells which killed its captain, Lieutenant Commander Young, and destroyed the engine. The survivors got away in a small dinghy, having sunk their launch. Without her guide, *Thetis* steamed blind into the harbour, coming under fire from the guns on the end of the mole. She replied, opened up to full speed and tried to ram a barge which was secured to the end of the mole. She missed it, but then managed to sink it with gunfire. Unfortunately, she then strayed a little from the clear channel and fouled a heavy net which formed a part of the harbour defences. Dragging the net with her, she carried on to within sight of the lock when her engines both stopped, the propellers being tangled in the net. Helpless and still under fire she ran on a mudbank on the port side of the channel where she stuck fast. Her captain, Commander Sneyd, signalled *Intrepid* and *Iphigenia* to pass her, made one more desperate effort to restart his engines, then detonated the scuttling charges, abandoned ship and scrambled into a cutter to be picked up by a launch which was close at hand. *Intrepid* meanwhile, using *Thetis* as a port hand marker, steamed straight towards the lock. She could probably have reached the lock gates where *Thetis* was supposed to be, but, following the original operational orders, her captain, Lieutenant

Bonham Carter, slewed her hard to port in the approach channel and scuttled her in the intended position. This was a wrong decision; the ship would have been far more effective if she had rammed the gates or scuttled herself in the lock itself. However, it is difficult to blame Bonham Carter, who was not aware of the state of *Thetis* and had only seconds, under constant heavy gunfire, to make his decision. *Iphigenia* followed *Intrepid* as intended but rammed into a barge on her way and got slightly off course, veering into the port hand side of the approach channel and striking the stern of *Intrepid*. However, with a lot of backing and filling she eventually was able to get into the correct position so that she and *Intrepid* completely blocked the channel. Although the ship had been under fire from all directions, including from the 8-inch guns of the *Goeben* battery ashore, there were too many survivors for all of them to get into the launch detailed to evacuate them, so the remainder rowed a cutter into the main channel and the launch towed them out of the harbour. The launch's commander was extremely glad to be able to get his craft out of harm's way, having stood by under machine gun fire while *Iphigenia* manoeuvred into position. 'It seemed,' he said afterwards, 'that the damned fellow was never going to stop juggling with his engines. Overloaded and riddled as she was, and full of casualties, the launch was lucky to encounter *Warwick* outside the harbour. The men transferred to the destroyer and the boat was scuttled. Part of the overcrowding experienced was of course due to the brave stokers who had refused to be taken off the blockships before they reached the harbour.

There was still time for one final disaster. *Iris*, attending *Vindictive* alongside the mole had not landed her landing party, as by the time she was able to get up to the mole the recall signal had been given. She was ordered to rendezvous some distance from the harbour, but on the way ran into a gap in the smokescreen and came under very heavy fire. Seventy-seven men were killed and 105 badly wounded, including most of the sailors and marines on deck who had been ready to go onto the mole. This was indeed a tragic outcome for a party of brave men who had not even been able to join in the fighting.

Warwick, with Keyes aboard, had been standing close to the end of the mole throughout the operation, exchanging fire with the enemy and attempting to co-ordinate operations, although with the poor visibility and primitive radio systems then available there was not very much she could do. She was able to pick up the surviving launches as they struggled out of the harbour and to make arrangements for evacuating the wounded. It soon became clear that the casualty rate, though severe, was not as dire as had been expected: 635 men had been killed or seriously wounded, a relatively small loss compared to the terrible battles raging in France at the time. The Germans lost twenty-four. One British warship, the destroyer *North Star,* and three small motor-boats had fallen victim to the German artillery, the guns on the mole itself proving particularly effective. As the armada returned across the North Sea a picture of what had and had not been achieved began to emerge:

> Two of the three blockships had been sunk in position blocking, at least for a time, the canal entrance and confining an unknown number of submarines and destroyers to Bruges where they could do no harm.
>
> The mole had been effectively cut off from the land by *C-3*'s exploit although this did not severely inconvenience the Germans.
>
> The mole's defences remained intact.
>
> Neither of the enemy destroyers alongside the mole had been severely damaged, but some dredgers and barges had been sunk.
>
> An attack by aircraft on the ships and U-boats which would be stranded in Bruges did not take place. This was due to the newly-formed Royal Air Force having taken control of the Royal Navy's bombers and very poor communication between the Navy and the RAF.

Hearty cheers greeted each ship as she staggered back into Dover. Eva Keyes arranged for flowers to be given to the wounded and special arrangements were made for their care.

On 9 May the final phase of the campaign to block the ports took place. *Vindictive* had been got ready for another hazardous voyage, this time to act as a blockship in Ostend harbour. She was accompanied by another old cruiser, *Sappho.* Once again monitors sailed from Dunkirk to provide diversionary fire on the coastal batteries while the blockading force assembled at Dover. The admiral, in *Warwick,* had interrupted a meeting with the King and Queen of Belgium – two of his most ardent admirers – to lead the expedition. From the start things went badly. News was received that the navigation marks off Ostend had been removed, suggesting that the Germans were expecting an attack; then *Sappho* suffered an engine failure and had to limp back to Dover. The expedition forged on and the monitors opened fire as arranged. Shortly afterwards two CMBs fired their torpedoes at the Ostend pier-heads, hoping that by doing so they would disrupt the guns mounted on them. The torpedoes found their mark but do not seem to have been effective. *Vindictive* then became shrouded in a patch of sea mist and had great difficulty in locating the harbour entrance. She blundered about for some time, then the mist cleared and she came under intense fire from the land which wrecked most of the superstructure and killed her captain and navigator. With no one in control, the ship plunged towards the eastern side of the channel and became stuck in the mud there. A junior officer took control and tried to slew the ship into the centre of the channel but she would not budge and was scuttled where she was, blocking less than half the fairway. Many of the crew were badly wounded and the launches designated to take them off were also severely damaged by gunfire; nevertheless, most of the men were rescued. One of the two boats limped out to where *Warwick* was waiting, shrouded in mist. Fearing that at any moment the mist would lift, exposing the ship to the coastal batteries, *Warwick*'s crew quickly helped the survivors aboard. Keyes was questioning the officers of *Vindictive* when there was a terrific explosion aft as *Warwick* hit a stray mine. At first it seemed she must sink but Keyes ordered *Velox* to secure alongside to keep her afloat and *Whirlwind* took her in tow so that she made her way slowly back to Dover. (*Warwick* was repaired and survived the war. Eventually, she succumbed to a German torpedo in 1944.) Luckily the German destroyers normally stationed on the Belgian coast were deployed to Germany at the time and could not intervene. It is easy to imagine how Keyes must have relished being involved in this destroyer work. As an experienced destroyer man himself, he would have been in his element and delighted by the 'can do' attitude of his three destroyer captains. The second rescue launch was picked up by a returning monitor in the morning. This had not been a successful operation, although the official communique issued by the Admiralty claimed that the harbour had been rendered unusable. Keyes was furious about this as he and the participants in the raid knew that it was untrue; however, the original announcement was never revoked.

One more attempt on Ostend was actually planned, this time using the old battleship *Swiftsure* as a blockship. The idea was that she would get herself as far into the harbour mouth as she could, then she would be rammed from behind by an ancient cruiser which would slew her round to block the channel completely. Both ships would then be scuttled. *Swiftsure* was made ready for the task, but Keyes cancelled the operation at the last minute having been informed by Room 40 that Ostend was no longer being used by submarines. Destroyers had not used the port for some time.

Keyes returned home to find himself a hero. The Royal Navy, so destitute of successes since 1914, determined to make the most of this one victory and it came as a timely boost to national morale amid the terrible reverses still being suffered by the army in France and Flanders. A British force had landed on the supposedly impregnable enemy coast, pulled the nose of the Huns, cut their U-boats off from the open sea and returned to England! Hurray! What a victory and what an admiral! Up there with his men and in the thick of the fighting! Every propaganda button possessed by the Admiralty and by the government was firmly pressed. Keyes was awarded an immediate knighthood and was flooded with congratulatory letters from his Naval colleagues, civilian dignitaries, outposts of the Empire and from allies everywhere. Some typical comments included:

From Lord Fisher:

> You have earned the gratitude of the whole Navy. We feel vindicated. We can put our heads up again ...

Interestingly Fisher changed his tune later. He wrote of the Zeebrugge affair in his *Memoirs*:

> Brock (the pyrotechnics expert) was lost to us at the Massacre of Zeebrugge – lost uselessly; for no such folly was ever devised by fools as such an operation as that of Zeebrugge (sic) divorced from military co-operation on land. What were the bravest massacred for? Was it Glory? Is the British Navy a young Navy requiring glory? ... It's murder and it's criminal.

From Murray Stewart, a City bigwig:

> I have today received the following telegram from Hong Kong 'Pay £1,000 Vice Admiral Keyes from Hong Kong war charities for benefit of his wounded in Zeebrugge action'. It is

easy to imagine how deeply the story of the heroism displayed at Zeebrugge must have stirred the hearts of those living in distant parts of the Empire ... I count it a privilege to be thus associated with the Colony's evident admiration of the actors in an exploit whose fame, as long as England lives, assuredly will not die.

From the Archbishop of Canterbury:

Dear Admiral Keyes
The news which tonight's paper gives us is of the sort which makes a man 'hold his breath' in admiration of the magnificent courage and skill involved in such an enterprise. I should like, on St George's day, to say to you and your brave men how intensely we appreciate the heroism of such deeds, and how proud we are of those who are thus adding lustre to the long and varied record of English seamanship and Naval prowess ... .

Admiral Lord Charles Beresford to Lady Keyes:

Your husband's brilliant action sent a thrill of pride throughout the whole Empire...

From the French Admiral Ronarc'h:

Proud to serve under the same commander as the British ships whose dash and courage they have witnessed at Ostend, and deeply honoured at his high praise. The French units will be happy to fight again in their ranks and to strive to equal their bravery. I send you their thanks.

In parliament Geddes revelled in the Navy's success. He announced:

'A Signal Success' under the leadership of Vice Admiral Roger Keyes (cheers) in an extremely gallant and hazardous operation ... . The men on the blockships and in the storming and demolition parties were bluejackets and Royal Marines, volunteers from the Grand Fleet (loud cheers) and from naval and Marine depots (cheers).

The next day, under the heading 'Well Done *Vindictive*', *The Times* announced:

> Above all (these events) tell us of the coolness and seamanship of our officers and of the unsurpassed daring of all ranks. *Vindictive* and her gallant consorts have reaped fresh laurels for the Navy and have renewed once again its splendid traditions in the hour of danger and of trial. Well Done *Vindictive*.

Churchill dubbed the Raid 'The finest feat of arms in the Great War, and certainly unsurpassed in the history of the Royal Navy'.

High praise indeed. But how successful was the action in the cold light of day? Is there some substance in Fisher's charge of stupidity and murder? The objective had been to make it impossible for submarines to use the Bruges-Zeebrugge canal. This was certainly not achieved. German records show that in the subsequent two months an average of two submarines per day moved out of the Belgian ports – the same frequency as before the raids. It had been quite easy to dredge a channel large enough for U-boats to pass around the blockships at high tide without serious inconvenience. Destroyers had more difficulty and the main destroyer force was redeployed to Germany, with the result that there were no more raids on the defenders of the Channel barrage like the successful foray which had occurred in February, causing so much damage to the drifters and minesweepers. In fact, at the end of the war, seven destroyers were stranded in Bruges and sunk by their retreating crews. The damage to the mole achieved by *C-3* was nothing more than a nuisance. On the positive side, the impact of the raid on morale in Britain and especially in naval circles was, as we have seen, remarkable considering the rather modest achievements and the terrible losses suffered by the brave marines and sailors. Strangely, it seems to have been effective in Germany as well. The submarine campaign was already beginning to go badly wrong and the Channel route to the killing grounds in the Western Approaches was now too dangerous to be much used. The British, hitherto seen as being concerned purely with defensive action, had shown that they could mount quite an effective aggressive strike well behind the lines on the Western Front. In June and July, the German Navy began to retrench, withdrawing their ships from the Belgian coast into home waters, leaving only a small contingent still based at Bruges. Gone were the days when lightning destroyer attacks could be launched against the Dover Patrol and when U-boats could make a night passage down-

Channel. Now they must either confine themselves to the North Sea or make the long passage round the north of Scotland to reach their hunting grounds. Even then, the convoy system ensured that victims were harder to find and far better defended. The U-boat war, which had seemed likely to deliver a speedy German victory, was turning distinctly sour. The German press scoffed at chaotic attack on their sea ports and loudly sang the praises of the Pope of the Mole and his men but, in reality, the confidence of the Imperial Navy had been shaken. Furbringer, the U-boat commander whose hazardous voyage up Channel has been described, was in no doubt that the tide had turned. He wrote:

> By July 1918 it had become extremely difficult for a U-boat to get in an attack … .In the last 12 months the British had made unbelievable strides towards improving their submarine defences … . In the month of May 1918 the Entente succeeded for the first time in launching more tonnage than the U-boats destroyed. Accordingly we were no longer convinced that the U-boat alone was capable of bringing about a decisive change in our fortunes.

That same month he took his new boat, *UB-110*, to sea from Zeebrugge. It was his last voyage, ending with his boat being rammed and sunk before his eventual transportation to a prisoner of war camp.

The Zeebrugge and Ostend raids in themselves achieved little, but they were an important part of an aggressive, and ultimately successful, naval campaign against the U-boat menace. Keyes's achievement – and it was a considerable one – was to bring the war to the enemy on many fronts, in the Channel, in his use of the monitors against coastal artillery, in the air, and against the forward bases in Belgium.

Strangely, Keyes himself never fully accepted the fact that the blockships had been so ineffective. Perhaps he could not force himself to believe that all the slaughter of the fine fellows he had selected for the raids had been in vain. He always maintained that Zeebrugge had been closed for a long period to any but the very smallest submarines, in spite of the ample evidence that this was not the case. The public continued to laud his achievement and official propaganda, as well as the newspapers, ignored the evidence until some years after the war. This reveals an aspect of his mentality which unfortunately became more prominent as time went on – a capacity to deny facts which contradicted his own theories.

It is interesting to consider whether Bacon's scheme for assaulting Zeebrugge, using monitors to put the assault force on the mole and to bombard the lock gates, might have been more effective than the tactics devised by Keyes. The scheme was rejected because Keyes and others thought that it would be impossible to moor a monitor head-on to the mole and disembark the assault troops using ramps, because the tidal stream would make the clumsy ship impossible to manage. This may well be so, but Keyes's method didn't work either and the landing on the mole was in any case useless except in that it distracted the defenders for a brief period. Bacon's attempt could hardly have been less successful than Keyes's proved to be. The idea of using two monitors close to the pier-head to bombard the lock gates at close range was also abandoned by Keyes as he did not think that the heavy shells from the monitors would penetrate the massive concrete-and-stone housing of the lock gates. Bacon was far more expert in all aspects of gunnery and ballistics than Keyes and he disagreed. A 12-inch shell at 2,000 yards is a projectile travelling at over 1,500 mph and weighing half a ton. A 15-inch projectile is twice as heavy and far from easy to stop. Certainly the monitors would have been exposed to some heavy fire from the mole and from the coastal guns and might well have been lost in the action, but they were cheap ships designed to be expendable and it is difficult to believe that their fire would not have been effective. Furthermore, in Bacon's plan, a group of destroyers were to fire continuously on the mole to distract the attention of the guns there from the monitors and the blockships. Even if the monitors had failed, the blockships in Bacon's plan would have had as good a prospect of getting into position as they had in Keyes's scheme. Altogether, it does look as though the changes introduced by Keyes were detrimental, if anything. Bacon certainly thought so until the end of his days.

After the battle Keyes had another campaign to fight, in this instance against subtle foes in the Admiralty. The bone of contention was who got what decorations for their participation in the raids. He was furious when men he had recommended were passed over. Tellingly he wrote:

> I suppose the change is due to the influx of KCs [barristers] and politicians which wise generals get on their staffs to help them fight – not the enemy but attacks such as those from which I am suffering – I am afraid not too patiently. I do feel so strongly that all one's energies should be devoted to fighting the enemy, and that I waste a good deal of time, since I am

hopelessly slow and stupid on paper, and far too incoherent
and lose my temper too easily, about things that really don't
matter. But the Admiralty are so infernally rude … .

This passage is typical of a dyslexic letter writer lamenting the trials of a
political minefield which he was totally unsuitable to navigate. Eventually,
King George V got involved in the decorations affair and it was sorted
generally in accordance with Keyes's wishes.

There was certainly still no shortage of tough fighting for the Dover
Patrol to do. The destroyers had to work particularly hard, escorting supply
ships and troop-carriers across the Channel by day and patrolling the nets
and minefields by night. Keyes had been able to increase his destroyer
force considerably since January and had lured some of the best destroyer
officers down from the Grand Fleet. As the prospect of another fleet action
in the North Sea diminished, Keyes was able to promise keen young officers
plenty of excitement with the Dover Patrol. Work continued on the barriers,
the towers and minefields across the Channel and new technology was
introduced, including acoustic indicator loops which could detect the sound
of a U-boat's engine underwater. *U-55* was the first boat to fall victim to
this system in April, and in May *UB-31* and *UB-78* were forced to dive and
struck mines, having been spotted and bombed by a small naval airship.
Another of the mounting list of casualties was *U-109*. She was cunningly
passing through the swept channel almost directly underneath a freighter,
hoping thus to avoid detection. A smart acoustic loop operator recognised
the distinctive note of the sub's diesel above the sound of the freighter's
steam engine and detonated his mine directly under the submarine. Another
new technology consisted of magnetic mines. A field of those were laid off
Zeebrugge and immediately proved deadly to a destroyer and to sweepers
sent to clear them. Whatever his shortcomings in other areas Keyes, with
his boundless energy and dynamism, had breathed new life into the Dover
Patrol and the crucial battle with the U-boats was, as Furbringer said, won
by early summer 1918.

In mid-May 1918, Keyes was asked to a meeting with Haig and General
Plumer, the army commander at Cassel, near the Allied front line. The
mood was all gloom. So far the enemy advance appeared unstoppable and
the French army seemed worn out and despondent. Keyes argued strongly
that Dunkirk must be held at all costs. Without it the Navy would be unable
to handle the U-boat menace or protect cross-Channel traffic so vital to
the BEF and to France (most of France's coal supply was imported from

England). Plans were made in secret for the Navy to disable all the French ports east of Cherbourg (the French were not informed of this) and to move the Channel barrage westward. A depressed Keyes returned to Dover by way of the French Admiral Ronarc'h's headquarters in Dunkirk, where he was much heartened by the admiral's determination to use his own men as infantry to hold the line if need be. As it happened, Keyes need not have been so worried. Starved of raw materials, food and vital imports, the German army had advanced further than its rear echelons could support. At the same time fresh troops from the Empire and Dominions were moving into line in place of the exhausted British formations. Well fed, fit and tough, they were more than a match for the storm-troopers.

Keyes had his own battles to fight on the home front at this time. No sooner had the matter of decorations been resolved than a bitter fight began about the deployment of aircraft. This was a battle which he would wage for the rest of his life. The RAF had been formed in April 1918 and rapidly took control of the fighting aircraft which had previously belonged to the Royal Navy. At the end of May, Sir Roger, as we must now call him, wrote to the Admiralty protesting that, whereas the Navy had until recently had its own aircraft with maintenance, training and communications facilities, this had now been absorbed into the RAF which showed little concern for the needs of the Navy. He now had no authority even over those units designated for use in support of the fleet. He expressed himself in the strongest, albeit ungrammatical, terms:

> Whilst fully appreciating the great value of aerial warfare in co-operation with the Armies in the Field I desire to impress on their Lordships that the formation of the Royal Air Force has, up to the present, resulted in a most detrimental manner, as regards co-operation with Naval forces under my command. The correspondence alluded to, shows that but little consideration is being given to the work of the Navy on the Belgian Coast; and displays a complete failure to appreciate our requirements. Although the Port of Bruges has been closed to traffic since 23rd of April and a very large number of TBDs, TBs and submarines have been locked up either in the harbour of Bruges or in the Canel (sic) yet having only a few Handley-Page machines, and practically no day-bombing machines until quite recently, the full fruits resulting from these operations have certainly not been gathered, owing to the inadequacy of the bombing force at my disposal.

This was one of the early shots in the battle between the Royal Navy and the Royal Air Force which was to blight the defence establishment after the war and indeed still rages today. It is difficult to imagine this rather ill-constructed letter from Keyes having a very positive effect.

Astonishingly, at this time Keyes raised again the possibility of a naval assault in the Dardanelles and asked to lead it himself. Once again, some of the old pre-dreadnought battleships would be used, escorted by CMBs and destroyers fitted with the newly-introduced paravanes to sweep the mines. The fleet would sail into the Marmara and threaten Constantinople. He was pacified with a promise from Wemyss that if such a venture ever did take place he would be in command.

By August and September, the German offensive in France had exhausted itself and the British Army at last went into the attack. Haig and Keyes met again and decided that the Navy should not attempt a landing on the German flank, but should pretend they might do so, thus sapping enemy morale and speeding the German withdrawal. The monitors intensified their bombardment of the coast and Bacon's enormous barges, built for the abortive 'Great Landing', were towed ostentatiously about where they could be spotted by German aircraft. The fight was rapidly going out of the German army and soon they were streaming back through the lands they had ruined in France and Belgium. As the enemy visibly crumbled, Keyes became determined to be in at the kill. He now had at his disposal the very-long-range guns of *Gorgon,* a sister ship to the ill-fated *Glatton*; also, two old monitors had been fitted with 18-inch guns, the largest ever mounted on a warship, having a maximum range of about 36,000 yards (20.5 miles). These harassed the German retreat through Belgium, unmolested by the shore batteries which could not match their range.

Chapter 12

Victory in Sight

Keyes had met King Albert and Queen Elizabeth of Belgium on several occasions during the war and there was obviously a high degree of mutual respect. Significantly, the two men shared a high opinion of Winston Churchill, who had instigated the British intervention at Antwerp in 1914, which the king regarded as having been extremely successful. He had been delighted to hear that Churchill was once again in the Cabinet in 1918 as Minister of Munitions and was not surprised to hear from Haig and Keyes that the supply situation for the fighting services had improved dramatically since he had become involved. The two Belgian princes, Leopold and Charles, were at Eton and Dartmouth respectively and would stay with the Keyes family at Dover on their journeys to and from school. The king and General Degoutte, his army commander, were deeply involved with Sir Roger in planning the naval offensive which was to accompany the British and Belgian armies' advance, harrying the retreating German army. This involved many trips by air to and fro across the Channel. Keyes seems to have enjoyed flying, although rather surprisingly, unlike Churchill, he never became a pilot.

One story related to these flights illustrates why Keyes was so popular with men under his command. His own small plane had taken him to Belgium for a morning conference. It had then got diverted onto other duties and he had to find another plane and pilot to take him home in the evening. The young pilot selected did not realise that his distinguished passenger had no warm flying gear with him and climbed to 10,000 feet during the crossing where it was terribly cold, then made a very bumpy landing in the gathering darkness at Dover. Most senior officers would have reprimanded the pilot severely. Not Keyes. Instead he invited the young fellow to dinner at his home with his family. Before they sat down, however, he found out that his guest had recently got married and his wife lived nearby. Knowing that the poor man would much prefer to be with his new wife, and that his life expectancy as a pilot on the Western Front was only a few weeks, Keyes cancelled dinner and instead provided a car to take him to his home and his new wife. (The pilot was in fact shot down a few weeks later; fortunately, he was taken prisoner and survived.) Another story in a similar vein relates to an earlier occasion when Keyes was sitting next to a junior officer who had been called to a conference on the flagship of the formidable Beatty. Beatty, as was his custom, glossed quickly through the agenda, spending no time on the subject on which the junior was an expert and had an important point to make. Keyes could see the young fellow was upset, feeling overwhelmed by all the brass hats around him and, when Beatty was about to close the meeting, said to him, 'Go on, tell him all about it'. Emboldened, the young fellow said his piece and Beatty welcomed his contribution. 'I quite agree,' he said, 'Why didn't you say that before?'. This is the sort of little act of kindness which made Roger such a popular leader and such a fine man.

The Belgian Royals were frequently in the front line of the advance. They kept in close touch with Keyes throughout the first phase of the advance into Flanders. During this period British aircraft sustained the Belgian army's advance by dropping supplies to the forward troops while monitors pounded Germans using the coastal roadways. Sir Roger took it upon himself to brief the War Office and Haig on progress of the Belgians. As ever, he pressed the army to agree to more offensive action and pleaded that the 100,000 troops stationed in East Anglia for home defence, quite unnecessarily, should be loaded into monitors and used to liberate Ostend and Zeebrugge, cutting into the flank of the retreating German army. In reality it was far too late to organise such a venture as he knew perfectly well. In any case, the harbour at Ostend was blocked by the retreating enemy. Keyes was not alone in bemoaning the waste of manpower on home defence. This had been a particular bugbear of his for a long time and he frequently complained about it. He hated seeing Allied forces being used in a static, defensive role.

Typically, he was still aching to get in on the action himself. He wrote to Beatty complaining bitterly that he was having to shuffle about having meetings and making reports while the soldiers ashore were storming into Flanders and having all the fun. Beatty, whose Grand Fleet had done almost nothing since June 1916, must have known how he felt. On 14 October, the armies on land called for a coastal bombardment and reconnaissance to discover the status of the German coastal heavy gun positions before they advanced further into Flanders. Keyes himself led a force of three large monitors and a host of small craft along the coast, close inshore. At first he hoisted his flag in the large new destroyer *Douglass* but she drew too much water for his liking, so he transferred to *Termagant* which drew three feet less. Her captain was Andrew Cunningham, a favourite of Keyes's, recently lured down from the Grand Fleet by the promise some real fighting; he was to achieve great things twenty-five years later. As they moved along the coast they shelled the enemy gun positions. At first they received no reply – the forward positions had been abandoned. The destroyers and the new monitor *Gorgon* soon drew a long way ahead of the slower 12-inch monitors and got very close to the four 11-inch guns of the Tirpitz Battery which had been the bane of the monitors' lives for years. These suddenly sprang into action. *Gorgon* was immediately straddled and showered with bits of exploded shell. Luckily, she was fast and handy and could reply with her after turret as she beat a hasty retreat, while Keyes and the escort dashed about making covering smoke.

On the 17th, General Degoutte asked Keyes to make another coastal reconnaissance the next day. He set off in *Termagant* with three other destroyers and cruised as far as Ostend without incident. When they were close to the harbour someone noticed that the escorting aircraft were looping the loop crazily over the town. Moving in closer they saw that the Belgian flag was flying. This could only mean that the Germans had abandoned the town. The approach was not without danger, however; *Termagant* almost ran into a shallow minefield off the town and would have been lost if some local fishermen had not given warning. Once past this hazard, Keyes telegraphed Dunkirk inviting King Albert and Queen Elizabeth to be among the first to enter the city. He himself with Tomkinson, Godfrey (his coxswain) and Morgan (his flag lieutenant) got into a whaler and pulled for the shore. Finding the harbour blocked, they scrambled up a ladder to be heartily kissed by a large unshaven man smelling strongly of garlic, and applauded by an excited crowd. All seemed well until a woman shouted that the Germans had re-appeared and immediately two shells smashed into the harbour. Shouting to the crowds to disperse Keyes's party rowed back to *Termagant*, the destroyers got under way just as the massive 12-inch guns of the Knoke Battery, which had not been evacuated, opened fire. The destroyers sped off, *Termagant* in the rear. A well-aimed salvo burst a few yards ahead of her. 'That's the end of *Termagant*,' said an officer on the bridge of the destroyer ahead. Fortunately, he was wrong; everyone on the bridge and on deck was soaked but the ship was not damaged.

Keyes had sent a message to cancel the king and queen's trip to Ostend, but the royals had reached his office in Dunkirk before the cancellation and made a great fuss about not being able to visit the city. Eventually Keyes relented because he had heard from the commander of the motor launches still in the area that all was now quiet. Once again, *Termagant* set off for Ostend, this time with the royals on board, arriving there in the dark and at dead low water. The royal party rowed ashore and had to face a long slippery climb up a ladder to the quayside. The king and queen managed it well, but their ADC slipped and got a good soaking. The town was quite dark as the retreating Germans had wrecked the local generating plant, but the little party made for the town hall and soon were overwhelmed by excited crowds. After thus making their mark with their own citizens, the king and queen set off back to Dunkirk. To arrive as soon as possible Keyes transferred them and his own entourage from *Termagant* into a CMB, a high-speed coastal motor boat. During the transfer the ADC got his second ducking, then off set the little boat at 40 knots. Behind them the still hostile Knoke Battery opened fire on the destroyers but achieved no hits. To add to the excitement, Keyes's CMB broke down halfway to Dunkirk. After drifting for about an hour, the party were lucky enough to be picked up by another passing CMB which took them to Dunkirk, but not before the ADC managed his third immersion in the North Sea. As the queen said to her husband, 'Albert, we could only do such things with *our* Admiral'.

The next morning, Keyes was again in Ostend and listening to complaints about the damage done locally by British shelling. To counter this he arranged for supplies of flour and canned milk to be sent to the town, which was in a near starving condition, and got the mayor to pay a visit to King Albert's villa in la Panne, where the king had spent the war, right up on the front line. There, he was able to see the far greater destruction caused to the town by German artillery. On the 19th, Keyes intended to carry on eastward up the coast in *Termagant* with some French officers, but hardly had they started when the minesweeper *Plumpton* hit a mine. For safety, Keyes transferred to a CMB which itself only just avoided a floating mine whilst travelling at 30 knots. The destination of the party was Zeebrugge which Sir Roger hoped to 'liberate'. They reached the harbour safely, only to find that some French CMBs had got there first. A little disappointed not to be the first into the harbour, Keyes returned to Dunkirk.

There was still a lot to do on the coast, however. The next day, for a change, Keyes and his party set off by car to Ostend, accompanied by another car carrying Belgian officers. Unfortunately, Keyes's car ran into a ditch, slightly injuring some of the occupants; however, they all squeezed into the Belgian car and arrived to survey the condition of the harbour. As his car had been wrecked, Keyes sent a signal to Dunkirk calling for a destroyer to take him back that evening and another to the monitor *Terror,* standing off the harbour, to send in a boat to collect him and take him to the destroyer. As darkness began to fall no boat arrived from *Terror* so he signalled one of the MLs standing off to send in a dinghy. With three of his staff and two seamen he set off in the dinghy, only to find a very heavy sea running outside the harbour. The voyage became very uncomfortable but, even worse, they spotted the small monitor *M-21* sinking in the roadstead. She had struck a mine. Several boats, including *Terror*'s, were at hand to take off the crew and eventually Keyes and his party were able to transfer from the dinghy to one of these, a naval cutter, which took him to the waiting destroyer. After a most harrowing day he must have been glad to get back to Dunkirk. The dinghy which he had abandoned, with two men aboard, capsized and sank on its way back; both men became lost in the darkness and the rough sea but somehow managed to struggle ashore. The mines protecting Ostend seem to have been extremely difficult to sweep; they claimed another victim, *ML-561,* which had been trying to explode any visible mines on the surface at low water with gunfire the next day. The minefield had been laid specifically to prevent another 'Zeebrugge Raid' on the harbour and eventually had to be cleared by a specialist team from Britain.

As soon as Bruges was liberated from the Germans, King Albert invited Keyes to join him in a triumphal entry into the city. He was congratulated on all sides on the efficiency of the British air attacks on the German port facilities, which, he was told, completely avoided hitting civilian areas.

His mission on the coast accomplished, the admiral returned to Dover for the mighty celebration of the end of hostilities on 11 November. Some sailors had procured a bell which had been brought from Zeebrugge mole and hung it on a cart outside his house, ringing it so lustily that conversation and sleep were impossible.

What had Keyes himself done to contribute to the great victory? Certainly, his period as Vice Admiral Dover had been outstandingly important and had played a significant part in the defeat of the U-boats. Where his predecessor, Bacon, had adopted a secretive and defensive management style, Keyes was more open, accepting advice and help wherever he could get it. Room 40 is an excellent example. Whereas Bacon distrusted and often ignored its advice, Keyes frequently called on his friend 'Blinker' Hall, the Director of Naval Intelligence, and employed the matchless skills of the experts in his team extensively. He used his network of friends and contacts in all spheres of government and the armed services to get what he wanted for the Dover Patrol. The outcome was a most severe, perhaps even decisive, series of blows struck at the U-boat offensive as witnessed by Furbringer.

Almost as important, his appearance as a fearless leader of the supposedly triumphant Zeebrugge Raid put new heart into a nation which had grown depressed and demoralised by news from the terrible war on land. He deserved the laurels which were to be awarded to him. However, the story of his activity in the last days of the war once again raises questions about his maturity and judgement. Was it really right for a vice admiral with responsibility for some 250 ships, numerous aircraft and large numbers of men, to be paddling about in the dark on an enemy-infested shore in an overloaded dinghy? Should he have dashed about in potentially hostile waters in an unreliable motor boat with the King and Queen of Belgium? Should he have been in *Termagant* testing the reactions of enemy heavy batteries? It seems that he never got over the thrill of adventure and danger. He had not learnt that conduct that is altogether laudable in a junior officer is not appropriate for an admiral. A flag officer's role is to plan, command and communicate, not to engage in exciting skirmishes in the front line. The years to come were to test him in new, more complex, roles. He had shown the courage of the lion: he must learn the subtlety of the serpent.

Chapter 13

Between the Wars

After the Armistice there was no shortage of work for the Dover Patrol, including ferrying VIPs to and fro across the Channel, sweeping the enormous minefields and generally tidying up. Most of the RNMR minesweeper crews wanted only to get home and go back to fishing and some were on the brink of mutiny when made to stay on in the service. Keyes dealt with them tactfully; he went aboard the most intractable trawler and spoke to the crew. 'How would you feel, he asked 'if some of our wonderful soldiers, who have fought so well, were blown up on their way home by mines you didn't want to sweep?' The men went back to work with no further trouble. On 19 December King George V arranged a welcome in London for all the senior generals from France. He wrote to Keyes asking him to be sure that they all crossed the Channel in time for lunch in London at 1 o'clock. Keyes himself set out to collect them in the faithful *Termagant*. Arriving at Boulogne, where the generals were assembled, he found a brisk north-westerly gale blowing and such a heavy swell running into the harbour mouth that it was unsafe for the destroyer to enter. Cunningham anchored her in the lee of the breakwater while the admiral went ashore in a pilot boat. To spare the brass hats a passage in heavy seas in the destroyer, Keyes commandeered a powerful Belgian ferry-boat and the party put to sea into the ferocious weather. At first, they tried to follow the swept channel, running due north clear of the minefields, but once outside the harbour the ship could make no progress into the teeth of the December gale. Keyes enquired as to the draft of the ferry and learned that it was only about seven feet. Realising that this was about the same as the trawlers which had worked in the minefields throughout the war and that it was high tide, he ordered the skipper to steam north-east, straight over the unswept mines; this brought the sea broad on the port bow and the ship rolled horribly but was able to make good progress. They spotted a few floating mines on their way but arrived safely at Dover in time for the special train awaiting them. How much the generals felt like eating lunch after this ordeal is not recorded. General Byng, commander of

146

the British Third Army and hero of the Battle of Vimy Ridge, chaffed Keyes about the risks he had run and accused him of wanting to kill off some top brass to accelerate the promotion of young army officers.

The end of the war found Keyes, now loaded with decorations bestowed by British, French and Belgian heads of state and promoted to the rank of baronet by King George V, a popular hero. Universities showered him with honorary degrees and towns honoured him with Freedom of the City status. He was on familiar terms with the British and the Belgian royal families and acquainted with senior military and naval officers and with the leading politicians in Britain, France, the USA and Belgium. He had, however, never commanded big ships in battle and had always longed to serve in battle-cruisers, the fastest and most glamorous of the dreadnoughts. His wish was fulfilled when he was given command of the Battle Cruiser Squadron, then based at Scapa, flying his flag at first in Beatty's old flagship *Lion* and later in the newest and most formidable of the battle-cruisers, *Hood.* With the war over, there was not much for the great ships to do. Their only faintly warlike activity was a cruise into the Baltic designed to subdue the Bolshevik navy, which was successfully humbled, then to make a grand tour of Scandinavian capitals 'showing the flag' in the traditional manner.

The family did not move to Scotland on this occasion but found a comfortable house in Devon. The children were delighted when their pony, Jenny, was delivered from where she had been kept in Scotland, by the battlecruiser *Lion.* Jenny was used as a substitute for a pram for the two small boys, Geoffrey and Roger. When he was at home their father would take the five children up a hill near Plymouth and point out the warships in the sound. He made a special point of showing them *Hood,* which he assured them was the most splendid vessel in the fleet.

After an uneventful two years with the battle-cruisers he hauled down his flag and was told that his next posting would be to the Admiralty as Deputy Chief of the Naval Staff (DCNS). This was rather a strange post, created during the war. It was effectively deputy to the First Sea Lord who was none other than his old friend David Beatty. The post, however, was not going to be vacant for a further twelve months; in the meantime he would be on half pay and could take some time to be with his wife and family. Some of that summer of 1921 was spent with his friend King Albert of Belgium. While the king was visiting England, Keyes took him to a polo match at Hurlingham. It so happened that Churchill was playing that day and Keyes introduced the two men. Albert had been a great admirer of Churchill because of his intervention at Antwerp in 1914 and the three seem to have got on famously. Soon after this meeting it transpired that the current DCNS was unwell and Keyes's appointment had to be brought forward so that he assumed his post in November 1921.

The inter-war period, which is appropriately often known as 'the Long Weekend', marked a time in which wishful thinking and groundless optimism persuaded many nations, particularly the UK, that war was no longer a possibility and deep cuts could be made in public expenditure on the armed forces. Certainly economy was necessary. Public sector debt was £7.6 bn against GDP of £6.2 bn and much of this debt had been incurred in building up the armed forces during the war. For example the Royal Navy had commissioned sixteen new dreadnoughts and over 200 destroyers of various classes between 1914 and 1918. Disarmament on a grand scale was inevitable as soon as hostilities ended. Geddes, now the minister responsible for making vast savings in public expenditure, began to sharpen his famous axe, which was to fall in 1922. The Ten Year Rule, proposed by Lloyd George and adopted by Parliament, required defence policy to be based on the assumption that no war could possibly occur for the next ten years, the stipulation rolling forward year after year unless specifically revoked. At the same time the conflict between the Royal Navy and the Royal Air Force about who should control aircraft operating over the sea was in full swing, wasting everyone's time and resulting in a string of unsatisfactory compromises, eventually leading to disastrous operational outcomes. As DCNS, Sir Roger was in the midst of these murky waters.

From the start he was plunged into the deep end as Beatty had to travel to Washington to maintain the Royal Navy's position in the Washington naval treaty negotiations. These turned out badly for Britain. Battleship construction was outlawed, except that Britain was allowed to complete two ships, *Nelson* and *Rodney*, already on the stocks, provided that they conformed to limitations on size and weight. This resulted in two of the most extraordinary warships ever built. More seriously, Britain was unsuccessful in trying to get submarines outlawed altogether and worst of all her mutual treaty with Japan, which had been concluded in 1902, was scrapped and Japanese naval strength was limited to three-fifths that of Britain and the USA. This was the cause of Japanese loss of faith in Britain and became a factor in the rise of Japanese militarism and the terrible Pacific war twenty-two years later. While Beatty was fighting these battles in Washington, Keyes was locked in conflict with his wife's brother-in-law, Trenchard, the 'Father of the RAF', over the future of Naval aviation. Trenchard was a far more canny opponent than Keyes, and the eventual solution, described as

'The Compromise' forbade the Navy from having or training any aircrew. 'Air,' said Trenchard, 'is one and indivisible'. Trenchard continued to be a bête noire for the Navy throughout the 1920s. There were more meetings and more compromises. In practice the outcome was that neither force devoted any significant resources to the development of Naval aviation, a field in which Britain was far superior to all other nations in 1918. This vital sector of defence fell into a disastrous decline, struggling with reduced budgets, inadequate training and woefully obsolete and unsuitable aircraft.

By November 1922 a savage war between Greece, supported by the Allies, and Turkey had died down enough for a conference to be established in Switzerland to settle a question on which Keyes was generally considered an expert – the free navigation of the Dardanelles. It was natural that he should be chosen by Lord Curzon, head of the British delegation, to chair the technical committee of the conference. The Turkish side, led by the cunning Ismet Pasha, knew perfectly well that the Allies had no intention or will to go to war over the future of the Dardanelles or the border disputes between Greece and Turkey, and came prepared to drive a hard bargain. In the technical committee, things soon became completely deadlocked and Keyes eventually decided that he was wasting his time and resolved to go home. This rather shocked the Turks, who always revelled in protracted negotiations. At first, they refused to believe the threat, but when Keyes actually boarded the train, they began to climb down. Mysteriously things which had been impossible the day before became possible after all and the technical committee managed to reach complete agreement. The rest of the negotiations droned on for months and, after various adjournments and disagreements between Britain and France, the conference achieved a reasonable compromise. In order to get the Turks to agree to the final draft, Curzon had to follow Keyes's example and had his bags packed and loaded onto the Orient Express, the departure of which had to be delayed for half an hour, in order to convince Ismet Pasha that it was a matter of 'now or never' for his signature. Keyes joked later that in the end he had forced the Dardanelles after all because the Treaty of Lausanne, which concluded the negotiations, did indeed stipulate that complete freedom of navigation of the straits was guaranteed.

After over three years as DCNS, Keyes landed the most prestigious post afloat that the Royal Navy had to offer – Commander of the Mediterranean Fleet. He was now fifty-two-years old and seemed to be at the peak of his seagoing career. Previous 'Cs-in-C Med' had gone on to be First Sea Lord, professional head of the Royal Navy. His appointment was not uncontroversial: his accelerated promotion, achieved in China, meant that he was several years younger than was usual for the post, and his high public profile had made him enemies in naval circles where old grudges and the feud between Fisher and Beresford still rankled. It was also argued that Keyes had almost no battleship experience. As if this was not enough, there had developed a most unpleasant conflict between supporters of Jellicoe, who had left the service to become Governor General of New Zealand, and Beatty. Beatty was furious when the first draft of the history of the war at sea, commissioned by the Admiralty and prepared by Sir Julian Corbett, criticised his conduct in the Battle of Jutland and endorsed Jellicoe's more cautious approach. He demanded that the draft should be drastically revised, and even insisted that a note should be inserted in the final version stating on behalf of the Lords of the Admiralty:

> Their Lordships find that some of the principles advocated in
> the book, especially the tendency to minimise the importance
> of seeking battle and of forcing it to a conclusion, are directly
> in conflict with their views.

Politicians and Naval officers began to take sides in the conflict, one party arguing that the duty of the fleet was to preserve British interests by remaining intact at all costs and the other that a much more aggressive approach to the German fleet should have been adopted. Keyes naturally sided with his friend Beatty. Supporters of the cautious approach worried that if Keyes eventually became First Sea Lord their prospects in the service would be blighted. Churchill, of course, was a strong supporter of Beatty and Keyes's views of the battle. He wrote to Keyes, 'One feels as one studies them [reports of the battle] that a shrinking hand and an anxious doubting spirit guided the British fleet that melancholy day and night'.

Chapter 14

C.-in-C. Mediterranean

The Mediterranean Fleet was at the time the largest naval formation in the world and it had the primary task of safeguarding the key routes from the Atlantic to British colonies and dominions in the Far East and to Australasia. The fleet consisted of eight battleships, ten cruisers, two aircraft carriers and thirty-six destroyers, together with numerous ancillary vessels. The C-in-C had a lovely house for his family in Malta and was expected to entertain royally. This suited Eva perfectly. She happily moved her family there early in the summer of 1925.

Soon after her arrival an event occurred which nearly brought an end to her husband's career. He had been on an inspection visit to the aircraft carrier *Eagle* and decided to be flown ashore after the visit. His plane took off normally, then suffered engine failure at a height of only 200 feet. It crashed headlong into the rough sea with Keyes trapped in his seat and badly injured. The two crew members were not seriously hurt and managed to get their passenger out of the plane before it sank; they then supported him until a destroyer picked them up twenty minutes later. Keyes was unconscious and the destroyer made straight for Malta where there was a good naval hospital. Conditions in the Grand Harbour were difficult as a strong wind was blowing, bumping the destroyer badly as she went alongside. This somehow aroused the unconscious admiral who growled at the helmsman for being 'no seaman' before lapsing back into oblivion. He recovered quickly in hospital where he received numerous letters from friends, among them one from Churchill:

> My Dear Roger,
> I have been moved by reading your letter to Johnny Hamilton describing your providential escape. I am indeed thankful that all ended well. Don't presume too much on good luck. It wears out gradually. I gave up flying after my last crash, and although in your position I suppose it is occasionally a duty, I am sure it should not become a habit in a C-in-C.

Churchill was becoming gradually closer to the Keyes family at the time. Eva had been working hard on his parliamentary election team in Epping, a seat which he won. Also, the two men grumbled together in frequent letters about the abandonment of the Gallipoli campaign.

Another condolence came from his old colleague and opponent, de Robeck:

> My dear C-in-C,
> It was only last week that I heard what a nasty accident you had when flying off Malta. Believe me these aircraft are bad mounts; they are as bad as an unbred horse, fall into the middle of a brook and then try to drown you. You stick to the polo pony – not so far to fall and not so heavy on you. However, trust you have now recovered and got the salt water out of you.

Once recovered, Sir Roger seems to have taken at least some of de Robeck's advice. He had three polo ponies sent out from England and started his own polo team, the Centurions. Patronage of the admiral soon got a very active polo scene established on Malta, with special arrangements to make it and other sports available to junior officers and midshipmen. With the help of Eva, who seems to have been in her element, the hospitality at Admiralty House was generous and encompassed almost every officer of the Fleet at one time or another. Every midshipman joining the fleet would get an invitation to tea and to chat about his home life, interests and pastimes, with the C-in-C, who had the knack of making youngsters feel relaxed and comfortable. The Keyes children – the oldest of them then barely teenagers – were required, to their embarrassment, to join in these tea parties. Sometimes these evolved into lively games round the house. 'Bear' was the most popular of the games, involving children and midshipmen marching round the rooms calling 'Where's that bear?' At the appropriate moment the 'bear' would leap out and capture one of the hunters.

A rather innovative social activity organised by Eva and her sister, who was a frequent house guest, was the Admiralty House Ladies' Polo Team. This consisted of herself, her two daughters, and some visiting girlfriend or Naval wife. They would play teams of novices, usually midshipmen, starting in the early morning and convening at Admiralty House for a hearty breakfast after play. When the Mountbatten family was in Malta, Lady Mountbatten got up a rival team. Unlike the Keyes family the Mountbatten ladies were fully made up and the team gained the title of the 'Painted Ladies'. Possibly the Keyes family took their enthusiasm for polo a little too far. Even in the 1920s it was an expensive sport and officers who could not afford to participate sometimes resented the easy access to the C-in-C which it provided. This accusation was not without substance and was to plague Sir Roger later in his career. There was also the suspicion in some quarters that the C-in-C was spending too much time on the polo field and too little afloat or in his office. This, too, surfaced later.

He did not forget, in the midst of all these pleasant activities, to keep up pressure on people of influence on the issue of Naval aviation. He wrote, for example, to Churchill in January 1926:

> My Dear Winston
> I would very much like to have a few hours talk with you about 101 things. We really must get on with unfettered development of our Air Arm. We have to fight for one thing after another to establish it and improve its efficiency, and these fights which can only have one end, even if the Government does not give it to us, [sic] are becoming tiresome. It looks as if we will need a war to put things in their right perspective in this country .... However, I suppose this is a subject on which we will never agree. And you are one of the villains of the piece.

Churchill had supported the introduction of the Ten Year Rule, and was a champion of the RAF.

As well as polo playing the five Keyes children enjoyed an idyllic life in Malta. The family were continually invited to parties on board ships where the sailors would lay on wonderful games and entertainments. The C-in-C Med had the sloop *Bryony* to use almost as if she was a private yacht, giving the two small boys and their sisters an opportunity to experience shipboard life and the chance to steer the ship in good weather. On one occasion Eva thought her children were suffering from too much Maltese sun and took them off in *Bryony* to Yugoslavia, where they stayed in a hotel in the Dolomites and got used to some vigorous hill-walking, little Roger being carried by donkey or on his mother's back.

While Keyes was enjoying his command in the Mediterranean, the political battles at home raged more and more furiously. Beatty's prestige and popularity with the public made it difficult for the cost-cutters in government to make the reductions they wanted in the Navy's budget.

This led to a hope in certain quarters that he might be forced to retire early as First Sea Lord. If this were to happen they calculated that Keyes, who was expected to be at least as awkward, would still be employed as C-in-C Med, and not available to replace him and so the opportunity would arise to select a more pliable candidate. After a short illness, Beatty came out to visit Keyes in his wife's steam yacht *Sheelah* and the two admirals discussed the future. They agreed that Beatty should stay on at the Admiralty for another year at least, then he would resign and fight the Navy's battles from the House of Lords. He would support Admiral Madden's claim to succeed him as First Sea Lord while Keyes remained in the Med. Madden was regarded as a somewhat weak figure but he was due to retire two years later, which would coincide nicely with Sir Roger's return from the Med, so he could immediately take over from Madden.

Another visitor to Malta was Churchill, who arrived with his son Randolph and his brother Jack. Churchill was at the time Chancellor of the Exchequer, wrestling with the problems associated with the resumption of the gold standard and with the drastic reductions in national expenditure required to achieve a promised reduction in income tax. He was wont to describe himself as a 'naval person' and greatly enjoyed his association with the service, so the break in Malta must have been especially pleasant for him. Certainly, he wrote a most charming 'Thank you' letter to his host and hostess. Among subjects discussed must have been the two men's differing views regarding Japan. Keyes had earlier sent Churchill a book by Stephen King-Hall which convinced him that Japan was preparing to drive Europeans out of China and South-east Asia. Churchill would have none of it. He wrote, 'I do not believe that Japan has any idea of attacking the British Empire or that there is any danger of her doing so for at least a generation to come'. (Did he remember these words in 1942?) This was an important question at the time because the Treasury was resisting naval demands for funding a strong force of cruisers to protect British interests in the Far East. Churchill fought bitter battles with the Admiralty over the number of cruisers required and the assumption of Japanese neutrality was central to his arguments.

Two naval colleagues featured strongly in Keyes's career. One was Dudley Pound, who was later to become First Sea Lord. Pound was his first chief of staff in the Mediterannean. He had been with Roger in *Opossum* and had been his flag captain in *Colossus,* then served with him in the Plans Department of the Admiralty. He was called home in 1927 for an important Admiralty posting. He was then replaced as CoS by none other than Wilfred

Tomkinson who had served with Sir Roger in China, the Dardanelles and in the Dover Patrol. Keyes was fortunate in having such congenial and able assistants as the entertaining connected to his job was formidable. He had to arrange polo for the Duke of York, later King George VI, pay visits to the loathsome Mussolini and extend the Fleet's hospitality to a continual stream of diplomats and potentates. There were also frequent contacts with French, Italian, Spanish and Greek navies to be managed and good relationships to be maintained. During Keyes's tenure there was no need for the Fleet to go to action stations, the only notable event being the despatch of a battleship to Alexandria after some trouble was reported ashore. The Fleet therefore was able to concentrate on high-speed manoeuvres, training in fleet deployments and anti-submarine warfare. Most reports indicate that in Keyes's time morale was generally good and efficiency high; certainly he was personally popular both with most of his officers and with the lower deck, although there were some complaints that he drove the seamen taking part in boat races too hard.

One absurd event, however, became a serious blot on his record. The 1920s were a long 'silly season' for the press who loved to focus on scandals of any kind. In March 1928, when Keyes's period of command was coming to an end, the *Royal Oak* incident made national newspaper headlines. The story is almost too trivial to relate. Rear Admiral Collard, commanding a battle squadron under Keyes, had as his flag captain Captain K. Dewar. The two did not get on. One evening a dance was being held aboard *Royal Oak* and Collard noticed that some ladies had no dancing partners. He summoned Dewar and stormed at him in public for not seeing that everyone had a partner. Later that same evening the Marine band was playing some rather smoochy American dance music. This infuriated Collard who ordered that the band should be dismissed and insulted the bandmaster: 'I won't have a bugger like that on my ship,' he said. The bandmaster immediately resigned from the service. A little later there was another incident surrounding a delay in providing the admiral with a gangway to go ashore. This time the dispute was so violent that Dewar and his executive officer, Commander Daniel, felt obliged to write a report which criticised the admiral's conduct generally. This set off a serious row. Keyes had to become involved and was forced to delay the planned departure of the Fleet to Gibraltar for important exercises. Collard, Dewar and Daniel were sent home in disgrace, the Fleet duly sailed and took part in planned exercises. When Dewar and Daniel arrived home, however, the cat was among the pigeons. A member of parliament asked if it was true that there had been a mutiny in the Fleet and that officers of *Royal Oak* had refused to sail with Collard aboard.

The Admiralty clumsily replied that 'It had no information'. The press had a field day. No criticism of Keyes was at first made and the Admiralty confirmed that the steps he had taken to nip the problem in the bud were approved of, but later his opponents were to use this incident very effectively as an indicator that he was unfit for high command. In truth, Keyes should probably have been aware of the issues between Collard and Dewar earlier and taken steps to separate them. Maybe he was a little too concerned in social and sporting activities to pay enough attention to personnel problems within the Fleet. Certainly, he was to regret the incident bitterly, as we shall see.

On expiry of his tenure as C-in-C Med, Sir Roger returned to England expecting to be on the unemployed list for a few months until Madden retired as First Sea Lord. He would then slot into the top job which Beatty had assured him would be waiting. He was distressed when he visited Madden to be told that the King (George V), who took a great interest in Naval affairs, was furious about the *Royal Oak* incident, and that he had ordered Keyes to report to him directly to discuss it. The meeting duly took place and the king made his displeasure very clear. It was hinted that he and Madden believed that too much polo and socialising had got in the way of proper management of the Fleet. Other bad omens became apparent. The Admiralty announced that, as there was to be a general election in spring 1929, Madden's appointment would be renewed for an extra year so that the new government could appoint his successor after due consideration. Also, it was rumoured that Madden would favour Admiral Sir Frank Field, Sir Roger's successor as C-in-C Med, for the post when Madden did eventually go. Worst of all the election resulted in the Labour party – committed to further disarmament – winning the most seats, although not an overall majority. Ramsay MacDonald became Prime Minister and A.V. Alexander, a leading pacifist, First Lord of the Admiralty. The new government lost little time in agreeing to the provisions of the London Naval Treaty, which yet further decreased the number of ships, especially cruisers, allowed to the Royal Navy. Keyes made his opposition to this very plain, which did not endear him to the new government. The last thing that Alexander wanted was a row with the professional officers of the Royal Navy and, had Keyes been in office as First Sea Lord, Alexander was afraid that he would have resigned in protest at the cuts and taken the rest of the board with him, creating a political crisis.

Soon after he had returned home from the Mediterranean, Keyes accepted the post of C-in-C Portsmouth which he regarded as no more than a stepping stone to his ultimate goal. The job kept him on full pay and provided a house for his family. Although no longer so short of cash (in addition to his salary he had received a £10,000 grant for his war service), he remained keen to earn as much as he could during the latter part of his service career. Almost as soon as Alexander was appointed, Keyes invited him to stay at Admiralty House, Portsmouth, and pleaded his case. Alexander replied that the *Royal Oak* affair had damaged his chances. Keyes replied by handing over all his documentation on the case which seemed to impress his visitor, but it was to no avail. In February 1930 Alexander wrote to Keyes to say that Field would indeed succeed Madden as First Sea Lord. Obviously the government wanted to have a more pliable character than Sir Roger in the top position. Beatty and Keyes were both thunderstruck. Keyes protested to Alexander and to the prime minister. There were extraordinary examples of politicians wriggling and lying their way out of responsibility for the decision, but they would not reverse it. ('The King has approved Field's appointment so we can do nothing'. 'The press release has been prepared, it is too late to change it'. 'It was not my decision, it was the view of the Cabinet'. etc., etc.) Keyes actually visited the Prime Minister himself, at Chequers, thereby achieving nothing except to further antagonise Alexander. As a small compensation for his dashed expectations Keyes was promoted Admiral of the Fleet – the highest rank in the Royal Navy, but indeed this was an empty gesture as Field wrote to tell him in November 1930 that his tenure of the Portsmouth job was over and he must therefore retire, hauling down his flag in June 1931. By this time the naval treaties to which he so strongly objected had been signed by the UK, the USA and Japan. France and Italy had refused to sign, making the reductions called for even more objectionable to Keyes and to his friends Beatty and Jellicoe, both of whom spoke strongly in the House of Lords against them. Now that he was no longer at the Treasury, Churchill led a small but vocal anti-treaty party in the Commons.

The Keyes family bought a house in Tingewick, Buckinghamshire, where Sir Roger resolved to occupy himself with hunting and writing his memoirs. The house is still there, although now divided into two. In Roger's time there were fourteen bedrooms as well as five outlying cottages which were rented out, and about 100 acres of land with extensive stabling for horses. The household consisted of Roger and Eva, two sons, Geoffrey and young Roger, three daughters, Diana, Katherine and Elizabeth, and three Irish maids – altogether a costly establishment to run. There is some evidence that Eva was a bit of a Tartar where the maids were concerned. Like many moderately well-off English families, the Keyes would import maids from the west of Ireland and train them to work in their houses. As these girls had no family members nearby they had no one to turn to if they were treated unfairly, exploited or bullied, and they seldom had enough money to flee back home, so they stuck it out, often for years. But there were limits. One morning the family were all at home and waking up as usual, but something was not as it should be. No one arrived to pull back the bedroom curtains with a 'Good morning, Sir Roger' or 'Good morning, Miss Elizabeth'. No one brought up basins of warm water for washing. There was no smell of breakfast wafting up from the kitchen and the breakfast bell did not sound. What could have happened? A quick inspection of the third floor, where the three Irish maids lived, revealed the awful truth. The poor girls could stand no more of Eva's bullying. They had packed their few things and left. No one knew where they had gone. It was an ominous pointer towards life as it would be when the 'long weekend' was over.

Sir Roger sorely needed the money and, apart from his naval pension, his only source of income came from his pen. Fortunately, there seems to have been a ready market for naval books at the time and his various publications sold well: *Naval Memoirs, Adventures Afloat and Ashore,* numerous articles for the press and a steady flow of publications and lectures brought in some welcome cash. The house was situated in excellent hunting country, so the family could enjoy plenty of sport. They made a splendid sight riding at full pelt across country. Usually there were at least six horses in the stables all needing to be cared for and fed. The five children, all at various boarding schools, were a heavy expense. Geoffrey, at Eton, showed great promise in spite of various illnesses which unfortunately affected his eyesight, making it impossible for him to enter the Navy. Young Roger was at a special prep school which prepared him for Dartmouth. The two boys and their youngest sister, Elizabeth, were extremely close friends and undertook all sorts of adventures together, building a motorbike, shooting at pigeons and enjoying an idyllic rural existence. As the children got older there were skiing parties to Switzerland and Austria and visits to London where they stayed with their formidable maternal grandmother who had a large house in Lowndes Square. Almost next door lived another formidable lady, the grandmother of their cousins, the Dorrien Smiths. Both houses were full of teenagers for major occasions like the Derby and the Eton-Harrow match and there were parties and riotous games for everyone. Keyes seems to have been an indulgent father, always taking a great interest in the progress of his offspring and encouraging them in their various exploits. Certainly he and Eva were the centre of an exceptionally lively and happy family, enjoying life with a wide circle of friends and relations. There were occasional visits to the old family stomping grounds in Donegal. On one such visit, Sir Roger was walking with his young nephew, Patrick. He managed to fall into a deep pool and found himself unable to scramble out. A passing tramp came to the rescue and saved the unfortunate admiral. Patrick felt the tramp should be rewarded and gave him a half-crown (12.5p). The tramp grumbled as he walked away 'I suppose that's all the little bugger had'.

Shortage of parental cash is seldom a setback for vigorous children and in the case of the Keyes family it seems to have been a stimulus to invention and resourcefulness. They had to buy or borrow 'difficult' horses that no one else could handle, for example, thus learning a lot about animal management and horsemanship. The motorbike seems to have been a challenge to everyone's mechanical skills. They were clearly a very close family. Sir Roger's youngest daughter, Elizabeth, remembered how she was allowed to stand with her father while he was shaving in the morning and take pot shots out of the window with a .22 rifle at pigeons on the lawn. She also recalled that, when living in Portsmouth, he had kept a box of failed light bulbs beside the bathroom window to hurl at noisy cats. Later on, he took her with him for a visit to his old battleground, the Gallipoli peninsula. But money always remained a problem. Geoffrey had to leave Eton a year early to save the fees, thus never progressing to the highest ranks in the school hierarchy. He went on to Sandhurst where he distinguished himself and was commissioned into the Royal Scots Greys, a cavalry regiment in which one of his uncles had served. Tellingly, he had to make do with his uncle's cast-off uniform, as a new one could not be afforded.

Though retired, Sir Roger could not avoid getting tied up in naval politics, and especially in trying to help old friends and allies in the scramble for senior postings in the service. There were discussions with Churchill as to how he might be able to be of use politically. Churchill wrote to him in May 1931:

> You are absolutely right not to accept any of the proposals which have been made. As soon as you are free let us consult together upon the most convenient means of your taking part in public affairs ....

There was even an appeal to be considered again for the post of First Sea Lord when Field's tenure was over. Soon, however, a more pressing issue arose which is generally referred to as the Invergordon Mutiny. In a desperate attempt to reduce public expenditure the government imposed a 10 per cent pay cut on all public servants, including the Royal Navy. The cut fell especially hard on senior ratings and, to make matters worse, the Admiralty made a shockingly poor job of communicating its decision to the

Fleet, so that most of the lower deck first heard about it from the newspapers. The Atlantic Fleet, commanded by Admiral Sir Michael Hodges, was due to sail from Invergordon to carry out exercises in the North Atlantic but the lower deck were so disgusted by their treatment that they refused to sail. Just before the fleet was due to put to sea Hodges fell ill and was relieved by Keyes's old friend and shipmate Wilfred Tomkinson. Tomkinson had been commander of the Battle Cruiser Squadron and found himself suddenly confronted with a mutiny in his new command in which neither he nor the ships which he had commanded had taken any part. He cancelled the exercise and the Admiralty, struggling frantically to avoid any blame for the situation which their own clumsiness had caused, ordered the ships involved to return to their home ports pending an investigation. The First Lord cabled Tomkinson approving of his action and the situation settled down until questions were tabled in the Commons criticising Tomkinson's action as not being firm enough. The new First Lord, Eyres-Monsell, immediately moved to protect the Admiralty from criticism by dismissing Tomkinson, who had by then returned to his cruisers and was operating in the West Indies. That was the end of the fine career of a brave and resourceful officer and Keyes was not alone in finding it grossly unfair. All his resentment about Tomkinson's treatment and his own flowed out in correspondence with the First Lord and with Baldwin, the Prime Minister. One letter to Eyres-Monsell is typical of the dispute:

> No one who knows me can doubt that I share with practically the whole Navy, and those who have its interests at heart, a strong feeling that the weakness of the Sea Lords and the influence of the permanent civilian officials within the Admiralty have thoroughly undermined the discipline of the Navy and its confidence in its administration ... I have been repeatedly asked to write and speak and also to stand for Parliament in the interests of the Navy, up to the present I have refrained ...

This was a threat to take action on a political level against the people he believed had treated not only Tomkinson, but Keyes himself, and other officers whom he respected, unfairly. These same people, he thought, had undermined the Navy he loved by allowing a grossly unfair treaty to reduce the strength of the service to such a level that it could not properly protect the trade routes or the Empire. Sir Roger was beginning to embark on a political career for which he was spectacularly unsuited. Churchill had persuaded him to become a member of the 'Other Club' which was famously a meeting place for politicians and notable people from many walks of life who were prepared to gather socially around Churchill. Many members were aristocratic and wealthy but Sir Roger complained to his friend that he would have difficulty finding the £5 entry fee. A few years later he found that club members were being expected to contribute no less than £15 towards the cost of a fine new Daimler car which was to be a present to Churchill to celebrate his recovery from a traffic accident in New York; some wealthy members must have contributed a great deal more. Keyes duly stumped up. He was convinced that by networking with the great and good in such an environment he could achieve political influence. Certainly membership brought contacts, but influence is an entirely different thing. In spring 1934 he stood for the parliamentary seat of Portsmouth which he won easily, in spite of showing himself to be a poor and nervous public speaker. Keyes was already quite a well-known public figure partly because of his achievements as commander of the Dover Patrol, and partly because of a filmed speech which he had made, and which was widely distributed, lamenting the reduction in naval strength. He had also burst into print with the publication of his book *Naval Memoirs*. Again, this naturally supported Churchill's views and his own regarding the Dardanelles and was published that same year, receiving very favourable reviews and selling well. Churchill sponsored his entry into the House of Commons. His maiden speech was a stuttering performance concerning the Naval Estimates; it was followed by a vain attempt to get the House to intervene in the Tomkinson affair. In May 1935 he was formally retired from the active list of the Royal Navy which gave him more freedom to speak in public on naval affairs.

That summer, during the recess, he made his first trip to Canada and the USA. He made speeches in Canada about the vital need for a larger British Navy (the Royal Canadian Navy had almost ceased to exist at the time) and in the USA he learned a little about the rate of American progress in naval aviation. He also managed to meet President F.D. Roosevelt, whom he had conveyed across the Channel during the war. This visit seems to have reinvigorated his interest in the parlous state of the Fleet Air Arm and he formed an alliance with Churchill to try to improve matters which had not moved forward much since the days of the Keyes-Trenchard Agreement of 1923. Eventually some progress was made on this front. In 1937 Baldwin, the new prime minister, was swayed by the Navy's arguments and decided to hand over control of Naval aviation to the Admiralty, although Coastal Command, including all flying boats, remained part of the RAF. In public,

Keyes got a great deal of the credit for this development; Churchill was in fact much more effective than Keyes in bringing it about but he was still out of office and unpopular in many quarters, so kept a lower profile. The other critical figure in the controversy was Chatfield, once Beatty's flag captain, now First Sea Lord and a figure much more to Keyes's taste than Madden or Field. Twice he went so far as to threaten to embarrass the government by resigning over the Fleet Air Arm issue and would have done so if he had not eventually won at least a partial victory. He wrote to Keyes:

> Trenchard was allowed to state … on Baldwin's authority that there would be no alteration in the control of the RAF, of the FAA, or the Coastal Areas. So I then enlisted Churchill and Guest – not too easy as they both took a hand in defeating us in 1923. Churchill's intervention in May 1936 was of great value … . Nevertheless as I told you Baldwin angrily told me to let sleeping dogs lie … . A man very much in Baldwin's confidence told me that the only way to move him was to get the public on our side.

'Getting the public on our side' was the part which Sir Roger was able to play as Chatfield generously acknowledged, writing 'I realise and value most sincerely the gallant fight you have put up and the immense help to the Navy it has been'. In spite of his lack of aptitude for politics, Sir Roger was by now a well-known public figure. He had been re-elected as MP for Portsmouth with an increased majority in 1935 and continually pressed the case for re-armament, which was gaining momentum as the public looked in dismay at the developments in Germany. Churchill, still on the backbenches, but extremely active in the press and in the Commons, was the strongest voice in politics calling for rearmament and asked Keyes to be a member of a parliamentary delegation urging more effort and cash to be expended on the armed forces. Churchill, outside the Cabinet, led a small group of MPs constantly harassing the government to increase defence spending and to take the terrible threat posed by Nazi Germany seriously. Keyes was now a loyal member of this small splinter group of the Tory party opposing Baldwin, and later Chamberlain, on foreign policy issues.

Keyes's strident criticism of what he considered to be a spineless administration caused him to distance himself from the Naval establishment in the late 1930s and become more of a political figure, used somewhat as a talisman by Churchill and others to promote their ideas. He was, however, quite unsuited for the subtleties of politics and very much inclined to 'go over the top', making demands which would have no hope of being satisfied. His style of speaking was ineffective in the House, so although he commanded great personal respect because of his service record, he cut no ice in serious debates. Harold Nicolson commented sourly on his ability to empty the House as soon as he got up to speak. One can almost hear the civil servants in the Treasury, the Admiralty, the Air Ministry and the War Office sighing with boredom as they warded off his assaults on their parsimony and incompetence. In the events leading up to the Second World War, Sir Roger sided with Churchill, Eden and a handful of other MPs in not voting in favour of Chamberlain's 'Peace for our time' speech after Munich. Eva, who was at the time writing a family newsletter to her five offspring, was disappointed that her husband was not called to speak in the debate on Chamberlain's deal with Hitler as he had a speech prepared. Given his poor parliamentary performances up to that date it seems unlikely that his contribution would have had much effect. He did, however, produce a statement for the press which was widely reported, making the case against further appeasement. He was convinced that war with Germany was inevitable and determined that, although he was a retired admiral of the fleet aged sixty-seven, a frequent critic of the Board of the Admiralty, and out of favour with the government, he was going play a part in the fighting. He also believed that the sooner the nettle was grasped the better. This was an unpopular stance to adopt after the joy and relief which swept over the country after Munich. He wrote to his daughter Elizabeth:

> Personally I think we are going down a slippery slope from one surrender to the next, accepting one insult after another provided we can get peace. I don't think Chamberlain and Halifax should be allowed to go to Rome bent on agreeing almost anything provided they can stave off war.

The Keyes family were all primed to participate in the conflict which was to come. The family now consisted of:

Daughter Diana, married to Captain James Johnson, Royal Welch Fusiliers.

Daughter Katherine, married to Peter William-Powlett, 7th Queen's Own Hussars.

Son Geoffrey, serving in the Royal Scots Greys.

Son Roger, sub lieutenant RN.

Daughter Elizabeth, unmarried.

Chapter 15

A Frustrated Mission

In spite of Sir Roger's unpopularity in official circles the possibility of active employment increased when Churchill was made First Lord of the Admiralty in September 1939, just as Hitler was flinging his forces against Poland and Russia was sitting on the eastern border of that unfortunate country, waiting to scavenge in its ruins. Keyes wrote on 5 September:

> Winston Churchill volunteered yesterday that as soon as he has looked round he will find a 'mission' for me, so I live in hope. It was bad luck for me being too junior to have a big command in the last war and too senior to have one in this. However ... I have faith in my star.

From the first things did not go well. In the first few weeks of the war Keyes found himself again in serious conflict with the First Sea Lord, Dudley Pound, who had been his long-term friend and subordinate and whose appointment he himself had strongly supported. At the outbreak of the First World War Churchill had concentrated the Royal Navy at Scapa Flow and the Mediterranean Fleet at Malta, ready for immediate action, and within a few weeks the very successful action in the Heligoland Bight had been fought and won. Not so in 1939. The Mediterranean Fleet was scattered about the sea, with one of its most powerful battleships, *Barham*, actually paying a curtesy visit to Naples when Mussolini massed his forces to invade Albania. Britain was thus unable to make anything but feeble protests about this naked aggression. At that moment, determined action might have deterred the Fascist dictator. Perhaps he would then have been less ready to go to war with Britain in 1940. Worse still, in Keyes's opinion, was the failure to do anything at all to use the Fleet to help Poland which the Germans were bombarding from the air and by sea, actually using two pre-dreadnought battleships considered obsolete in 1914. As ever, he was in favour of immediate aggressive action, but nothing seemed to be happening.

Like almost all senior British commanders, he grossly underestimated the devastating effect of air power on Naval operations close to shore, so the British naval intervention in Poland which he urged would have probably have resulted in heavy losses. As we shall see, many of his ideas were hare-brained but in the case of Italy there was some substance in his criticism. Pound, whom he blamed for the inaction, was indeed to prove a weak leader, generally taking a pessimistic view and totally unable to stand up to bullying by Churchill. As Keyes had feared, he was an excellent staff officer but a timid and unimaginative commander. The unfortunate Pound had some excuses for his shortcomings. He had only been appointed in June 1939 and had inherited an Admiralty much diminished after years of disarmament. He was suffering nagging pain from a degenerating hip which prevented him from sleeping and he was to die in agony from a brain tumour in 1943. Constant chiding from his former chief must have been yet another burden for him to bear. He fought against any involvement of Keyes in Naval affairs. To make matters even more complicated, Keyes returned to the contentious subject of the Fleet Air Arm. Affairs in the Admiralty and at the Air Ministry were certainly fraught enough already with the Battle of Britain to be won and submarines and magnetic mines to be conquered, so there could be no question of yet another re-organisation of the two services. Keyes kept the matter on the boil, however, by writing to the newspapers, speaking in Parliament and badgering Pound, Churchill, Chamberlain, or anyone else he thought might listen. The only effect was to worsen his relations with service chiefs and lessen his influence on politicians.

Luckily for Pound, Churchill was as good as his word. He did find Keyes suitable employment, although it was far away from anything concerning the Royal Navy. The neutrality of Belgium had been a crucial part of Allied policy between the wars. It was guaranteed by Britain and France and even Hitler had given an undertaking to respect its status as long as the small country committed no acts of aggression. Nevertheless, the Allies were suspicious that Germany would launch an attack through Belgium exactly as they had in 1914. The British and French tried desperately to arrange for military staff consultations with Belgium but the Belgians had seen what happened to Poland regardless of Allied guarantees of assistance and decided that it would be foolish to antagonise Germany by holding staff talks with the Allies. With an astonishingly bold stroke of wishful thinking the Belgian government convinced itself that doing nothing was the best protection against German aggression. King Leopold, however, thought otherwise. He was convinced that it was important to start discussions with Britain and France on how resistance to a German assault could be organised. Churchill and Keyes were both on the friendliest terms with the Belgian royal family and it was to them that the king appealed when Belgian official channels were closed. Churchill immediately seized the opportunity. A secret message was conveyed to Keyes asking him to pay a 'private' visit to the royal palace, taking with him details of Allied plans for defending the left wing of the Allied armies in France. On 17 October 1939 Keyes, armed with details of Allied plans, set out for his visit to Brussels. Leopold expressed the belief that his forces were strong enough to hold up the German army for long enough to allow British and French forces to enter the country and take up defensive positions. Keyes stated that the Allies needed a clear idea of Belgian defensive plans before they finalised their own tactical dispositions. He persuaded the king to allow detailed and highly confidential discussions to take place between the British military attaché in Brussels, Colonel Blake, and General van Overstraten, Leopold's own military adviser. Under the Belgian constitution the king would become supreme commander of the armed forces as soon as war was declared, but until the country was at war he had to be careful not to take any action which might seem to be contrary to the policy of the government, or to provoke the Germans. Keyes briefed the Cabinet on his visit and the arrangements for sharing military intelligence were approved.

Pleased with the results of this visit, the War Office asked Keyes to make another visit to Leopold in January 1940. By this time the sentiment in the country had changed because a German aircraft had made a forced landing in Belgium and happened to be carrying plans for a German advance straight through the country; these were immediately seized by Belgian military intelligence. The plans caused an upsurge of hostility to Germany but nevertheless increased the general feeling of nervousness, making Keyes's work increasingly difficult. The situation was complicated by the British refusal to give Belgium guarantees of her territorial integrity or that of her colonies unless she immediately opened her western frontier to allow the British and French armies to take up defensive positions inside the country. The Belgian government steadfastly continued to refuse to allow British or French forces to move forward. In spite of this, Keyes did gain permission for a military staff visit to view Belgian defensive positions, provided that the officers involved were in civilian clothes. The inspections took place but were to prove of little avail against the might of the assault which was to come.

Scarcely had this mission come to an end than, on 7 April, the German invasion of Denmark and Norway took place. Brilliantly planned and executed, the invasion happened to coincide with an extremely ill-conceived plan, the brainchild of Churchill himself, to occupy northern Norway and cut off German supplies of iron ore from the mines in northern Sweden. As a self-professed expert in amphibious warfare, Keyes was especially keen to become involved in planning a counter-attack to smother German forces flooding into southern Norway. He rapidly put together a plan for an operation using the battleships of the Home Fleet to cover a landing of troops at Trondheim to seize the airfield there and fall upon the German occupiers before they could build up a strong force in the country. Naturally, he insisted that he himself should lead the expedition. Like an over-excited gun-dog he longed for a mission and kept nagging at his master to be sent off after this elusive quarry. He wrote long personal letters to Churchill constantly referring to the Zeebrugge affair and did manage to arrange to see him on the 16th, by which time the Admiralty had convinced the First Lord that a naval attack would be too risky as the Home Fleet might suffer serious losses. It seems unlikely that Churchill ever read most of Keyes's proposals, begging to be put in command of a task force to make an immediate attack using the obsolete First World War battleships and pouring scorn on what he thought was the Admiralty's over-cautious approach. Churchill refused to let him become involved and Keyes complained bitterly at being passed over for command. After the meeting he wrote to Churchill: 'I was very offensive at our meeting - but I am very devoted to you and I only wanted to help. But you won't let me'. He continued to harass Churchill and Pound throughout the campaign, demanding to be given a leadership role in various hazardous raiding operations; the pair must have been heartily sick of having him constantly nagging them while they were in the midst of so many difficulties and dangers. Churchill wrote of him later, 'Of course there was at hand, in passionate ardour for action and glory, Sir Roger Keyes'. In truth, Keyes's wild half-planned ventures would certainly have been doomed to failure. Such British troops as were available to be landed in Norway were mostly new recruits or territorials, totally untrained in mountain warfare and hopelessly ill-equipped for fighting in a land still covered in winter's snow. The force that did land put up a poor performance against well-led German forces equipped with obsolete but still formidable tanks and massively superior airpower. For the Allies, the whole affair was a ghastly waste of time and resources and a casebook study of bad planning and shoddy staff work. Keyes's plan, scrambled together in a few days, would have been no different and far more costly in ships and men. Both sides lost significant numbers of warships in the conflict – the only redeeming feature of the whole sorry operation from the Allied point of view was that the German surface fleet was so reduced that it was able to do very little to disrupt the Dunkirk evacuation a month later. Geoffrey Keyes, Sir Roger's eldest son, was by chance involved in the final part of the Norway campaign, working with by far the most effective troops employed there by the Allies, the Chasseurs Alpins – French mountain forces fully equipped for fighting in deep snow. They re-took Narvik from the invaders, only to be withdrawn to fight in France.

There was one other positive outcome from the Norwegian campaign. Churchill, who had been its primary advocate and architect, managed to use its failure to oust Prime Minister Chamberlain and succeed him. In this astonishing exercise in the arts of Houdini, he was assisted by Keyes in Parliament, who attended in full uniform and made an astonishing speech in which he claimed to represent the men of the fighting forces who, he said, had been so let down by their leaders. He decried the lack of determination and courage of the government and the loss of fighting spirit. Harold Nicolson described this speech as 'by far the most dramatic I have ever heard'. Somehow, this oration did seem to touch the hearts of the members, eroding any confidence left in Chamberlain. Members applauded Keyes's intervention wildly although some considered it 'rather vulgar'. Keyes then joined a chorus of members shouting 'For God's sake, go' at the ailing Prime Minister. He resigned in favour of his longtime bête noire, Winston Churchill.

Keyes was by this time back in Belgium. On 10 May, German forces, without a word of warning or a thought for their treaty obligations, crashed into Belgium and Holland. Churchill sent for Keyes and despatched him at once, with full diplomatic status, to be the British Prime Minister's liaison officer with the King of the Belgians. He was flown to the BEF's HQ near Arras to meet the GOC, Lord Gort, and then set off by car for Brussels. The journey was difficult as he was frequently mistaken by the police for a German in his naval uniform, but on the morning of the 11th he was able to meet the king who was exercising his role as head of the armed forces. The picture, Leopold said, was grim. Paratroopers and glider-borne forces had seized the most powerful fortresses and the strategic crossing points over the Albert Canal, which had been intended to be a formidable obstacle. All but seven of the air force's fighters had been destroyed on the ground and enemy aircraft were busily machine-gunning refugees fleeing westward and troops in defensive positions. Unless the situation could be stabilised by British or French aircraft the whole country would be overrun in a few days. Keyes rushed back to Brussels and telephoned of the Chief of Air Staff asking for help. The CAS was not co-operative, so he called Churchill's office. The very next day RAF did appear over the country and briefly had a field day; the Luftwaffe got a nasty surprise after their unchallenged operations in the past few days. This allowed the Belgian line to be stabilised somewhat and British and French troops began to move forward to support them. At Leopold's prompting, Keyes visited the British and French embassies in Brussels and persuaded their ambassadors not to flee the capital. The respite was temporary, however. The main thrust of the German assault was actually much farther south, through the Ardennes, and there the Panzer divisions advanced almost unchecked, crashing through feeble defences, overrunning Sedan and swinging north towards the English Channel. They threatened to cut off the Allied forces in Flanders completely. It was a brilliant, bold, plan and it was working perfectly. For some time neither Leopold, Keyes, Gort, nor the French General Giraud realised the peril of their situation but, in reality, the ice was breaking all a round them and French armies were showing little inclination to fight. Brussels fell and the Germans appeared in Antwerp. What was left of the Belgian army pulled further and further back towards the French border. Leopold established a temporary headquarters in Bruges while his government retreated to le Havre. Churchill at least realised the seriousness of the situation and began contemplating the evacuation of the BEF. Even Keyes became downhearted. He felt strongly that the Belgian army had not been defeated and was still full of fight but that the French had 'sold the pass' at Sedan, letting their Allies down. He hated the sight of roads crammed with innocent refugees, mercilessly machine-gunned from the air. He was asked by Leopold to confer with Gort on 19 May and then to brief him on British plans. Keyes's visit coincided with a visit by the CIGS, General Ironside. Gort and Ironside decided that they would co-operate in a final French attempt to break through the German lines, striking south-east from Arras to cut off the head of the German advance. If this failed there would be no alternative to evacuation. It did fail. Although two British divisions made some progress the French made only feeble efforts and there was no air support. The Belgian and British forces tried to re-group on the line of the river Yser, but this was indefensible in the long term. By this time Leopold seems to have become very dependent on Keyes for counsel and comfort as well as for liaison with the British army. He described the admiral as 'the best friend a man ever had'. Ever since he was a schoolboy staying with the Keyes family at Dover he had looked up to him as an authority figure and friend; now he found him an invaluable ally who could keep him in close touch with the British army, the French, and with Churchill himself. Unfortunately, the Allied armies had a poor opinion of Belgian forces and were reluctant to co-operate with them. Only Keyes, with his direct contact to the British prime minister, was able to gain some grudging support from the BEF. One of Keyes's concerns at this time was, ironically, the blockading of the ports of Ostend and Zeebrugge. Blockships were sent from Dover but these were mistakenly fired on by French forces occupying the towns. Keyes himself arrived and, while under furious attack by the Luftwaffe, managed to destroy the outer lock gates and block the canals. This time his blockade seems to have been 100 per cent successful.

By the last week in May both men realised that there was no fight left in the French army and the British forces were exhausted after their attempted counter-attack. Leopold had told Keyes that when his army was forced to surrender, as surely it soon would be, he himself would not join any sort of government in exile but would stay in Belgium and share the discomfort suffered by his people. As the Germans hammered at the Belgian positions east of Dunkirk, he rallied his troops with the stirring message 'Quoi qu'il arrive mon sort sera la votre' (Whatever happens my fate will be as yours). By 25 May it was finally clear that the best Britain could hope for was the withdrawal of at least a part of the BEF from Dunkirk, leaving the remains of the Belgian army at the mercy of the invaders. Keyes had assured Leopold that, in this event, Britain would fight on alone against Germany. He respected the king's decision to remain with his people but found himself at cross-purposes with Churchill, who sent Keyes the following message on the 27th:

> Certainly we cannot serve Belgium's cause by being hemmed in and starved out. Our only hope is victory and England will never quit the war whatever happens until Hitler is beat or we cease to be a state. Trust you will make sure he returns with you by aeroplane before too late … .

This message never actually got through to Keyes but it would have made no difference. Late on 27 May the Belgian army, its morale broken by constant and unchallenged air attacks and by devastating assaults from superior German forces, blew the bridges across the Yser, flooded the surrounding land, and asked Germany for an armistice. By this time the evacuation was in full swing. The Belgian army had certainly delayed the German advance by several days and helped enormously in giving the BEF time to fall back on Dunkirk, but they were no match for the German army and had no defence against the Luftwaffe. Nevertheless, they had formed a key part of the forces holding back the north-eastern jaw of the pincer movement which the Germans were using to encircle Dunkirk. (Unaccountably, the other jaw was held back on the direct orders of Hitler himself.) The evacuation of the BEF, some French and a few Belgian troops was now underway. A British force moved into the defensive line around Dunkirk to replace the Belgians. Tellingly, in the midst of perhaps the worst crisis in British history, Churchill found time to pen a personal letter to Lady Eva Keyes:

> My Dear Eva,
> This is only to let you know that I talk to Roger every day. He is doing wonderful work, I thought you would like to know.
> Yours very sincerely

On the very same day he was writing to Keyes:

> By present decision [to remain in Belgium] the King is dividing the nation and delivering it into Hitler's protection. Please convey these considerations to the King and impress on him the disastrous consequences to the Allies and to Belgium of his present choice.

Keyes had some difficulty at this point in finding Leopold, but eventually the two had a meeting at which Keyes delivered Churchill's message and dutifully urged him to escape capture by boarding a British ship at Ostend. He pointed out that Belgium had undertaken not to make a separate peace with Germany, and that was exactly what it was now doing. His pleas were of no avail, so he and the remaining British staff made for Ostend by themselves. Their journeying was quite eventful: at one stage they found themselves shooting with rifles at enemy paratroopers who were landing nearby. On reaching the port, they took some time to find a fishing boat with enough fuel to get them to Dover, then luckily an MTB arrived out of the mist and picked them up. The British party privately agreed that Leopold was doing the right thing in staying with his people in defiance of Churchill and they had felt uncomfortable in obeying London's orders and trying to encourage him to escape. What would the Belgian forces have thought if, after his promise to remain, their king had deserted them in the very hour of defeat?

In the later stages of the campaign Keyes had found himself in the difficult situation of being used by Gort as a means of communication to Churchill. Communications between the BEF and London were poor, but Keyes had found a reasonably secure telephone line running from la Panne under the sea to England. He wrote to Gort after his return home:

> On 21st May and during the next few days I motored hundreds of miles in order to speak to Churchill from la Panne and did my utmost to make him understand the gravity of your position. He would not listen and even abused me for the statements in the military appreciation you gave me. If I only had been free to say it was really yours I might have been more successful ... .

His closeness to Churchill, though envied by some military commanders, certainly seems to have brought some problems.

Throughout his ordeal, dashing between Belgian, French and British command posts whilst constantly keeping in touch with the king and with Downing Street, Keyes found time to write voluminous letters to Eva telling her of his true feelings about the situation and the characters involved.

Keyes justifiably thought that he had made himself extremely useful while in Belgium and that the Belgians had done a sterling job, with his help and encouragement, in delaying the German advance. He was, therefore, appalled when the French premier, Reynaud, accused Leopold of cowardice and treachery. This was probably simply a clumsy ploy intended to hearten his own armies, but Keyes felt obliged to speak strongly in Parliament, calling for judgement to be suspended, at least until all the facts were known. His parliamentary speech, delivered when he was exhausted, having just returned from Belgium, was halting and ineffective. Churchill followed Reynaud's lead, criticising Belgian weakness and irresolution. Meanwhile the British press launched quite unjustified attacks on the nation's erstwhile ally. Even British generals (Gort, who should have known better, among them) publicly accused the Belgian army of letting them down. *The Daily Mirror* went so far as to criticise Keyes himself, accusing him of being an accomplice in a cowardly act. This was too much for Sir Roger. He sued the paper and in June 1941 an out-of-court settlement in his favour was agreed. The *Mirror* published a fulsome apology, not just to Keyes, but also to King Leopold. The judge in the case, Mr Justice Tucker, stated that the action had 'served a most useful purpose and resulted in statements which will give very wide satisfaction'.

Chapter 16

The First Commandos

The evacuation from Dunkirk had been planned and directed brilliantly by Admiral Sir Bertram Ramsay, who had commanded a monitor and a destroyer under Keyes in 1918 and who had taken part in the Ostend raid. Over the following five years he was to show himself a master in the arts of planning and amphibious warfare. Keyes must have frequently envied his erstwhile subordinate and his crucial role in many of the most important operations of the war. Unlike Keyes, Ramsay never tried to get himself put in the front line of the operations he planned; he understood the need for detailed, meticulous planning and staff-work and a proper command structure.

After returning from Belgium, Sir Roger once more set about badgering Churchill and Pound to give him a job involving active service. Before long a suitable vacancy materialised. After Dunkirk, Churchill lost no time in demanding that 'Commando' raids across the Channel should be organised to disrupt the occupying German forces. Major General Bourne of the Royal Marines was charged with creating a special force of up to 5,000 highly trained and properly equipped men to undertake these hazardous operations. In June and July the first recruits to this force did indeed make two attacks, one on le Touquet and one on Guernsey, neither of which produced any significant results. This disappointing performance provided an opportunity to give Keyes a job which might suit him, although it was quite inappropriate to his exalted rank. He was appointed to the new post of Director of Combined Operations, with Bourne continuing to serve as his subordinate. Churchill waxed lyrical about what might be achieved by 'specially trained troops of the hunter class who can lead a reign of terror up and down the coasts of Europe'. He envisaged the capture of Calais or Boulogne and all kinds of feats of derring - do. Plenty of ambitious soldiers applied to join the show; even Montgomery wrote to him saying 'If you want a good fighting corps to hit someone a crack overseas, I hope you won't forget me'. Unfortunately, no one had got around to defining what the role of the director was. Bourne's job had been primarily training and provision of equipment: Keyes wanted, and believed he had been given, full planning and operational control of the Commandos as well, reporting directly to Churchill and demanding ships, aircraft and whatever else he required from the appropriate service chiefs. This would have been a short-circuiting of the normal command structures which neither the Army nor the Navy could possibly accept. To make matters worse, one of his first actions was to move his HQ out of the Admiralty building into other offices in Whitehall, creating a quite unnecessary barrier between his operations and the Navy. Thus, the ground was laid for bitter conflict between him, the Admiralty, the Air Ministry and the War Office. Nevertheless, he wrote to Churchill:

> I must tell you how happy I am – and that I am most grateful to you for giving me this opportunity of proving that I am not as useless as my detractors, whoever they may be, would have you think. I am going slow as you advised me: and when I have got both feet in the stirrups and my knees well dug in, I will come and tell you.

He wrote even more excitedly to his son Geoffrey:

> I spent the day in the Pytchley [hunt] country with W. [Churchill] inspecting an armoured brigade and its support troops. Lunched and dined with him in the train – I am so very happy.

Churchill instructed him to make plans for two or three large raids involving 5,000 to 10,000 men in the next three or four months. At a meeting of the joint planning committee shortly afterwards, Churchill remarked, 'I make myself detestable to everybody except for Roger (Whose dupe I am)'. He then suggested a further raid on the Channel Islands which Keyes said he thought would be easy to arrange. It wasn't and failed to materialise. Keyes went on to suggest a raid on Casablanca as an adjunct to de Gaulle's forthcoming descent on Dakar. This idea was rejected by the Chiefs of Staff. Unfortunately, both Churchill and Keyes were living in a fantasy world. Wishful thinking has no place in modern warfare. An alert and powerful enemy like the Wehrmacht can easily swat little flea bites on its flanks. Churchill learnt this lesson quickly, thanks to the realism of his Chiefs of Staff. Keyes probably never learnt it at all.

Both Roger's sons, Geoffrey and young Roger, had been brought up by their parents to be as daring and as vigorous as their father. They joined the commandos and held high hopes of action. Geoffrey was by then a captain in the Royal Scots Greys and Roger a sub-lieutenant serving one of the two MTB's which were allocated to the Commando force. Their father was proud to see them both performing well in various environments, including rigorous training exercises, and, by contrast, at a grand ball given by the Duchess of Montrose. The duchess was extremely kind to the Commandos, allowing the officers access to her shooting and stalking, both of which they took advantage of in their free time.

It was not until August that the first whiff active service for the commandos appeared. General de Gaulle led his expedition to Dakar to try to persuade the French administration there to throw in their lot with the Fighting French. Keyes immediately volunteered to contribute a force of 2,300 highly-trained commandos to the expedition and to lead it himself; it would have been interesting to see how he got on with the famously awkward de Gaulle. It was fortunate for Keyes and his commandos that nothing came of the suggestion as de Gaulle's expedition was a comprehensive failure. In the meantime, the volunteers continued training at Inveraray in Scotland under Bourne while the Keyes family were living in their son-in-law's house in Saint Leonard's Terrace, Chelsea. This was the worst period of the Blitz: German bombers arrived over London in daytime during September and almost every night during the winter, delivering their deadly cargo. Eva was running a substantial household with several domestic staff for whose safety she felt responsible. On one occasion an incendiary bomb landed on the roof next door. Eva, Roger and their daughter Elizabeth were at home. Eva wrote:

> Daddy and Elizabeth and I rushed up to the top back bedroom with the stirrup pump and cans of water, and I got out of the window and along the balustrade with the end of the hose while Daddy and Elizabeth pumped till we got it out at last …. a tremendous barrage was going on and a good deal of shrapnel so I was glad when they handed out my tin helmet … . The reason why I had gone out with the hose was because I knew my way about the roofs having gone out before in daylight to prospect for a way down in case the house ever caught fire.

Both houses were saved from destruction, although molten lead from a roof caused some damage. The lady who had put her husband's horsemanship to shame on the day of their engagement certainly had lost none of her pluck.

While the training progressed in Scotland, Keyes himself spent his time in badgering the Admiralty for the landing craft he needed to practise amphibious landings and the Air Ministry for aircraft to train his paratroopers. When thwarted, he often relied on his personal friendship with Churchill to appeal for help. This was hardly the way to make himself popular with the senior officers of both services, who were occupied in the struggle for national survival. They clearly decided to ostracise Keyes to the greatest extent possible; this was exactly the situation which the directorship of combined operations intended to avoid. At one stage there was a scheme to use the commandos to capture the Spanish-held islands in the Atlantic, Canaries and the Cape Verde Islands, in the event of Franco joining the Axis powers. Keyes immediately made a bid to command this operation himself but was firmly put down by the Chiefs of Staff. As it happened, Franco was far too cunning to fall in with Hitler and Spain remained neutral, so the project was aborted. Unfortunately, this affair rumbled on for several months during which the commandos had to stand in readiness to fall upon the islands, so there was no question of their being diverted to any other activity.

More serious was Operation WORKSHOP, plan to capture the Italian island of Pantellaria. This rocky island lies about seventy miles north-west of Malta, directly between Sicily and the Tunisian coast. The island had an airfield and underground hangars for keeping aircraft safe from enemy bombing. It was thus perfectly situated to interrupt Axis communications between Italy and their armies in North Africa. Churchill strongly supported the idea of a commando raid to capture the island, insisting at first that it should be a joint services operation commanded in person by Sir Roger Keyes. The service chiefs were appalled at this suggestion. When the Chiefs of Staff, looking for reasons to scuttle the project, asked that the C in C Mediterranean (Keyes's former protégée, Andrew Cunningham) should be allowed to review the plan, Churchill exploded:

> Why, to put another committee on to find all the reasons why it should not be done? Consulted NO! Tell them we propose to do it. Have they any remarks to offer?

The Admiralty was not convinced and continued to infuriate Keyes with reasons for delay or why it couldn't be done. Meanwhile, Sir Roger had lost no time in telling his force that there was something big afoot and they should prepare for action. The idea of the capture of the island was eventually accepted in principle by the Chiefs of Staff. However, when detailed planning began they put every possible obstruction in its way – the destroyers needed could not be spared; the island would be subject to ferocious air attack; there were insufficient air and naval resources to hold Pantellaria long term; it would be impossible to re-supply the island with food, water, aviation fuel and ammunition. Most potent of all was the argument that it was absurd for an admiral of the fleet, almost seventy years old, with little experience of modern air/sea warfare, to be planning and leading a complex expedition regardless of normal military practices and protocols.

Andrew Cunningham, who had previously been a staunch friend and ally wrote:

> Although I knew well Lord Keyes's ardent fighting spirit I felt quite sure that to have an officer of his seniority operating independently within the area of my command would lead to difficulties.

Churchill, however, was still adamant and insisted that Keyes should lead the operation in person. In spite of all the opposition planning progressed and on 30 December the commandos were ready in their ships when the order came for postponement, the principal reasons being that German aircraft were beginning to operate out of Sardinia and Sicily, making the whole venture too risky. Also, the Navy had no destroyers available to cover the landing. By 21 January it was cancelled altogether. Even before this disappointment, the morale of the commandos had been eroded by the constant delays and lack of any serious action. Numerous officers and men had applied to leave the force and return to their units. Geoffrey Keyes himself wrote to his father in November:

> The men are longing for a show … one troop has gone away for a boating holiday (training with landing craft) and the rest are pretty jealous and excited. If we have to wait until January it will be a flop for an absolute certainty. Men are asking to go back to their units so that they can go to the Middle East and fight. It is all disappointing so please fix us up Pop.

Eventually the remaining commandos, including young Roger and Geoffrey, commanding a commando troop, were shipped out to Egypt where they came under the authority of C.-in-C. Mediterranean and the GOC Middle East Command in Cairo respectively. Keyes had no control over them.

Keyes was furious and heartbroken, especially as Churchill had stated that he refused to discuss the matter further and at first deliberately prevented Keyes from seeing him. Sir Roger wrote a furious letter accusing Churchill of giving in to 'craven hearted advisors' and complaining that his own position was intolerable. Churchill, in the midst of his incredibly heavy workload found time to write:

> I do not think you ought to write me letters of this kind in matters which affect those under whom you are serving. It is not possible for me to argue out with you privately, either by letter or in conversation, every decision of the Defence Committee which affects your command. My burdens would become intolerable if I were to attempt such a thing. You and your commandos will have to obey orders like other people and that is all there is to be said about it.

In fact, Churchill was never quite convinced that he had done the right thing in allowing the Admiralty to cancel WORKSHOP. He grumbled when the cruiser *Southampton* was sunk by German dive-bombers from Sicily on 11 January 1941 that this would not have happened if he had stuck to his guns and allowed Keyes to go ahead.

By this time Churchill's staff were totally fed up with Keyes's badgering of their chief. Colville, the PM's secretary, actually described him as a 'megalomaniac'. He seems to have been delighted when asked to send Keyes a 'snubbing' telegram saying that he was not to be invited to a high-level planning meeting with the prime minister at Ditchley House, Churchill's country retreat, lent to him by Ronald Tree. To the general dismay, Keyes arrived anyway and attacked Churchill for the cancellation of his Pantellaria project. He was soon sent unceremoniously home.

In fact there is little doubt that the capture of Pantellaria, had it been achieved, would have been of negative military value. The Luftwaffe soon established strong forces in Sicily and would have made the island impossible to hold. Britain famously had great difficulty holding and supplying Malta in fact, Pound strongly recommended that the island should be abandoned as it was consuming a disproportionate amount of naval and air resources. The very last thing the British required was another island to defend and there were certainly no aircraft or ships to do so. Churchill's advisors were not 'craven-hearted'; they were realists who by this time did know something of modern warfare and of the terrible effectiveness of a well-trained and equipped air force. The island was captured in July 1943, by which time the Allies had overwhelming air and sea superiority with the vast resources of the USA available. There was a single casualty – a British soldier was badly bitten by a local donkey.

Through January and February 1941, the volume and tone of Keyes's letters to Churchill became quite apoplectic. On one occasion he even suggested that he should be made Under Secretary for Defence, so that he could help the PM do away with all the committees and meetings which he believed were getting in the way of any effective action. Churchill must have been far too busy to read most of these missives but one especially provoked him and he replied, 'It is quite impossible for me to receive a letter of this character … . I therefore return it to you with its enclosures'.

Keyes was, however, retained for the time being as Director of Combined Operations and he set about raising and training another batch of commandos in Scotland. On 4 March some of his men did briefly see action. The German forces occupying Norway had established an operation producing fish oil in the Lofoten Islands. Some Norwegian collaborators there operated the plant, protected by a small body of German troops. Fish oil was an important ingredient in the manufacture of vitamin-rich foods. A surprise action was planned to put a stop to this operation. The raid was commanded by one of Keyes's staff – Brigadier Haydon. Keyes's youngest son, Roger, was by now serving in *Arethusa*, one of the supporting cruisers. The raid turned out to be a quick, surgical, affair during which most of the German garrison were made prisoners together with the collaborators. Some 20,000 tons of precious German merchant shipping was destroyed as well as the oil factory. The operation, in spite of its small scale, was a useful morale booster for Sir Roger and his men, but seemed scant reward for all the effort put into developing and training the force. It was not until long after the war was over that the real purpose of the raid, which probably not even Keyes himself knew about, became public knowledge. The garrison on the islands had an Enigma machine and the attackers managed to capture an important set of coding wheels and documents associated with this, thus making a most important contribution to the work of the decoders at Bletchley Park.

Ever more frustrated and disappointed, Keyes continued in his role until October. By then it had been decided that any amphibious activity undertaken should be under command of GHQ Home Forces, not Keyes.

His role was redefined as one involving training, development of equipment and giving advice only. This he would not tolerate. He fired off a further tirade of letters to which Churchill replied: 'I have to consider my first duty to the State which ranks above personal friendship. In all the circumstances I have no choice but to arrange for your relief'.

He resigned at Churchill's request on 19 October 1941, his place being taken by Lord Louis Mountbatten, who at once set about mending fences with the many military and civilian organisations whom Keyes had offended so deeply. Ironically, Mountbatten's first major operation was the Dieppe adventure which took place in August 1942 when 68 per cent of those involved were killed, wounded, or captured, due to appallingly bad planning and chronic underestimation of the enemy's strength.

Churchill certainly felt sad to have to sack a close personal friend and fellow member of the 'Other Club'. The two of them had fought together in 1914 to get the submarine force the resources it required, in 1915 to breathe some aggressive spirit into the Navy in the Dardanelles and in the inter-war years to demand re-armament against Hitler. Each admired the other's courage and resolution, but Churchill, as he said, had responsibilities more pressing than the ties of friendship.

The seemingly modest achievements of Sir Roger's period in command of Special Forces should not be dismissed too lightly. He had set up a tough training programme which had produced fighting units equal to any in the world. His newly-developed amphibious forces were trained to operate in stormy Scottish waters, night and day, to be ready for immediate action even in the most difficult conditions. Keyes never really grasped fully the complexity of amphibious warfare, or the devastating effectiveness of air power, and had no proper understanding of the disciplines of long-term military strategy, but he had developed and procured some useful types of landing craft for infantry (LCIs) and for tanks (LCTs) which were to play a vital role later in the war. He was to see a little later in his life, in the Pacific, how a really effective air/sea landing operation could be equipped and organised. Closer to home, British special forces, drawing on his training methods, were soon to achieve some notable successes such as the Bruneval raid, in February 1942, and the brilliant St Nazaire raid in March 1942. His vision and training certainly contributed to these superb achievements. It is important to understand, however, that these were not the kind of 'piratical' operation which Keyes, and at first Churchill himself, had envisaged; they were hit-and-run actions with limited and well-defined objectives. Keyes remained bitter and resentful of his treatment by Churchill and by the Admiralty. His mood is well illustrated in a long letter written to General Ismay, Churchill's chief military assistant, on 14 November. In it he fulminated against people whom he thought had undermined him by accusing him of using his relationship with Churchill to bypass proper service procedures. He wrote:

> Meanwhile the seeds of intrigue he had sown against me in the Naval Staff were bearing fruit. They had never forgiven me for my exposure of the Norwegian fiasco and considered the office the Prime Minister had given me – with the object of prosecuting Combined Operations more effectively and offensively – was a reflection on them.

The 'he' in this case was Captain Maund who had been on General Bourne's staff when the Combined Operations team had first been set up. Keyes had him transferred away from the commandos to the Admiralty, where he believed that Maund had started a campaign against him. In fact, Maund, by the time this had been written, had left the Admiralty to become captain of *Ark Royal,* the carrier which, under his command, played such a gallant and vital role in the destruction of the *Bismarck.*

Later in the same letter he wrote: 'I think the Prime Minister owes me very considerable amends for my humiliating downfall and all the slanders I have suffered on his account.'

One is inclined to believe that Churchill had more pressing things to worry about than the feelings of a retired and bitter Admiral of the Fleet.

The autumn of 1941 and the early months of 1942 were the blackest in the war for the UK. The loss of Singapore, the *Prince of Wales* and *Repulse*, and the successes of the *Afrikakorps* in Libya seemed to call into question the competence of the government and indeed the fighting spirit of British forces in general. Keyes's commandos, having arrived in Egypt, were deployed to Crete, just in time to witness the disastrous British withdrawal from the island and to suffer heavy casualties themselves. One small glimmer of light for the commandos was provided by young Geoffrey Keyes, then a Major and second in command of a Scottish commando unit. British forces were gradually pushing into Vichy-held areas of the Middle East and had been held up by well dug-in Vichy French forces on the Litani river. The idea was to land commandos from the sea at night on the north bank of the river to roll up the flank of the defenders. Poor navigation resulted in the landing taking place on the wrong bank. The enemy detected the landing and opened fire, killing the commanding officer and causing other serious casualties. Keyes nevertheless rallied the remaining men and charged across the river, crossing a minefield on the other side and destroying the enemy strongpoint which had been holding up the advance. This opened the way for regular forces to cross the river and continue their progress. To his father's delight, Keyes was given an immediate MC and promoted to Lieutenant Colonel at the tender age of twenty-four. Gradually, however, Middle East Command allowed the fine commando force which they had been sent to become split up and dissipated, completely destroying its esprit de corps and morale.

Chapter 17

Politics

Sir Roger himself, now without any official appointment and with no hope of being given any favours by Churchill, had time to concentrate on his parliamentary activities. On 25 November he made a personal statement to the House. In this, he decried the passive stance adopted by Britain and the lack of aggressive action. He said,

> Today we have a fighting Prime Minister, but the essence of success in war is speedy action and surprise … I have unbounded faith in our ultimate victory, but victory will be delayed while – in Whitehall phraseology 'every stone is turned and every avenue is explored'- for imaginary dangers and difficulties to avoid action being taken, and the glorious vista of the goal beyond is shrouded in a fog of indecision.

As ever his speech was poorly delivered, halting and tense, producing little effect on members except to evoke some sympathy for the obvious sincerity of the speaker. By a cruel stroke of misfortune, at the very time that Keyes was addressing the House his beloved Geoffrey was lying dead in a grave in North Africa. He had led a raid on a building wrongly thought to be housing Rommel, far behind enemy lines in Libya. The raiders landed from a submarine, losing much of their equipment in a heavy sea. Unfortunately, the intelligence regarding Rommel's whereabouts was wrong and Geoffrey's party attacked a building of little importance. During a confused assault on the building he was shot dead while leading a small body of commandos. For his brave action he was awarded a posthumous Victoria Cross.

The first months of 1942 found Keyes still in a bitter mood. He was particularly distressed by the thought that the Admiralty, and especially his former friend and protégé Pound, had been the main cause of his troubles and continued unemployment. Pound had, he heard, deeply resented his supposed influence on Churchill and was stung by his intemperate remarks about the cowardice of the Admiralty planners. He strenuously resisted any suggestion that Roger should take any active role. Keyes kept himself occupied by getting involved again in the bitter debates about naval aviation, in which he found a powerful ally in Admiral Ramsay, one of the few senior officers in the Navy who really understood air power. The middle of a world war, however, was not the time to be tinkering with inter-service politics and the debate gradually petered out in the Commons, to be revived later, as we shall see, in the House of Lords.

A more useful occupation for Sir Roger, with his high standing in public esteem, was to go up and down the country making speeches in support of the war loan programme. He took advantage of such occasions to lambast the previous Labour-led government which had signed the naval treaties during the inter-war period and also to condemn the supposed laziness and greed of shipyard workers, who, he thought, were being morally damaged by a combination of too high wages and too little discipline. In particular, he attacked the 'cost plus' system of awarding contracts to arms suppliers which he believed led to complacency and inefficiency. On at least one occasion, when he had criticised an incident in a shipyard in which a trade union had insisted on a young worker being sacked for working unauthorised overtime, he went himself to address a mass meeting of the workers. This was expected to cause a riot, but his personal charm saved the situation and he parted from the site good friends with both management and the trade union. This friendship with organised labour did not last, however, and the following months saw many broadsides fired at 'overpaid, lazy, unpatriotic' shipbuilders by Sir Roger. He was even more scathing in his attacks on Herbert Morrison and Ernest Bevin, Labour members of the war cabinet, whom he despised for their rabble-rousing and supposed lack of patriotism.

His parliamentary appearances were occasionally downright bizarre. The most extreme case occurred when he allied himself with Sir John Sidney Wardlaw-Milne in a vote of censure on the conduct of the war. The disasters of 1941 and early 1942 were so grave that Churchill's competence to lead the war effort was being seriously questioned. The leader of the doubters was Wardlaw-Milne, an almost comically right-wing Conservative MP, who introduced a motion which suggested that Churchill should go and be replaced by a 'dominating figure to run the war and also a generalissimo to command the armed forces'. For this daunting role he proposed no less a person than the Duke of Gloucester, the king's younger brother, a man with no administrative and experience and whose military activities were for the most part limited to enjoying the messes of the many regiments of

POLITICS

which he was Colonel-in-Chief. Keyes, for some reason, allied himself to
Wardlaw-Milne and undertook to go into the parliamentary lobby to support
the motion. This was actually a very serious threat to Churchill as many left-
wing MPs joined in and, had they won, Churchill, who defined himself above
all as 'the servant of the House', would have had to resign. In his speech in
support of the motion, Keyes fulminated not at Churchill himself but against

> A Home Secretary [Morrison], once a conscientious objector
> who uses his powers to free strikers who have been imprisoned
> for breaking the law. A Minister of Labour [Bevin], formerly a
> strike leader, who cannot stop strikes which discredit the nation
> when the Empire is in danger, and a First Lord of the Admiralty
> [Alexander], who is responsible for the disarmament which
> has cost us command of the sea.

Alexander was a Labour politician who had actively supported naval arms
limitation in the 1920s and 1930s. A very special place in his particular
hell was reserved for poor Dudley Pound, still the First Sea Lord. (The
feeling was mutual. Pound wrote to Cunningham, 'I am sorry to say it
but RK is just out for his own glorification. Nothing else matters.') For
Churchill himself he had nothing but praise, except insofar as he was letting
himself be manipulated by cowardly, incompetent or unpatriotic, advisors.
There was a comical moment when Keyes found himself welcomed
into the parliamentary lobby supporting Wardlaw-Milne's motion by the
very socialist politicians that he most loathed – he tried to ignore them.
The motion of censure was lost by 476 votes to 25. Keyes was generally
considered to have made a fool of himself by being associated with such an
absurd motion and with Wardlaw-Milne.

Churchill emerged unscathed form the debate and does not seem to have
held the affair against Keyes, although on one occasion he did taunt him with
a reference to it. He did, however, feel that Keyes was an embarrassment
in the House of Commons and offered him a peerage. Sir Roger was in
two minds about accepting it but eventually was persuaded, partly because
his bitter rival in the debate about the Fleet Air Arm, Trenchard, was a
member of the House of Lords and naval aviation was to be debated there.
The other factor was that Churchill hinted that it would be easier to find a
job for him as a lord than in his present role as an MP. On New Year's Day
1943 he accepted the honour, taking the title of Baron Keyes of Zeebrugge
and Dover. As soon as he was introduced into the House, he plunged into

185

battle with Trenchard, who had once again proposed that the Royal Air Force should take total control of naval aviation. By this stage of the war, it was evident that British naval aviation was miles behind that of the USA and Japan, with poor equipment and tactics, a scarcity of modern fighters and inadequate patrol and strike aircraft. This was inexcusable because, in 1919, Britain had by far the largest and best-equipped maritime aviation in the world. In the end Keyes, supported by Chatfield – Beatty's old flag captain and now, like Keyes, a peer – eventually agreed that no organisational changes should be made until the war was over. In the meantime, American naval fighters and attack aircraft would have to be purchased.

Keyes still hoped for some role in the conduct of the war but 1943 brought nothing but further calls on his services for fundraising and some lecturing appointments. Among the latter were the Lees-Knowles Lectures at Cambridge which he used to decry the over-cautious approach, as he saw it, adopted by the War Cabinet at the behest of the Chiefs of Staff. Ironically, he also held forth in these lectures on his theories regarding amphibious warfare to an audience which included many American officers. The Americans claimed to have profited from the experience, although their expertise in this branch of warfare was to prove far superior to anything their lecturer could have imagined. In between these activities he found himself frequently concerned with the welfare of individual sailors who had served under him and who continued to turn to him for help in time of personal or financial difficulty. Always diligent and humane, the admiral expended many hours on these frequently tedious issues. He learnt of the successful Allied amphibious landing in Sicily in July, masterfully planned and organised by Admiral Ramsay, who he generously congratulated, but bewailed the decision not to land commandos behind enemy lines when invading forces were delayed around Catania. It must have been galling for him to see the branch of warfare in which he particularly specialised being planned and carried out without any reference to him whatever.

A further call on his attention was a campaign on behalf of Admiral Dudley North. North had been the Flag Officer North Atlantic in 1940 while Operation MENACE, de Gaulle's assault on Dakar, was taking place. He had been based at Gibraltar, together with Admiral Somerville who commanded Force H, also based at Gib. Orders from the Admiralty had forced North and Somerville to detach all but one of their heavy ships to support MENACE, leaving only one battle-cruiser, *Renown*, and six destroyers to guard the straits. At that very moment news came that six modern Vichy French warships were heading west towards Gibraltar. This was reported to the Admiralty, but no response was received. The French force proceeded through the straits and turned south, first stopping at Casablanca, then onwards to Gabon. The Admiralty was furious that no attempt had been made to intercept this French squadron, which they feared, wrongly, might have been a threat to MENACE. Typically, they hunted for a scapegoat and fastened the blame on North. This was entirely unjust. North was not even in overall command at Gibraltar; his position vis a vis Somerville had never been defined. Vichy France was in any case a neutral state, so their ships had a right to sail through the straits whenever they wanted. The French force was actually much stronger than the one capital ship and handful of destroyers available at Gib. In the absence of any orders from London how could it be argued that North had done wrong? However, he had been recalled, censured and never again employed in any seagoing capacity. Keyes was infuriated by the treatment meted out to North, and the affair gave him another stick with which to beat the Sea Lords in general and Dudley Pound in particular. He wrote to North:

> It is really difficult to write temperately about the matter. It is a shocking story - much worse than I thought and I knew it was pretty bad. I would much like to help you vindicate your professional reputation when you decide to act.

The Admiralty stubbornly stuck to its version of events, however, and the issue of North's reputation was still being disputed long after the war was over.

In February 1944, Keyes found himself driving up to London from the family home in Tingewick when he found that something strange was happening to the sight in his right eye. A specialist soon diagnosed a detached retina, probably the result of a blow on the head, perhaps caused by falling off a horse, or possibly by his flying accident in 1925. His sight, he was told, could perhaps be restored by an operation but the chances of success were only fifty/fifty. He opted for the operation which was performed at St Mary's Hospital, Paddington. At first it seemed to have been successful but the healing process required him to lie still for three weeks with his head bandaged. When the bandages were first removed the patient was delighted to find that he could see perfectly, so it seemed that the problem was being resolved. Unfortunately, a few days later, a heavy bomb exploded close to the hospital and the shock caused the retina to become detached again. After a rest at home he returned for a second operation but this was not successful: Keyes was forced to abandon the struggle and became resigned to losing the sight in his right eye.

Chapter 18

With the Pacific Fleet

Thus handicapped he set off on yet another speechmaking tour of Britain while Eva continued her rather dreary war work in London. However, they were soon both able to look forward to a new adventure. It had been agreed shortly before the accident that Keyes should make a visit to Canada, Australia and New Zealand to drum up enthusiasm for the war effort, accompanied by Eva in the role of secretary. The visit had been postponed while the eye problem was being dealt with and this fortunately provided a chance for Roger to be taken on a visit to the Normandy beaches early in July, just before his departure. This was a wonderful opportunity to see the progress of history's greatest amphibious operation, brilliantly planned by the redoubtable Admiral Ramsay. Commanders on the spot were generous in their praise for the training and equipment designed and provided by Keyes's Combined Operations team, giving him a much-needed morale boost before the long trip to Australia.

Roger was, of course, only one of a series of VIP visitors to the Normandy beaches. Churchill himself made an expedition to Montgomery's HQ in Normandy, coming ashore as soon as the army commanders were convinced that it would be safe for him to do so. He had actually wanted to cross the Channel with the leading landing craft. He was only dissuaded from this by King George VI who insisted that if his Prime Minister was going, he, as King, would go with him. To the great relief of his military staff, and of Admiral Ramsay, the whole idea was then dropped. This affair illustrates how very alike, in some respects, Keyes and Churchill were. Both heroes of wars fought long ago, they yearned, at their advanced age, to be in the forefront of battle again and refused to understand that as old men they would be nothing but a nuisance anywhere near the front line. Just as they both felt ashamed of their failure to press forward in the Gallipoli campaign, they both convinced themselves that the opportunity for a heroic act would somehow come their way.

Lord and Lady Keyes sailed first to New York in the liner *Queen Elizabeth*. Once in the USA, Keyes seems to have lost none of his skills in networking. Within a few days he was in the White House talking to President Roosevelt, whom he had known since 1918 when he had ferried him across the English Channel. The two seem to have got on well and the president arranged for Keyes to meet the formidable Admiral King, head of the US Navy. King was famous for his savage temper and for his dislike of the British in general and of the Royal Navy in particular, but he obviously took to Keyes and admired his aggressive spirit. The US Navy in the Pacific at the time was in the process of successfully reversing the Japanese advances of 1942 by deploying its massive air and maritime superiority. Japanese naval aviation had never really recovered from the Battle of Midway in June 1942, allowing the US to perfect the art of amphibious warfare, strongly supported by naval aircraft – the very area in which Keyes considered himself an expert. He longed to see some of the action. Roger particularly commended himself to King by his attitude to the thorny question of control of naval aviation. There was a strong US Army-led party endeavouring to set up a separate all-embracing air service along the lines of the RAF, which would wrest control of naval aviation from the US Navy. King was fighting this tooth and nail. Keyes undertook to share all the arguments which had been deployed in the UK against such a move and it was not difficult for him to provide plenty of evidence showing what a devastating effect such a move had had on British naval air capability. (The USAF was established as a separate entity in 1947, but the Navy retained control of its own air operations and even the US Marines had their own Air Corps.) When King made arrangements, things buzzed. Eva was recruited as an honorary WAVE, the US equivalent of the WRNS, so that she could be carried in US Navy aircraft, and arrangements were made for the pair to visit the combined operations training centre in San Diego. A US Navy officer was assigned to escort them and General MacArthur and Admiral Nimitz, respectively army and navy commanders in the Pacific, were ordered to provide help and hospitality. Whilst in New York, Keyes also found time to pay his respects to General Pershing, commander of the US Army in France in the First World War. Pershing was a long-time, personal friend, who was by now unfortunately very frail and sometimes incoherent. The visit was a typically thoughtful act of kindness on the part of the admiral. After his scheduled visit to Canada, which involved many speaking engagements and dinners, Lord and Lady Keyes were taken fully in hand by the US Navy. Their assigned guide, Captain Rees, escorted them as they flew down the Pacific coast to San Diego. Roger Keyes wrote to Churchill (At last! A letter not full of complaints and pleadings), detailing the massive warship building yards they passed over and the airfields ready with literally thousands of combat aircraft waiting to be delivered to the carriers in the Pacific.

In San Diego, Keyes was treated with the greatest respect and generous hospitality. He was shown the extensive combined operations training activities which he was told were derived from what US officers had seen of the commando training programmes in Scotland which he himself had devised. He was taken to sea in one of the vast new aircraft carriers which by that time had replaced battleships as the principal striking force of the navy. He was particularly impressed by the Alligator tracked amphibious troop-carriers, or LVTs (landing vehicles, tracked), which were to be the keystone of the assaults on enemy-held islands. He could not help contrasting the superb equipment now available to the rowing boats and mules he had had to use only thirty years earlier at Gallipoli. At this time planning for the liberation of the Philippines was in full swing, Admiral Nimitz, in command of naval forces in the Pacific, hinted that he might be able to let his visitor see something of the action.

Roger and Eva then set off in a US transport aircraft for Brisbane, Australia. Roger made a series of broadcasts and public speeches, then received the unusual honour of being asked to sit with the Speaker of the Australian parliament and listen to tributes from all sides of the House. Hardly had this finished than he received an urgent message from General MacArthur asking him to visit Admiral Kinkaid at his Pacific headquarters, where he was planning a major assault which was soon to take place. The operation consisted of the landing of 100,000 US troops on the Japanese-held Leyte Island in the Philippines. This, in turn, precipitated what was to be the biggest sea battle of the war, and was almost certainly the last time in history in which battleships on both sides would fight each other in line. The order of battle on each side gives an idea of the scale of this historic encounter:

	Japan	US
Battleships	7	12
Aircraft carriers	6	32
Cruisers	16	23
Destroyers	36	100
Submarines	11	22

This is not the place to describe the course of the battle. Vast US superiority in numbers of ships and aircraft and in technology ensured eventual victory in spite of deadly Japanese *Kamikaze* aircraft which managed to strike three US escort carriers, and some tactical errors on the part of the Americans. Keyes was allotted a berth in *Appalachian,* the command ship, which was to oversee the landing of the US troops on Leyte itself. Her station was just off the landing beach. He was able to observe at close hand as the battleships and cruisers bombarded the Japanese defenders on shore. As usual the beaches seemed deserted as the enemy sheltered in bunkers and foxholes, invulnerable to shelling, ready to emerge with deadly machine-gun and mortar fire as soon as the bombardment ceased to allow the attackers ashore. The Japanese were using exactly the same tactics as the Turks had employed at Gallipoli, bringing back memories of the terrible carnage there caused by a handful of well-placed machine guns when the British and Commonwealth forces had endeavoured to land. But this time there was a nasty surprise ready for the defenders. The bombardment lifted and, sure enough, landing craft appeared in the shallows off the beaches, but just as the Japanese left their bunkers and prepared to open fire some of those craft pulled ahead then sprouted a hideous array of rocket-launcher tubes which sent their missiles crashing into the now exposed Japanese on the beaches. This fearful surprise bombardment was immediately followed by the infantry assault which swept away the opposition, sending them scuttling for the jungle in the rear. It was not only foot soldiers who came ashore; in the first wave of the attackers were the very LVTs which Roger had seen practising in California. These 14-ton monsters were armed with heavy machine guns and each one carried fourteen fully-armed infantrymen. As they were fully amphibious, they could deposit their loads on shore then lumber back, crossing reefs and sandbars, to collect another load. To see this successful landing against strong and well-disciplined opposition was a major revelation for Keyes. He did have a suggestion, however, which he explained when he reached MacArthur's headquarters after the landing. He had seen that, although there were not many casualties among the infantry ashore, many of the landing craft got shot up as they approached the beaches. Why, he asked, was the landing not made at night? This would, in his opinion, have saved many lives as the landing craft would have been virtually invisible. The answer given was that US troops were not trained for night fighting and experience had taught them that the Japanese were much more formidable at night than US infantry or marines. Keyes countered this by suggesting that a 'commando' unit should be formed and rapidly trained for night fighting. Perhaps he hoped that he would be asked to help train it. He was looking forward to a meeting with MacArthur himself to discuss his proposals when fate intervened.

Shortly after the Leyte landing he was to suffer an unfortunate accident. Japanese land-based torpedo planes were menacing the fleet anchorage, so the US admiral ordered a huge number of smoke floats to be launched to provide some protection. Some of these proved to be of a new type which produced highly toxic smoke. Keyes and several US officers on the bridge of *Appalachian* inhaled this and suffered nausea and serious lung damage, unpleasant for a young man and doubly so for a seventy-year-old. Confined to a sick berth, he missed his meeting with MacArthur and also a planned transfer to the old battleship *Tennessee,* thus missing what must surely have been the last battle in history between columns of rival fleets of battleships. It would also have been the only chance in his life to witness a major fleet action. A Japanese task-force under Admiral Nishimura had been assembled to assault the continuing landing operations on Leyte and force the American troops to withdraw. This would be achieved by steaming at night up the Surigao Strait and attacking the landing beaches at first light. The operation was badly planned and executed. During the night of 24/25 October, unaware of American strength in the Surigao Strait, two squadrons of heavy Japanese ships ran a gauntlet of US torpedo boats, one of which held the future President Kennedy, and destroyers. After suffering severe damage, they got within radar range of a line of old US battleships, including *Tennessee.* Most of those veterans had been sunk at Pearl Harbor, then repaired, modernised and fitted with gun-directing radar, far superior to the rudimentary radar sets installed on a few Japanese ships. In the pitch darkness of the tropical night this gave the Americans an overwhelming advantage. In two columns the task-force approached the American battle line, strung out across their path. The US ships had perfectly crossed the Japanese T. They opened fire at 22,000 yards. One Japanese column was totally destroyed. The other, badly damaged, fled back down the strait, most of its scattered ships falling victim to US submarines and aircraft during the next few days.

The damage to his lungs notwithstanding, Keyes flew in a US aircraft back to Australia to continue his speaking tour and immediately got involved in political battle. The cruiser *Australia,* attached to the US Pacific Fleet, had been damaged in action and needed urgent repairs. To his disgust, and that of the ship's crew, these repairs were carried out in an US fleet repair base, not in civilian yards in Australia. The reason given for this was that the US Navy yard, under naval discipline, worked twenty-four hours a day, but the Australian labour unions would not allow this in their own civilian yards. Keyes had a conversation about this which a journalist overheard and then reported that Keyes didn't think that Australian workers were putting their backs into the war effort. A furious row ensued which led to him stating that he had said much the same about British labour unions. He went out of his way to praise the conduct of Australian fighting forces, but continued to compare the dockyard workforce's efforts unfavourably with those of their soldiers and sailors. He went on to quote another example, that of the cruiser *Hobart*, which had been out of action for eighteen months due to labour problems in Australia. A meeting was arranged between union bosses and Keyes which seems to have calmed things down a little, but the clash rather spoilt the lecture tour and certainly strained the admiral's already damaged constitution. An extract from one of his lectures, this one delivered at a youth rally, gives a flavour of his theme:

> In late years many people seem to have lost their religion, and with it their consciences and have put pleasure before duty and worked as little as possible for the highest possible wage. But people who have been in the front line in this war have, I think, learnt better now and have realised that selfishness doesn't pay and that no country can prosper unless we all work together. Your country's future is in your hands. Do your best to be worthy of its traditions so that you will be able to hand over the torch to your children in their turn.

All worthy sentiments, but it is hard to imagine them going down too well with the famously cynical Australian labour force.

Shortly before Christmas 1944, Eva and Roger set off by air for New Zealand. Like almost all passenger planes in those days, theirs was unpressurised, so breathing when at altitude placed a considerable strain on the heart and lungs. Keyes had been told by doctors not to fly at more than 10,000 feet, but on this occasion the pilot climbed to 13,000 feet to take advantage of a tail wind. Keyes became very distressed and Eva asked for oxygen but there was none on board. The pilot came down as quickly as he could but the damage had been done.

Once again Roger set about giving his lectures but suffered constant asthma attacks. He saw a local doctor, who subsequently turned out to be unqualified, who told him that nothing was wrong, so he continued his busy schedule of travel and speaking engagements, returning to Australia at the end of January. After a few weeks he collapsed totally and was seen by a lung specialist who confirmed that his heart and lungs were badly damaged and ordered a complete rest in bed for at least a month. Instead of a hospital he was accommodated at Government House in Adelaide where he seemed to make at least a partial recovery. By mid-March he was well enough to start his long trek home by air with numerous stops on the way, including one at Mountbatten's headquarters in Sri Lanka, then called Ceylon, and one in Egypt, where Roger and Eva visited the grave of their son, Geoffrey.

On his return to Britain, Keyes was clearly a very sick man. Nevertheless, he quickly plunged into the knotty problems of Belgian politics and the return of King Leopold to his own country, the war in Europe now being over. The king had been held captive in Germany, having successfully made enemies of his own government in exile, of the Allies, and of the Germans. Keyes had strongly vindicated Leopold's actions in staying in Belgium after his ministers had fled to France and then to Britain in 1940, so he now joined the ranks of those who wanted him to return to his kingdom. Leopold had, however, been seen as a traitor by both the French and the British when he remained in Nazi-dominated Belgium, rather than heading the exile government in London. The British press named him 'King Rat' for his conduct. His return home was also bitterly opposed by the Belgian left, who threatened civil war should the king be restored to his throne. Keyes tried hard to arrange a visit to Salzburg, where the King was residing, but was pronounced too ill to travel. He had to content himself with writing to newspapers and to anyone he thought might have influence, pointing out that had Leopold not been with his army in May 1940, after his ministers had all fled to safety, the Dunkirk evacuation could never have taken place. His loyalty to his old friend and protégé was admirable, but this was an ill-judged campaign by Keyes, who knew little about the subtleties of Belgian politics and was doomed to failure. Leopold did briefly return long after Keyes's death, in 1950, but was never accepted by the people and was forced to abdicate to avoid civil chaos.

This was to be the old hero's last campaign. Finding himself too weak and sick to attend Parliament or meet his old friends in London he returned home to Tingewick, where he died on 26 December 1945. Churchill, now out of office, broadcast to the nation on the night of his death:

> We have lost one of the great sailors of the Royal Navy who embodied its traditions and renewed its glories. It was by men like him, in whom the fire and force of valiance burned

194

that our Island was guarded during perilous centuries. The fame of Zeebrugge will hold its place among our finest naval actions .... The Admiral's countrymen and friends salute his services and cherish his memory. Our hearts go out to his widow – always his comrade and champion.

Keyes's career was certainly colourful and it is impossible not to recognise him as a thoroughly decent man, scrupulously honest, fiercely loyal to his friends, passionate for justice and afraid of nothing. The bravery and initiative which he displayed in China and his magnificent feats of seamanship in small destroyers bear witness to a rich vein of courage which was the hallmark of his naval career, and which commended him especially to another superlatively courageous fighter, Churchill himself. He also possessed, in common with his lifetime hero, Nelson, that extraordinary gift called 'leadership', inspiring trust, devotion and even love, in men serving under him. Somehow he also commanded respect from audiences of all sorts including seamen, trade unionists, dock workers and, occasionally, even the House of Lords. These extraordinary qualities took him to the highest rank in the Royal Navy and established his place close to the heart of the British wartime government. It was typical of Churchill that he recognised Keyes's genius and became almost carried away by a romantic desire to use him to achieve some singular feat of arms. In this both men were disappointed.

Strangely, Keyes's most significant achievements were in logistical roles. The evacuation of the Gallipoli peninsula with almost no losses was recognised both in Britain and in Germany as a brilliant achievement requiring superb inter-service co-operation and immaculate planning. The naval component of this was very largely down to Keyes whose understanding of the practical problems surrounding evacuation of beaches at night time and in uncertain weather was masterful and can be credited with saving many thousands of lives. His other major contribution to victory in the First World War was his shaking up of the Dover Patrol to deny the passage of the English Channel to U-boats. It is no exaggeration to state that this, together with the introduction of the convoy system, saved Britain from being starved out of the war. Any inconvenience to the Germans caused by the Zeebrugge Raid pales into insignificance compared to this triumph. Neither of these achievements were superficially glorious or romantic. They were the result of excellent understanding of practical seamanship, meticulous planning and the ability to work with others – soldiers, industry, politicians and allies – in a friendly, 'can do' atmosphere. Unfortunately for Keyes, the qualities needed to achieve great things in such military operations are not those required for strategic planning or political manoeuvring.

It is impossible not to regard his career in the Second World War as pathetic. Having been disappointed when passed over for the post of First Sea Lord before the war and placed on the retired list, he felt certain that his qualities would be recognised and used. They were, however, essentially attributes appropriate to a mid-ranking officer, not to an Admiral of the Fleet. Over and over again, he showed himself to have poor judgement in strategic affairs and totally unrealistic ideas about what he personally could achieve in combat. He seems to have been under the impression that wars could be won by a series of brilliant, daring, actions which would somehow demonstrate moral superiority and cow the enemy into submission. He had little concept of the need to husband resources until the achievement of a crucial strategic objective could be assured. His conviction that he knew more than anyone else about combined operations was not shared by the Admiralty or by the War Cabinet, who wisely delegated planning of Dunkirk, the North African, Sicilian and Normandy landings to the genius of Admiral Ramsay. Typically, Keyes was generous in his praise of Ramsay but his exclusion from the planning process must have been extremely hurtful.

His woeful career in Parliament merits no examination. He was totally out of his depth.

It is a measure of Churchill's genius that he recognised Keyes's qualities and also, latterly, his limitations. It is difficult to imagine the prime minister tolerating the sort of criticism hurled at him by Keyes from anyone else and his patience must have been sorely tried by the endless stream of increasingly hysterical letters. Churchill was a big enough man, however, to overlook his friend's shortcomings and to celebrate his qualities of determination, courage, honesty and decency. Such men were rare enough in political circles – the great man must have been refreshed to encounter them in 'His' Admiral.

Bibliography

Many excellent books exist about the Royal Navy in the twentieth century. The following selection of books is particularly relevant to the career of Roger Keyes.

ASPINALL-OGLANDER, Cecil, *Roger Keyes,* The Hogarth Press, 1951.

BACON, Admiral Sir Reginald, *The Dover Patrol: 1915-1917* (2 Volumes), Hutchinson and Co., 1919.

CHALMERS, W.S, *The Life and Letters of David Beatty,* Hodder and Stoughton Ltd, 1951.

COCKER, Maurice, *Royal Navy Destroyers: 1893 to the Present Day,* The History Press, 2011.

COLVILLE, Jock, *The Fringes of Power: Downing Street Diaries 1939-1955,* Hodder and Stoughton Ltd, 1985.

CORBETT, Sir Julian S, *Naval Operations* (Vols 1-4)

EVERITT, Don, *K Boats: Steam-Powered Submarines in World War I,* Naval Institute Press, 1999.

FISHER, Lord John Arbuthnot, *Memoires,* Hodder and Stoughton Ltd, 1919.

FURBRINGER, Werner, *Fips: Legendary U-Boat Commander* (translated by Geoffrey Brooks), Naval Institute Press, 2000.

KEYES, Elizabeth, *Geoffrey Keyes*, George Newnes, 1956.

KEYES, Roger, *Adventures Ashore and Afloat,* George Harrap, 1939.

KEYES, Roger, *Outrageous Fortune: The Tragedy of Leopold III of the Belgians, 1902-1941,* Martin Secker & Warburg Ltd, 1984.

KEYES, Roger, *The Naval Memoirs: Scapa Flow to the Dover Straits 1916-1918,* Kessinger Publishing, 2010.

KEYES, Roger, *The Keyes Papers (Volumes 1-3), Naval Records Society.*

NICOLSON, *Diaries,* Weidenfeld & Nicolson, 2005.

MCGREAL, Stephen, *Zeebrugge and Ostend Raids,* Pen and Sword Books Ltd., Barnsley, 2007.

ROBERTS, Andrew, *Churchill,* Allen Lane, 2018.

WINTON, John, *Cunningham: The Greatest Admiral Since Nelson,* John Murray Pubs Ltd, 1999.

The author is most grateful to Mr and Mrs Anthony Houghton Brown for their valuable help in understanding the Keyes family life in Tingewick.

Index